SYRIA: A SHORT HISTORY

By Professor Hitti

HISTORY OF THE ARABS

HISTORY OF SYRIA INCLUDING
LEBANON AND PALESTINE

LEBANON IN HISTORY

THE ARABS: A SHORT HISTORY

SYRIA
A SHORT HISTORY

Being a condensation of the author's
'History of Syria including
Lebanon and Palestine'

BY

PHILIP K. HITTI

Professor Emeritus of Semitic Literature on the
William and Annie S. Paton Foundation
Princeton University

New York
THE MACMILLAN COMPANY
1959

First Printing

Printed in the United States of America

Library of Congress catalog card number: 59-8223

The Macmillan Company, New York
Brett-Macmillan Ltd., Galt, Ontario

PREFACE

Ever since the publication of *History of Syria including Lebanon and Palestine* (1951) the author has entertained the hope of compressing it into a small volume, minus footnotes and other critical apparatus, which would appeal to a wider and more varied audience. It would bear the same relation to the larger volume that the author's *The Arabs: A Short History* bears to *History of the Arabs*. But the present heightened interest in Syria and the Syrians and the curiosity aroused about what is happening there, together with its setting and background, called for immediate action which I found myself unable to undertake because of prior commitments. Hence I sought and received the co-operation of my former pupil and colleague, Harry W. Hazard. Dr. Hazard has produced a work worthy of his scholarship and, we trust, adequately satisfying to the needs of the student and the intelligent layman. Three of the maps were newly sketched by him.

The last chapter in the larger volume, dealing with the contemporary scene, has been expanded by the author into four chapters.

P. K. H.

March 1958

CONTENTS

LIST OF MAPS

PLACE IN HISTORY

SYRIA, using the term in its old, geographical sense, occupies a unique place in the annals of the world. Especially because of the inclusion of Palestine and Phoenicia within its ancient boundaries, it has made a more significant contribution to the moral and spiritual progress of mankind than any other comparable land. Small as it appears on a map or a globe, its historical importance is boundless, its influence universal.

As the cradle of Judaism and the birthplace of Christianity it originated two of the great monotheistic religions and prompted the rise and development of the third and last — Islam. The soul of the Christian, the Moslem and the Jew — wherever he may be — turns to some sacred spot in Syria for religious inspiration. Every thoughtful Western man can trace some of his most fundamental values and beliefs to that ancient land.

Closely associated with its religious contribution was the ethical message southern Syria — Palestine — conveyed. Its people were the first to insist that man is created in the image of God and that each is the brother of every other man under God's fatherhood. This doctrine supplied the basis of the democratic way of life. They were the first to emphasize the supremacy of spiritual values and to believe in the ultimate triumph of the forces of righteousness, and thereby they became the moral teachers of mankind.

Not only did the early Syrians furnish the ancient world with its finest and highest thought but they implemented it with the provision of those simple-looking magic-working signs, called alphabet, through which most of the major literatures of the world are preserved. No invention compares in importance with that of the alphabet, developed and disseminated by the merchants and scribes of ancient Lebanon. It was from these Phoenicians, who called themselves Canaanites, that the Greeks derived their letters, in turn passing them on to the Romans and Slavs, and hence to all the peoples of modern Europe. The Aramaeans likewise borrowed these symbols and passed them on to the Arabians, who transmitted them to the Persians and Indians and other peoples of Asia, as well as to the inhabitants of Africa. Had the people of Syria rendered no other service, this would have been enough to mark them out among the greatest benefactors of humanity.

Their contribution, however, did not stop there. In their narrow land more historical and cultural events, colourful and dynamic, occurred than in perhaps any area of comparable size — events that have made the history of Syria a replica in miniature of the history of most of the civilized world. In the Hellenistic and Roman periods some of the leading thinkers of the classical age were sons of this land, including teachers, historians and Stoic and Neo-Platonic philosophers. One of the greatest schools of Roman law flourished in Beirut, capital of modern Lebanon, and certain of its professors had their legal opinions embedded in the Code of Justinian, rightly considered the greatest gift of Rome to later generations.

Shortly after the spread of Islam, the Syrian capital Damascus became the seat of the illustrious Umayyad empire, whose conquests extended westward into Spain and France and eastward into India and Central Asia — an empire greater than that of Rome at its zenith. During the Abbasid caliphate at Baghdad, which ensued, the Arab world entered upon a period of intellectual activity, involving translation from Greek, that had hardly a parallel in history. Greek philosophy and thought was the most important legacy that the classical world had bequeathed to the medieval. In this process of transmitting Greek science and philosophy, the Christian Syrians took a leading part;

their language Syriac served as a stepping-stone by which Greek learning found its way into the Arabic tongue.

In the Middle Ages Syria was the scene of one of the most sensational dramas in the annals of contact between the Moslem East and the Christian West. From France and Flanders, Germany and Italy, Crusading hordes poured into the maritime plain of Syria and the highlands of Palestine, seeking to recover the Holy Land from its Moslem conquerors. Thus began a movement of far-reaching consequences in both Europe and Asia. The Crusades, however, were but an episode in the long and checquered military history of this land which, because of its position at the gateway of Asia on the crossroads of the nations, has been alternately an international battlefield and a busy thoroughfare of trade. Its unrivalled roster of invaders begins with Sargon and Thutmose, includes among others Alexander and Julius Caesar, and continues through Khalid ibn-al-Walid, Saladin and Baybars down to Napoleon and lesser men of recent decades.

In recent years the people of this country, after an eclipse of centuries under Mamluks and Turks, have provided the Arab East with its intellectual leadership. In the nineteenth century the Syrians, those of Lebanon in particular, were the first to establish vital contacts with the West through education, emigration and travel and thus served as the medium through which European and American influences seeped into the Near East. Their modern colonies in Cairo, Paris, New York, São Paulo and Sydney are living evidence of their industry and adventurousness.

The historical importance of Syria does not arise solely from its original contributions to the higher life of man. It results partly from its strategic position in relation to the three historic continents, Europe, Asia and Africa, and its functioning as a bridge for transmitting cultural influences from its neighbouring civilizations, together with commercial wares. As the core of the Near East, which itself lay at the centre of the ancient world, Syria early became the principal transmitter of culture. On one side stretched the valley of the two rivers, on the other the valley of the one river. No other region can vie in antiquity, activity and continuity with these three, in which we can observe more or less the same peoples for fifty centuries of uninterrupted history. Their civilization has been a going concern since the fourth millennium before Christ. The early culture of Europe was but a pale reflection of this civilization of the eastern Mediterranean.

Even in prehistory Syria looms high in significance, as recent archaeological investigation indicates that it was the probable scene of the first domestication of wheat and the discovery of copper, which combined with the local invention of pottery to effect a change from a nomadic hunting way of life to a sedentary agricultural pattern. This region, therefore, may possibly have experienced settled life in villages and towns before any other place. Earlier still, as we shall see in our third chapter, it may have served as the nursery of one of our direct ancestors, the emerging modern type of man (*Homo sapiens*). But before we consider the prehistoric period, let us inspect the land which was to be the stage for great events.

THE LAND AND CLIMATE

THE name Syria, until the end of the first World War, was primarily geographical, covering the lands between the Taurus and Sinai, the Mediterranean and the desert. The physical unity of this region has usually been reflected in a corresponding cultural unity — for it has constituted a roughly homogeneous area of civilization sharply distinguished from the adjacent areas — but not in ethnic or in political unity. Throughout its long history there have been only occasional brief interludes — notably the later Seleucid kingdom at Antioch from 301 to 141 B.C. and the Umayyad caliphate at Damascus from A.D. 661 to 750 — during which Syria in its entirety stood as an independent sovereign state, and even then the rulers were of Greek or Arabian rather than native Syrian origin. All the rest of the time it was either submerged in a larger whole or partitioned among native or foreign states.

At present, geographical Syria is in a phase of political partition, after emerging four decades ago from a four-hundred-year phase of political submergence in the Ottoman empire. One of the five states now ruling Syrian territory was, until February 1958, called the Republic of Syria, so that at present the name 'Syrian', formerly applied to any inhabitant of the whole of Syria, is restricted, as a political term, to a citizen of that republic, though it is still applied as a linguistic term to any Syriac-speaking individual, or as a religious term to any follower of the old Christian church of Syria.

Other portions of geographical Syria currently form the states of Lebanon, Israel and Jordan (for a short time in 1958 part of the Arab Federation); the region around

5

Antioch and Alexandretta is under Turkish rule. Due account will be taken of all these territories, but the principal focus of this short volume will be the land of Syria in its current narrow political sense. Excellent accounts of Palestine exist, while Lebanon deserves separate attention such as the present author has accorded it in *Lebanon in History*; both will therefore be treated here primarily as they participate in the general history of Syria as a whole.

The ruling feature of Syrian topography is an alternation of lowland and highland zones running roughly parallel to the eastern coast of the Mediterranean, in a generally north–south alignment. Five such longitudinal strips may be delineated.

On the west the first of these strips is the maritime plain stretching along the shore of the eastern Mediterranean from the Gulf of Alexandretta to the Sinai peninsula. Twenty miles wide in Palestine, the plain dwindles at the foot of Mount Lebanon to a mere ribbon less than four miles across. At the mouth of the Dog River (Nahr al-Kalb), north of Beirut, the mountain cliffs plunge straight into the sea, providing a strategic situation for ambushing invading armies. Again at Mount Carmel the promontory juts across the plain, leaving a passage barely a furlong wide. This obstacle deflected inland the great international highway of ancient times, which had its start in Egypt and followed the coast northward.

Most of the maritime plain originated in an uplifting of the old sea floor in the remote past. Its chalk deposits were later overlaid in places by alluvium dragged and spread by the running water from the mountainsides. Around Beirut an overlying sand deposit has been left by the waves of the Mediterranean, which in turn received it from the Nile. Thus formed of beaches and sea-beds and enriched by soil — as well as water — from the adjoining highlands, the plain is everywhere remarkably fertile. In the north it comprises the Nusayri littoral, in the middle the Sahil of Lebanon,

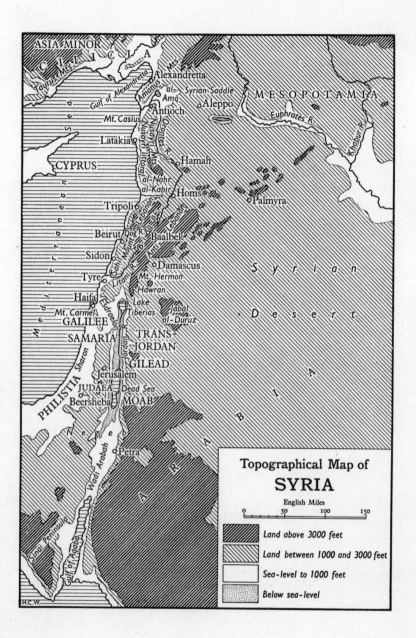

ASIA MINOR

C I L I C I A

Taurus Mts.

Gulf of Alexandretta

Alexandretta

Amanus Mts.

al- Syrian Saddle
Amq

Antioch

Aleppo

MESOPOTAMIA

Euphrates R.

Mt. Casius

Orontes R.

Khabur R.

Latakia

CYPRUS

Hamah

al-Nahr
al-Kabir

Djebel Ansarieh Mts.

Nosri Mts.

Homs

Palmyra

Tripoli

Mediterranean Sea

Beirut

Dog R.

Baalbek

Lebanon

Anti-Lebanon

Sidon

Nahr Mts.

Litani R.

Damascus

Tyre

Mt. Hermon

Haifa

Hawran

Lake
Tiberias

Jabal
al-Duruz

Mt. Carmel

Esdraelon

GALILEE

SAMARIA

Jordan R.

TRANS-
JORDAN

Sharon

GILEAD

Jerusalem

JUDAEA

Dead Sea

Beersheba

MOAB

PHILISTIA

N e g e b

Wadi Arabah

Petra

A

R

A

B

I

A

Syrian

Desert

Sinai Peninsula

Gulf of Aqaba

Topographical Map of
SYRIA

English Miles

0   50   100   150

Land above 3000 feet

Land between 1000 and 3000 feet

Sea-level to 1000 feet

Below sea-level

H.C.W.

and in the south the anciently renowned lowlands of Sharon and Philistia, from which the name Palestine is derived.

The entire coastline is one of the straightest in the world, with no deep estuary or gulf except at Alexandretta, at its northern end. From there to the Egyptian border, a distance of some 440 miles, there is hardly a natural harbour worthy of the name.

Overlooking the Syrian littoral, and often rising abruptly from it, is a line of mountains and plateaus which forms the second of the longitudinal strips. This barrier to communication between the sea and its eastern hinterland is breached at each end, east of Alexandretta and at the isthmus of Suez, and is pierced twice, by the valley of al-Nahr al-Kabir north-east of Tripoli and at the faulted plain of Esdraelon, east of Haifa.

From the Gulf of Alexandretta to the western bend of the Euphrates — a distance of about 100 miles — a grassy, elevated land forms a natural saddle between Mesopotamia and the Mediterranean. On the west a single low pass separates the Taurus mountains of Asia Minor from their Amanus offshoot in Syria. Over this easy saddle have passed countless invasions and migrations, as well as continuous cultural and economic interchanges of major significance.

The Amanus range extends along the Gulf of Alexandretta to the gorge of the Orontes river (al-Asi), and is crossed by roads to Antioch and Aleppo, the chief pass being the celebrated Syrian Gates (Baylan). The range is continued south of the mouth of the Orontes by the bald Mount Casius (al-Aqra), which rises to a height of 4500 feet and stretches down to the vicinity of Latakia (al-Ladhiqiyah), where it becomes the Nusayri range and continues south to the valley of al-Nahr al-Kabir. This chain is of limestone, with basaltic intrusions. It encloses several deep valleys, rugged ravines and steep cliffs which provided the Syrian branch of the Assassins in the Middle Ages with their stronghold, and the schismatic Nusayri Moslems with

9

their retreat. Some of its hills are still crowned with the imposing ruins of ancient Crusader castles. Al-Nahr al-Kabir marks the present political boundary between the republic of Lebanon and Syria.

The western range rises to alpine heights in the Lebanon massif, which extends more than 100 miles to the Litani river north of Tyre. The name Lebanon (Lubnan) comes from a Semitic root meaning 'to be white', and refers to the snow which now caps its peaks for about six months of every year. Mount Lebanon, of which the highest peak rises to over 11,000 feet, shelters the last surviving large grove of ancient cedars, resting in an amphitheatre representing the terminus of a prehistoric local glacier.

The rocks of Lebanon comprise an upper and a lower limestone series with an intermediate sandstone. The lower limestone forms the bottom of the deepest valleys, but elsewhere has been elevated by folding and reaches a height of about 9000 feet at Mount Hermon. On its surface are often found lumps of iron ore, the smelting of which has been carried on in rude furnaces up to recent times and has contributed to making Lebanon as bare of trees as it is. Mixed with clay and irrigated by water, this limestone provides fertile soil for the fruit and mulberry orchards on which much of the prosperity of the maritime plain around Beirut has been based.

The sandstone layers range in thickness from a few hundred to a thousand feet. They are devoid of fossils but have thin strata of lignite which has been mined in modern times to supply fuel for silk factories and for the railway during the first World War. This complex of sands and clays retains the rain water which seeps through the upper limestone and emerges in sparkling gushing springs that bestow their life-giving contents upon the slopes and valleys.

It is the limestone of the upper strata that has, through the ages, dominated the Lebanese scene, forming the summits and giving the landscape a greyish tone. Its erosion has yielded the soil for agriculture and rendered its roads dusty in summer. Its stones have provided building material. Its strata, being generally inclined, bent and twisted — often vertical and seldom horizontal — form a jumble of hills, cliffs and ravines that make communication difficult between one part of the country and another. This is further complicated by the fact that the whole region is broken by faults along which the different tracts of the country have pressed against and crumbled one another as the tormented crust was in ancient times being subjected to compression and folding.

This rugged terrain has, through the ages, provided refuge for communities and individuals with unpopular loyalties and peculiar beliefs, and has also afforded an unusually large proportion of high valleys and fertile tracts which have attracted the more enterprising and freedom-loving of the neighbouring peoples. Maronites, Druzes and Shiites (Matawilah) have taken shelter and maintained their identity in the fastnesses of Mount Lebanon. Armenians and Assyrians, fleeing from Ottoman misrule, were among the latest to find haven there. Christian hermits and anchorites preferred its caves to the pleasures of this world, and ancient robber tribes resorted to them for other reasons. A typical mountain home of lost causes, Mount Lebanon has always been the last part of Syria to succumb to foreign invaders.

Palestine is geologically a southward extension of Lebanon. The western Syrian range is continued, south of the Litani river, by the plateau and highlands of upper Galilee, virtually an outlier of Mount Lebanon ; these reach a height of nearly 4000 feet, the highest in Palestine, before tapering off in the chain of low hills termed lower Galilee. The range then suffers its greatest interruption at the plain of Esdraelon, which intersects the whole of Palestine, dividing the hill country of Galilee in the north from the hill country of Samaria and the rugged limestone tableland of

Judaea to the south. Jerusalem is 2550 feet above sea level. South of it the Judaean plateau rolls down in broad undulations to Beersheba and the barren southern region called the Negeb.

The widespread limestone formations which in Lebanon run out seaward in bold white promontories, hollowed in places by the surf into caves, are represented here by Mount Carmel, which rises 1742 feet above the sea. In its caves were discovered the earliest human skeletons yet found in the Near East. Such caves were inhabited by prehistoric men, who may have enlarged them, and, as in Lebanon, by later refugees from religious or political persecution; other grottoes served as burial places.

The third longitudinal strip in the structure of Syria is a long, narrow trough created by the subsidence of land in a rift between two great linear faults or fractures in the earth's crust in fairly recent geologic times. Starting north of the westward bend of the Orontes in a broad plain called al-Amq, the trough ascends at Hamah to more than 1000 feet above the sea, becomes the fertile Biqa valley between Mount Lebanon and Anti-Lebanon, and continues south through the Jordan to the Dead Sea and thence along Wadi al-Arabah to the Gulf of al-Aqabah, the north-east finger of the Red Sea.

This Biqa-Jordan-Arabah valley is one of the oddest features of the earth's surface. From 3770 feet above sea level near Baalbek, it drops to 685 feet below the sea at Lake Tiberias (the Sea of Galilee), and to 1292 feet below at the Dead Sea. Nowhere else in the world is such a depression visible.

From the Biqa, which varies in breadth from six to ten miles, the Orontes starts on its leisurely course northward and the Litani moves towards the south. Both at last turn abruptly westward, cutting through the western range to cross the maritime plain and reach the sea. The Biqa, drained by these twin streams, comprises the largest and best pastoral areas of all Syria. Blanketed with deposits of recent alluvium and loam, it also provides the most favourable soil for agriculture. Large irrigation works are planned for the Litani, but the Orontes' bed is so low that its water cannot readily be utilized. Therefore water wheels, for raising water to the level of the land, fill Hamah with their perpetual monotonous wailing.

The valley of the Jordan is some sixty-five miles in length and three to fourteen in width. This singular crevasse receives considerable streams from the west watershed — which makes Palestine the overdrained land that it is — and ultimately spreads its water into the bitterest lake in the world. The Dead Sea is unusually saline, with high concentrations of bromine, potash and magnesium chloride. Bituminous limestone and asphalt of excellent quality are found in and around the Dead Sea as well as south-west of Mount Hermon.

The faulted mountains of Lebanon and the long rift valley culminating in the Jordan-Dead Sea depression mark a zone of intense earthquake activity, which has not, however, been limited to the great fracture area. Part of the plateau east of Mount Hermon and south of Damascus is crossed by lines of extinct volcanoes and splotched by old lava fields, while thermal springs are scattered from Palmyra to the Dead Sea.

The history of Syria is more punctuated with earthquakes than its geography with volcanoes. At the northern extremity Antioch was scourged by earthquakes through the ages. In the first six centuries after Christ, they damaged it no less than ten times. The walls of the world-renowned temple of the sun at Baalbek bear scars of seismic disturbances, as do the extant Crusader castles. The sudden collapse of Jericho's walls on the occasion of the Israelite invasion as well as the spectacular destruction of Sodom and Gomorrah, at the south-western extremity of the Dead Sea, point to earthquakes, coupled in the latter instance

13

with fire from burning oil exudations and asphalt springs. The tidal waves which often accompany such disturbances have been especially destructive along the Phoenician coast, with Tyre and Sidon the principal victims. The last severe earthquake in northern Syria occurred in 1822 and converted Aleppo, among other cities, into a heap of ruins, destroying tens of thousands of human lives. The last in Palestine took place in 1837, utterly demolishing Safad.

The eastern range constitutes the fourth strip in the Syrian relief, but is absent north of Homs. The range called Anti-Lebanon rises opposite Mount Lebanon and almost equals it in length and height; it is divided by the plateau and gorge of the Barada river into a northern part, on the western flank of which there is hardly a village, and a southern part which includes Mount Hermon, one of the highest and most majestic peaks of Syria, with many flourishing villages on its western slope. Largely because its rainfall is lower and its vegetation sparser, Anti-Lebanon has a more scattered and less progressive population than that of Mount Lebanon.

Rising in a rich upland valley, the Barada flows east, reclaims for Syria a large portion of what otherwise would have been a desert, and creates Damascus, an oasis outpost of civilization. After irrigating the celebrated orchards called al-Ghutah, the river divides into five channels which serve the streets and homes of the ancient metropolis. The present Damascus water system derives from one installed at the behest of the Umayyad caliphs.

South and east of Damascus the eastern range is represented by the Hawran plateau, predominantly volcanic with basalt rocks and rich soil. To the south rises the mountain called Jabal al-Duruz, the occupation of which by the Druzes is a comparatively recent event, dating from the early eighteenth century. Although it has no trees and very few springs, the Hawran plateau bears abundant wheat and provides good pasture. The soil consists of disintegrated black lava and red loam, rich in plant food and retentive of moisture, overlying the limestone which elsewhere forms the surface rock. The archaeological remains range from great stones erected by primitive men to ruins of Roman and Byzantine roads, aqueducts, reservoirs, buildings and fortifications which testify to its once-thriving condition as a granary of the empire. Today it still provides Palestine and Lebanon with wheat as it did in the days of the Hebrews and the Phoenicians.

South of Hawran, in Transjordan proper, the eastern highlands continue through the hills of Gilead to the high tableland of Moab. East of Petra the sandstone strata attain a height of 4430 feet before merging with the stony desert of Arabia.

The great wasteland called the Syrian Desert is the fifth and last distinct zone in Syrian structure. The desert proper, which is separated from the highlands by a transition zone of steppes, volcanic tracts and sands, is a continuation of the great Arabian Desert, forming a huge triangular bay which separates settled Syria from the river valleys of Iraq. Its maximum width approximates 800 miles. Its nomadic denizens trade with the settled population on both sides, act as middlemen, guides and caravaneers, and in remote times built such cities as Palmyra, which lay on the trans-desert route between Syria and Mesopotamia. Their blood has always been a perennial reservoir of biological vitality to the urban population, supplying it with fresh infusion either through conquest or by peaceful penetration. But normally bedouins resist the temptation to settle down and, in quest of pasture for their flocks, they roam the desert plains, living off the grass which blankets it after every shower of rain. Bedouin hospitality to guests does not imply any corresponding hospitality to innovations. If the mainspring of progress in a settled community lies in the attempt to change and adapt the conditions of life and environment, the secret of survival in a nomadic community consists in accepting those conditions and adapting one's pursuits and attitudes to them.

Several of the streams which trickle down the eastern slopes of the Syrian eastern range are vanquished in the struggle with the desert and disappear into its barren soil. The struggle between the sown and the desert, old as time, is a central fact in the physical geography of that part of the country. The desert, which in many of its aspects resembles the sea, has in its movement through history behaved like a mighty one, endlessly repeating the pattern of ebb and flow. The struggle has its counterpart in the equally ancient conflict between the bedouins, the 'have-not' nomads of the desert, and the settled agriculturists, the 'haves' of the fertile plains. Centuries before and centuries after the Israelites, covetous eyes from the desert turned towards the neighbouring lands 'flowing with milk and honey'.

The ruling feature of Syrian climate is the alternation of a rainy season from mid-November to the end of March and a dry season covering the rest of the year. This is, in general, true of the whole Mediterranean region and is due to its location between two zones sharply contrasted in the amount of precipitation they receive: the dry trade-wind tract of Africa — largely desert — to the south, and Europe with its westerly winds on the north. It is these moisture-bearing westerlies which all the year round bring rain from the Atlantic to middle and northern Europe. They are in winter the prevailing winds in Syria; in summer the heat belt moves northward from the equator, and the country for months approaches the arid conditions of the Sahara. The variability of climate which characterizes the northern United States and is said to promote energy does not obtain anywhere there.

As the prevalent westerlies, at times associated with cyclonic storms, sweep over the Mediterranean they become more filled with moisture. They then encounter Mount Lebanon and the central hilly ridge of Palestine and rise.

In rising the air expands and discharges some of its moisture in the form of rain. The result is that the western slopes of the Syrian highlands annually receive the largest amount of precipitation, which decreases as one goes from west to east and from north to south. Thus Beirut averages about 36 inches of rain a year, Jerusalem about 26 and Damascus only 10. On the whole the Palestine-Lebanon coast receives more than twice as much precipitation as the corresponding coast of southern California.

The mean annual temperature in Beirut is 68° F., but temperatures above 107° and below 30° have been recorded there. Humidity reaches its maximum, strangely enough, in July with an average of 75 per cent, its minimum in December with an average of 60 per cent. In winter the dense, cold, dry anticyclonic influences of Central Asia spread over the eastern plateau region of Syria, giving it frost and snow, a phenomenon hardly ever experienced along the coast. There the temperature is moderated by the influence of the sea, which is warmer in winter and cooler in summer than the land. The mountains prevent the cooling sea breezes from reaching the interior, while dust-laden desert winds cause the summer heat in such cities as Damascus and Aleppo to become intense. Most dreaded of the hot winds from the east or south-east is the simoom, or sirocco, which is particularly oppressive and dry, with a humidity at times under 10 per cent, making it difficult to breathe. It is frequent through spring and autumn, when it often reaches the coast and announces the coming of rain. On the fringe of the desert it is often laden with fine penetrating sand, increasing the discomfort of man and beast.

Much of the rain water percolates through large expanses of limestone rock and is thus lost. Some of it gathers in subterranean channels and gushes out in the form of springs. The prevalence of limestone in Lebanon and Palestine thus introduces another unfavourable factor in addition to the minor one of a shimmering dusty landscape, mentioned above. It restricts the water supply and thus limits human settlement, especially on the slopes of Anti-Lebanon.

Whatever rain-water does not soak through the calcareous layers flows into streams and rivers, which swell into torrents after every heavy downpour, but shrink in the drought of summer to mere trickles or disappear altogether. The rush of water down the highlands, with its concomitant processes of erosion and denudation, has resulted through the ages in rendering barren many once-flourishing tracts of land. The perseverance without major modification of ancient crops, the persistence of tillage methods, and the preservation through the ages of virtually the same seasonal dates for ploughing and harvesting militate against any theory of desiccation through climatic changes. The real causes of decline in land productivity have been the denudation of the hillsides by the running rain water and winds, the failure of certain springs, deforestation and over-grazing which have deprived the loose soil of roots to hold it together, neglect of irrigation works and their destruction by barbarian invaders or attacking nomads, and possibly exhaustion of the soil in some places.

Three contrasting zones of vegetation are found in the Syrian area, in which two distinct floral regions meet: that of the Mediterranean and that of the western Asian steppeland. The position of Mount Lebanon introduces the complicating factor of altitude, making the transition from Mediterranean to continental influences unusually abrupt. Banana plantations, winter sports resorts and desert oases are therefore encountered within a mere sixty miles of the sea. But everywhere the contrast between the landscape in spring, when the foliage is at its best, and in summer, when the increased heat has burned up vegetation, is very striking.

The coastal plain and the lower levels of the western highlands have the ordinary vegetation of the Mediterranean littoral, characterized by evergreen shrubs and quickly flowering, strongly scented spring plants. The main food crops of Western man — wheat, barley and millet, all of which were first domesticated in or near Syria — still flourish, as do onions, garlic, cucumbers and other vegetables known from earliest times. Sugar cane was brought in from farther east by the Arab conquerors. Crops introduced from America in recent centuries include corn (maize), tomatoes, potatoes and tobacco, Latakia tobacco having become famous all over the world.

The ancient drought-resisting fruits — figs, olives, dates and grapes — have similarly been supplemented with banana and citrus trees, which in the absence of summer rains require irrigation. The baking Mediterranean sun, whose relentless rays strike the parched land almost daily throughout the dry season, ripens fruit to perfection. The olive tree in particular demands little and yields much. Its fruit was and is one of the main components in the diet of the lower classes. Olive oil was consumed in place of butter, which is more difficult to preserve, and was used for burning in lamps, for making ointments and perfumes, and for medicinal and ceremonial purposes. The pulpy residue of the fruit was fed to animals, and its stones were crushed and used for fuel. Ever since Noah's dove returned with an olive branch, its leaf has been a symbol of peace and happiness. To the south of Beirut one of the largest olive orchards in the world stretches for miles. Aside from fruit trees, the dominant trees in this littoral zone are the scrub oak, the Mediterranean pine, the beech and the mulberry, the leaves of which have been fed to imported silkworms, making silk manufacture possible. Since the first World War, however, the silk industry has been on the decline, and with it the mulberry orchards.

Along the crests of Mount Lebanon and Anti-Lebanon only such hardy trees as firs, cedars and other conifers are able to survive, constituting the second floral zone. The most magnificent and renowned of these is the cedar of Lebanon, noted for its majesty, strength, durability and suitability for carving. The cedar provided the Phoenicians with the finest of timber for constructing their ships, and was sought by kings from the treeless valleys of the Tigris, Euphrates and Nile. Unfortunately, after centuries of exploitation, culminating in use by the Ottoman Turks for railroad fuel from 1914 to 1918, the cedar survives only in small groves, the best known of which is that above Bisharri, where more than four hundred trees still grow. Some of these are perhaps a thousand years old, and eighty feet tall. One has been adopted as an emblem by the modern Republic of Lebanon.

The third floral zone comprises the canyon-like trough and the plateaus of eastern Syria, where intense heat and scanty rainfall combine to produce a steppe régime in which trees all but disappear, grasses tend to have a seasonal existence, and only coarse shrubs and thorny bushes survive. The Orontes and the Jordan flow in deep beds and are of little use for irrigation. The Hawran and Transjordan plateaus are sufficiently high to condense enough of the remaining westerly moisture to permit pasturage.

Goats and sheep, particularly goats, have furthered the process of erosion by eating up grass and young sprouts on the hillsides, leaving the soil loose and more exposed to the action of running water. Because of the relief of the Lebanon mountains and the over-drainage of the Palestinian highlands, Syria has always had scant natural grazing for cattle and horses, but sheep and goats can find enough forage.

Originally an American wild animal, the horse found its way into eastern Asia in remote prehistoric times and, while still in wild form, made its way as far as Palestine. It was domesticated in early antiquity somewhere east of the Caspian Sea by Indo-European nomads, and then imported into the Near East some two thousand years before Christ. The Hyksos introduced the horse into Syria and Egypt some eighteen centuries before the Christian era. From Syria it was also introduced before the beginning of our era into Arabia where, as the Arabian horse, it has succeeded more than anywhere else in keeping its blood free from admixture.

Like the horse the camel is of American origin and migrated to north-eastern Asia millions of years ago. It gradually made its way to north-western Arabia and on into southern Syria. The first known reference to the domesticated camel in literature is in Judges 6 : 5 (cf. Gen. 34: 64 — in Genesis the author was projecting backwards a condition then existing in his time), describing the Midianite invasion of Palestine in the eleventh century before Christ. Mesolithic drawings depict a small one-humped camel, still the typical Arabian camel of today.

Another animal introduced from arid Asia through Arabia is the ancient breed of broad fat-tailed, long-fleeced sheep, which is still the common type. Syrian draft animals include the donkey and mule, as well as the horse and camel, while domesticated animals comprise — in addition to goats and sheep — cows, dogs and cats.

PREHISTORIC ERAS

JUST as in an iceberg the part visible above the surface of the water is but a small fraction of the huge mass, so in the history of Syria and the Syrians the historic period is a still smaller portion of the whole, dating only from about 3000 B.C., a mere fifty centuries ago. The pre-literary period, for the knowledge of which we have to depend upon archaeological remains rather than written records, goes back through the New Stone Age (Neolithic) to the Old Stone Age (Palaeolithic) tens of thousands of years. Recent excavations in the uninhabited wastes of northern and eastern Syria, the caves of Lebanon, the tells of Palestine and the sand-buried cities of Transjordan leave no doubt that this archaeologically long-neglected and little-known region was much more advanced in the earliest ages than was previously suspected.

Throughout all or most of the early Palaeolithic Age, there were presumably human beings living in Syria, but their bones have not been found. By the end of the early Palaeolithic, however, some 150,000 years ago, man had progressed sufficiently to leave recognizable traces, in the form of stone implements found in cave deposits or scattered over the surface. These tools and weapons consist of roughly chipped or irregularly flaked flints — at first fist hatchets, then scrapers and choppers, and finally hand axes.

The humans who left these stone traces of their existence were presumably a primitive and unspecialized type of white man, whose culture was still undifferentiated. They lived — at least at times — in caves as a measure of protection against rain, wild animals and other enemies. The climate was rainy and tropical, producing luxuriant vegetation in which lived animals now largely extinct, among them early forms of the rhinoceros, the hippopotamus and an elephant-like creature. At this time Europe was suffering from the rigours of the Ice Age, allowing the Near East an earlier start as a human habitat.

The only other surviving traces of early Palaeolithic man are some fragments of charcoal from one of the lowest levels in a Mount Carmel cave. In his slow and arduous ascent from lower mental levels primitive man presumably stumbled by accident upon occasional discoveries which stimulated and developed his dormant inventive faculty. For instance, he must have witnessed, and eventually learned to utilize, fires engendered by lightning and other natural occurrences. Bits of fresh meat, green fruit, edible roots must have fallen accidentally into such fires. The resulting tenderness and improved flavour no doubt invited experimentation on the part of the intellectually alert or curious. He must, too, repeatedly have experienced sparks and even blazes as he chipped or flaked flints and other hard stones. After unguessable generations some genius pondered this phenomenon and, by trial and error, learned how to generate and control it, thus making one of the greatest single advances in the progressive march of mankind. The value of a blaze was gradually realized, not only for preparing new dishes but also as a measure of protection against cold and as a means of warding off wild beasts and driving game out of woods.

The earliest known human skeletal remains in the Near East were found in Palestine, and date from the middle Palaeolithic Age, at least 100,000 years ago. They present an entire series of skeletal material ranging from short, stocky Neanderthal man through progressively higher forms to some Mount Carmel skeletons which show certain anatomical features of *Homo sapiens*. They thus seem to constitute a significant link in the evolution of man and mark Syria as the habitat of an intermediate between the primitive and the modern man.

Man in the middle Palaeolithic still lived in caves and subsisted on plants and animals in their natural condition. Expertly cracked human bones from which the coveted marrow was extracted point to cannibalistic practices. His implements, as before, are irregular flakes and rough chunks of flint which he employed as hand axes, scrapers, choppers and hammers. Social organization was rudimentary, centring on family groups.

This culture developed in a climate which was gradually becoming drier. Animal remains include, in addition to the rhinoceros and hippopotamus, the gazelle, spotted hyena, bear, camel, river hog and deer. Though the weather was warm and dry, permanent rivers still watered the country and some woody or scrubby areas persisted. In the later portion of the middle Palaeolithic a drastic alteration in climatic conditions took place involving heavy rainfall. Another wet period ensued, and lasted for tens of thousands of years, during which the fauna begins to assume a modern aspect. The scanty human traces from this rainy epoch are associated with rock shelters in Lebanon.

Throughout the long span of the late or upper Palaeolithic there is evidence of increased dryness interrupted by one damper interlude; warm and cool Mediterranean climates alternated. The culture is known from recent cave excavations near the Dog River, which have yielded human skeletal remains as well as those of deer, hyenas, rhinoceros, foxes and goats, with gazelle remains assuming a dominant place. While the industry in this epoch does not radically vary from the preceding, the stone implements manifest a tendency to diminish in size, indicating that man had begun to mount his tools in wooden or bone hafts. The wood, being perishable, left no traces, but bones suspected of such use have been discovered.

The Old Stone Age shades off imperceptibly into the New Stone Age, in which man used polished stone implements. The transitional period — termed Mesolithic, or

Middle Stone Age — lasted some six thousand years beginning about 12,000 B.C. Not only did Mesolithic man polish flint, basalt and other stone weapons and tools and thus render them more effective, but for the first time he also exploited the resources of his environment to an appreciable extent. Mesolithic culture in Palestine — called Natufian after a wadi site — is associated with bones of a race smaller in stature than its Palaeolithic predecessors, slender and round-headed, evidently members of the same race to which the Hamites and Semites of later times belonged. Their industry is rich in worked and carved bones and notched arrow-heads.

The discovery of an almost complete skull of a large dog in a cave on Mount Carmel provides the first Syrian evidence of the domestication of animals — another major step in human progress. The dog was domesticated when man was still a food gatherer and hunter whose movements were dictated by those of the wild animals he sought for food. But Syria was the home of several animals adaptable for taming, which led to a life of herding with a more reliable supply of food than hunting. In this pastoral stage man remained a wanderer, but his movements now were governed by his quest of green pastures for his herds. The dog became the guardian of the flocks and the hearth and helped to dispose of offal.

Another innovation, which tended toward a sedentary mode of life and exercised an even more abiding influence on man, was the practice of agriculture, which began in the late Mesolithic or perhaps the early Neolithic period. Wheat and barley grew wild in North Syria and Palestine, and their nutritive value must have been discovered very early. Flint sickles and other implements left by Natufian cave-dwellers in considerable numbers prove that they and their North Syrian contemporaries were among the first in the Near East — and in the world — to till the ground. Agriculture in Syria presumably began before 6000 B.C.

as rude hoe culture, necessitating movement from place to place as the surface soil became exhausted. There is no evidence of agricultural practice by any other people so early in history; early Semitic migrants from Syria, for instance, evidently introduced both wheat and grape culture into Egypt. The principal cereals (wheat, barley and millet), fruits (olives, grapes and figs) and vegetables all were cultivated and improved before recorded history.

With the shift to stock and crop raising, the Mesolithic nomad became a settled villager. Caves and rock shelters in highlands were gradually abandoned in favour of clay huts or mud-brick houses in settlements on plains. Remnants of primitive habitations have been found in the earliest levels of the human occupation of Jericho, dating back to about 5000 B.C. No earlier settlements have been discovered anywhere else, so Jericho has perhaps the longest continuous existence of any city in the world.

Land ownership arose. Fixity of abode led to the accumulation of experience in the form of cultural tradition, and to the transmission of this tradition to subsequent generations. One important result of community life was the strong impetus it gave to the evolution of language, which Mesolithic man elaborated to an astounding degree. A comparison of modern colloquial Arabic, for example, with the reconstructed mother Semitic tongue reveals a continuing process of simplification from the high and remote prehistoric level.

Another relic of the higher life of Mesolithic man is belief in some deity or deities and a crude idea of some life for the departed person after death, as indicated by the presence of food vessels and offerings in burial places. The practice of agriculture and animal husbandry necessitated gods to watch over fields and flocks, instead of the spirits and magic on which hunters relied. Pastoral people were presumably devotees of the moon god, who in a warm country like Syria seemed more kindly disposed than did the sun. With the spread of agriculture, men came to associate growth with sunlight, and the sun began to take precedence over the moon. Besides the worship of the sun goddess, the worship of the Earth-Mother arose. Cultic symbolism and mythology associated with the goddess of fertility, which reached their full bloom later in the Adonis-Ishtar and the Osiris-Isis cycles of Phoenicia and Egypt, have their origins in this period.

Along with the religious growth of Mesolithic man went his artistic evolution. In its earliest manifestations art was closely linked with magic by representing animals to be hunted, by creating amulets of bone and stone for protection against forces man could not control and by making fertility and cult statuettes for use in rituals designed to increase by magic the produce of his herd or crop.

In the New Stone Age, which commenced around 6000 B.C. and lasted about two thousand years, marked advances were made in agriculture, animal breeding, the use of polished stone implements and settled life. This age also saw the invention of pottery and the discovery of metal. Pottery makes its appearance in Palestine in one of the lowest strata of Jericho, and may even have been invented there. Monochrome pottery in North Syria may date from about 5000 B.C. This was followed, after perhaps five centuries, by painted pottery from a mound north-east of Antioch. Prior to the invention of the potter's wheel, which must have antedated 4000 B.C., all pottery was hand-fashioned. The North Syrian ceramic artists were vase painters who evidently emulated the skilled products of basket makers and rug weavers. Technically and artistically their wares, including dishes, bowls, platters, jars and cups, rank among the finest hand-made fabrics of antiquity. They used intricate polychrome geometrical and floral designs which competent judges assert have never been surpassed in beauty. For this painted pottery era the largest number of settlements, the thickest deposits and the highest cultural remains come from North Syria and Mesopotamia, leaving no doubt that the main stream of civilization in western Asia flowed then through that region, leaving all surrounding zones relatively unaffected.

The invention of pottery was certainly a major step in man's cultural progress. Earthenware vessels soon replaced gourds, skins and hollowed-out pieces of stone or wood, enabling man to live some distance from the source of his water supply and — even more important — to store for future use any surplus food, as well as seeds. The food gatherer of the nomadic stage, who had turned food producer in the agricultural stage, now became, in addition, food conserver. This gave him respite from the constant time-consuming search for sustenance, and the resulting leisure was essential to the furtherance of human progress.

The addition of pottery to man's household goods serves incidentally a most useful scientific purpose. Pottery is imperishable, though it may be smashed into innumerable sherds. Its make and decoration reflect the tastes and fashions of the age as women's clothing does in our day; its distribution affords the best index of early trade relations. Therefore its study opens up before the modern scholar one of the widest windows through which he can peep into the obscure realm of the past. Metallurgy provides a later window. With ceramics and metallurgy we pass from prehistory to protohistory.

The actual discovery of metal may have been made in western Asia soon after the invention of pottery, but the supremacy of its first important representative, copper, must have been delayed a thousand years or so. In Syria copper began to be more or less widely used around 4000 B.C., but it did not displace stone as the dominant material for tools and weapons till after 3000 B.C. This millennium, the fourth, may be designated the Chalcolithic (copper-stone) Age; in it copper was utilized by the most progressive communities, but flint remained the principal material. Traces of Chalcolithic culture abound in Ugarit (near Latakia) and other sites in northern Syria and in Palestine. About 3000 B.C. the Copper Age begins, often wrongly designated the Bronze Age. The discovery about 2000 B.C. of ore deposits in Edom, south and east of the Dead Sea, completed the triumph of copper.

In the Chalcolithic as in the Neolithic period, northern Syria remains the main cultural focus of the entire Near East. From Syria the knowledge of copper was disseminated in all directions — to predynastic Egypt, to northern Mesopotamia and to Anatolia. The relics of man in this region indicate that he used first copper, later its harder alloy bronze, for the manufacture of weapons of war before he used it for tools of peaceful pursuit. Tribes or communities employing weapons of such malleable, ductile and tenacious metal obviously enjoyed a preponderant advantage over those employing stone. But the arts of peace benefited equally. The art of building markedly improved. Sizable structures make their appearance. Many Copper Age villages were encircled by a rude wall, for protection against enemies.

In the meantime impetus was given to agriculture and animal husbandry. The ox, sheep and goat, whose domestication began in the Neolithic, were now widely used, as evidenced by their frequent appearance on figurines. The pig was the preferred animal for sacrifice, and the dove was associated with the goddess of fertility. Almost all of the Chalcolithic settlements had their location in river valleys or alluvial plains and depended upon irrigation. In the realm of agriculture the outstanding Chalcolithic achievement thus came to be irrigation culture, involving the cultivation of several varieties of garden vegetables: lettuce, onions, garlic, chick-peas, horse-beans and condiments. This increase in the variety and quantity of available food is reflected in the noticeable rise of the median human stature in the late Chalcolithic. The ethnic composition of the population of the varied settlements, at this period before the arrival of the Semites, is not clear.

Art took a long stride forward when metal became available. Seals, jewelry articles and copper utensils from this period abound and manifest improved artistic quality. Sculpture flourished; mural paintings begin to appear. But it was ceramic decoration which continued to provide the artist with the best opportunity for the exercise of his talent. By the end of the fourth millennium the technique of glaze painting had reached early Minoan Crete and early dynastic Egypt from northern Syria. In a North Syria mound there has been found a hoard of cast copper statuettes, including a god and a goddess of fertility, the earliest known representation of the human form in metal.

The development of metallurgy and ceramics, which featured the late Chalcolithic and the early Copper Ages, gave rise to different trades, increased business relations between villages and towns and resulted in a higher degree of specialization in labour. Populous towns flourished in plains and valleys and in hitherto uninhabitable places. Trade began to assume international proportions. Expansion of commercial and cultural contacts between Syria, on the one hand, and Egypt and Babylonia, on the other, was a factor of primary significance for the further development of all these lands.

Only one great invention was lacking: writing. The first inscribed documents thus far discovered come from Sumer and date from about 3500 B.C. From lower Mesopotamia the art spread into northern Syria. It became well advanced in the early third millennium. With it and with the simultaneous arrival of the Semites, the historic period begins.

THE ANCIENT SEMITES

THE term Semite is derived from the name of Noah's eldest son, Shem, from whom the Semites were formerly assumed to be descended. In modern usage, however, the term is exclusively linguistic; a Semite is one who speaks — or spoke — any of the Semitic family of languages: Akkadian (Assyro-Babylonian), Canaanite (Amoritic and Phoenician), Aramaic (Syriac), Hebrew, Arabic and Ethiopic. Within this family the members manifest striking points of similarity, and as a group differ from other linguistic groups, the Hamitic being the nearest of kin. In all Semitic languages the basic words — such as personal pronouns, nouns denoting blood kinship, numbers and chief members of the body — are strikingly similar.

This linguistic kinship among the Semitic-speaking peoples is their principal but not their only bond. Comparisons of their social institutions, religious beliefs, psychological traits and physical features reveal impressive points of resemblance. The inference is inescapable: their common ancestors must have formed a single people speaking a single language and occupying a single region, presumably the Arabian peninsula. Whenever its population outgrew its meagre resources, the restless, half-starved desert nomads used their greater mobility and endurance to overrun the fertile fields and prosperous towns to the north. The Israelites of the Old Testament were neither the first nor the last Semites to seize and settle upon the tilled lands of Syria.

Such Semitic migrations northward were, indeed, continuous, reaching marked peaks at intervals of about a thousand years. Around 3500 B.C. such a wave spread

north-eastward over Sumeria and all Mesopotamia, pro-
ducing the Akkadians, later called Babylonians. As the
Semitic invaders intermarried with their predecessors on
the Euphrates and Tigris, they learned to build and live in
houses, to plant and irrigate the soil and to read and write.
Subsequent migrations, which went north-westward into
Syria and hence will be considered at greater length,
included the Amorites and Canaanites about 2500 B.C., the
Aramaeans and Hebrews between 1500 and 1200 B.C., the
Nabataeans about 500 B.C., and finally — between A.D. 630
and 650 — the Moslem Arabians, who spread the religion
and culture of Islam west across North Africa to Spain and
east across Persia to India and Central Asia. The modern
Arabians retain the purest Semitic traits, just as Arabic has
preserved the closest kinship to the mother Semitic speech,
of which all the Semitic languages were once dialects.

The first major Semitic people to settle in the Syrian
area was a group whose name for themselves is not known, but
who were called Amorites (westerners) by the Sumerians.
They presumably roamed northward from Arabia with their
flocks and herds about 2500 B.C., spreading out over northern
Syria, the Biqa and upper Mesopotamia in the next four
centuries, and making the transition from pastoral nomadism
to settled farming by the start of the second millennium.
It was during these centuries that Syria, exclusive of a few
pockets inhabited by Hurrians and other non-Semites, was
Semitized — permanently, as it turned out.

The Amorite capital Mari, on the Euphrates below the
mouth of the Khabur, has been excavated, yielding a notable
trove of over 20,000 cuneiform tablets, largely in Akkadian
but with characteristics reflecting the Amoritic speech of
those who wrote them before 1700 B.C. They are royal
archives of administrative and economic purport and mention horse-drawn chariots. Palace excavations have revealed
mural frescoes and bathrooms. The Amorites not only
established this state, called Amurru, and overran all Syria,

but also ruled a large part of Mesopotamia. Of the many local dynasties they set up there, the greatest was that of Babylon, to which belonged the earliest great lawgiver of antiquity, Hammurabi. It was he who conquered Amurru and destroyed Mari, but he did not overthrow the Amorite princes of Syria, at Aleppo, at Byblus, at Harran and elsewhere.

Gradually Amorite power came to focus on central Syria, and its princes made local conquests while seeking to evade or propitiate their two aggressive neighbours — the Hittites to the north and the Egyptians to the south-west. In the fourteenth century B.C. the latter — as revealed by tablets found in Egypt at Tell al-Amarnah — lost interest in Syrian affairs, and the Hittites took over all northern and central Syria, without eliminating the Semitic inhabitants. Meanwhile, the Amorites of Palestine were encountering a new group of Semitic invaders, the Aramaeans and Israelites, who found them in control of strategic sites and hilltops.

The Amorites were tall, powerful men with black beards and prominent noses. They hardened their copper spearheads and knives by hammering, then by alloying with tin to form bronze. Although they left few inscriptions, chiefly names of places and princes, there is no doubt that they worshipped a pantheon including martial and nature gods and a fertility goddess. They set up sacred poles and pillars, built megalithic high places and practised foundation sacrifice and sacrifice of the first-born. These institutions and practices were continued by their kinsmen and successors, the Canaanites or Phoenicians.

The Canaanites and Amorites belonged to the same migration, and thus were ethnically identical until the Canaanites intermarried with the natives of the Syrian littoral and the Amorites with those of the interior. Culturally, the Canaanites came under the influence of Egypt rather than of Mesopotamia, as the Amorites did. Minor differences in religion and dialect gradually developed, but the

33

real distinction remained geographical, as reflected in economic and political contrasts.

The name of the land, Canaan (in Hurrian) or Phoenicia (in Greek), refers to the purple dye which was the distinctive product of the Syrian littoral. This dye was extracted from a small mollusc and painstakingly distilled, and thus was rare and expensive. Purple robes became the mark of royal or pontifical dignity, or of great wealth, and remained so until the fall of the Byzantine empire. A scarlet dye made from insects dried and dissolved in acid was another article of Phoenician commerce, as was glass, at first of Egyptian origin but later of improved local manufacture. Ivories of exquisite workmanship and beauty, dishes and ornaments of silver and of gold, weapons and tools of bronze and of iron, cloth of wool and of linen, pottery turned on wheels and sometimes glazed with tin for special lustre — all these were manufactured by skilled Phoenician craftsmen organized in guilds, and were distributed throughout the Mediterranean by Phoenician merchants.

These craftsmen and merchants occupied a medial position in Canaanite society between an aristocracy of landed nobility and chariot warriors and a working class composed of agricultural serfs, fishermen, sailors and slaves. Canaanite farming utilized tools and methods, including dry-farming and extensive terracing, not very different from those still in use, and produced the same crops : grains, olives, grapes and other fruits, beans and nuts. Domesticated animals included cows, asses, sheep, goats and pigs, as well as dogs. Fish and salt were obtained from the sea, and humble artisans prepared pottery and cloth, buttons and needles, tools and weapons, ornaments and musical instruments for local consumption.

Commercially prosperous and culturally homogeneous, Canaan was never politically unified. The rural population was sparse, with the bulk of the populace crowded into tiny strongly walled towns, each self-sufficient and autonomous.

Certain of these — Aradus, Sidon, Tyre — were twin settlements, one on the mainland, where they traded and farmed, and the other on adjacent islets, to which they retired for defence. Other diminutive city-states lay at the foot of Mount Lebanon — Tripoli, Batrun, Byblus (modern Jubayl), Beirut — and in southern Syria — Acre, Ascalon and Gaza on the coast, Gezer, Jerusalem, Jericho and others inland. Occasionally several of these would form temporary defensive leagues when menaced by invasion, but usually each purchased immunity by payment of tribute, and concentrated on trade rather than on war. Ugarit, near Latakia, and Qadesh, on the Orontes, occasionally assumed an ephemeral leadership before 1400 B.C., and Byblus, Sidon or Tyre at times thereafter, but more often each stood, or fell, alone. Like their Amorite kinsmen they were pinched between Hittites and Egyptians and were attacked by Aramaean and Israelite invaders, as well as by Hyksos and Hurrians, but they maintained their pre-eminence until conquered by Assyria in the eighth pre-Christian century.

The basis of this prolonged prosperity was of course maritime and mercantile. The Phoenicians utilized Lebanese cedar to build ships powered by sails and oars. Their earliest sea routes were coastwise courses to Egypt and the Aegean, but they learned to navigate the open sea by the stars and established well-charted east-west trunk routes which remained their virtual monopoly. They furnished the whole Mediterranean with whatever each district lacked — timber, wheat, olive oil or wine — peddled tunny fish, glass, earthenware and other local products and developed markets for Canaanite cloth and metalwork, pitch and resin, horses and slaves. They distributed gold and incense, perfume and spices from southern Arabia, and brought back to Syria silver, iron, tin and lead from Spain, slaves and brass vessels from Ionia, linen from Egypt and lambs and goats from Arabia. Other items in Phoenician cargoes included the rose, palm, fig, pomegranate, plum and almond, which they disseminated over the whole Mediterranean, and the laurel, oleander, iris, ivy, mint and narcissus, which they introduced into Syria from Greece.

The Phoenicians were the first to venture beyond the Pillars of Hercules (the opposite promontories of the Strait of Gibraltar) into the Atlantic Ocean, though how much of this sea they traversed is not easy to ascertain. They may have reached the Scilly Isles and Cornwall to barter pottery, copper utensils and salt for tin. Their crowning nautical achievement was the clockwise circumnavigation of Africa about 600 B.C. at the direction of the Egyptian Pharaoh Necho, a voyage which required more than two years.

Wherever the Phoenicians went, they built trading factories, which developed into settlements and then into colonies. Especially after the thirteenth and twelfth centuries, when they were squeezed out of central Syria by the Aramaeans and out of southern Syria by the Israelites and Philistines, did the Canaanites turn their energies to overseas expansion. Cyprus and Cilicia, Crete and Samos, Corinth and Thrace, Malta and western Sicily, Sardinia and Corsica, the whole coast of North Africa, eastern and southern Spain — all fell under Phoenician sway. Cadiz in Spain and Utica in Tunisia were founded about 1000 B.C., and the most famous of all, Carthage, about 814. With the decline of Phoenicia, brought on by Greek competition and Assyrian invasion, Carthage took over commercial and political supremacy in the western Mediterranean until its destruction in 146 B.C. by the Romans.

The Phoenicians were the middlemen of the ancient world in intellectual and cultural matters as well as in commerce. The achievements of Egypt and Mesopotamia were carried by Syrians to all the Mediterranean peoples, serving as civilizing influences. The Greeks in particular became their pupils in navigation and colonization and borrowed from them in literature and religion.

First in significance among these borrowings was the alphabet. From a simplified form of Egyptian hieroglyphs presumably developed by uneducated workers in the turquoise mines of Sinai, the Phoenicians of Byblus derived a phonological script which they developed into a consonantal alphabet of twenty-two letters, thus effecting the greatest invention ever made by man. This occurred before 1500 B.C., and short Canaanite inscriptions in this alphabet date from only a century or two later, as do tablets from Ugarit written in a cuneiform version of this alphabet. Several non-alphabetic scripts were also in use in Syria during the second millennium. Such abundance of scripts indicates that the age was one of cultural pluralism and cross-fertilization in which Mesopotamian, Egyptian and Syrian ideas were freely exchanged and blended, though little of the relevant literature — written on perishable papyrus — has survived. Phoenician inscriptions died out by the time of Christ, though its Carthaginian form, Punic, was spoken until the Moslem conquest of North Africa. Meanwhile the Greeks had borrowed the alphabet before 750 B.C., inserted characters for vowels and passed it on to the Romans, through whom and the Slavs it reached all the peoples of Europe. The Aramaeans, too, had modified the Phoenician original before bequeathing it to the Arabs, Indians, Armenians, and other alphabet-using peoples of Asia.

Canaanite literature is known to us from two sources: the Hebrew Scriptures — in which lyrics, maxims and legends were embedded — and the tablets excavated at Ugarit since 1929. This material is mostly ritual and religious, representing an important portion of the lost Canaanite literature and exhibiting close parallels with the Book of Job, the Psalms and other Hebrew pieces from the common Semitic stock.

Basic in the Canaanite religion, as indicated by the meagre literary sources and the recent archaeological discoveries, was the worship of the forces of growth and reproduction, on which depended the very existence of an agricultural and stock-raising community in a land of limited and uncertain rainfall. This is generally true of all ancient Semitic religions. Its main features were mourning for the death of the vegetation deity Baal, rites to enable him to overcome his adversary (the god of death) and thereby to ensure enough rain to produce a new crop, and rejoicing at his resurrection and marriage to the fertility goddess Ishtar.

Associated with the idea of the periodic dying of the vegetation in the summer heat and its revival in spring, was that of the renewed vigour of the sun after its apparent defeat in winter, as embodied in the early Tammuz myth. This deity was called Adonis by the Greeks and afterwards was identified with the Egyptian Osiris. Rites in his honour included sacred prostitution, later commuted to the symbolic shearing off of women's hair, and self-castration, later reduced to circumcision, an ancient Semitic practice which was eventually abandoned by Syrians adopting Christianity. The paternal sky god and maternal earth goddess, with all lesser and localized deities, were honoured with sacrifices, with 'high places' (altars and sacred stones on hilltops), with temples, stone pillars and sacred poles or trees, with magical household images and with other symbols and rites repeatedly denounced by the Hebrew prophets.

Throughout the Amorite and Canaanite period relations between Egypt and Syria remained close. Byblus and other Syrian ports had sent cedar, wine and oils to Egypt even before the Semites had arrived, and had received in exchange gold, metalwork and papyrus. Gradually peaceful commerce led to military invasion as early as the twenty-third century and before 1600 B.C. southern and central Syria as far as Damascus and the Biqa were included in the Egyptian empire, then under Hyksos domination.

The Hyksos were a confused goulash of humanity which included Semitic Amorites and Canaanites as well as non-Semitic Hurrians and Hittites. Equipped with curving iron swords and horse-drawn chariots, they dominated Syria throughout the eighteenth and seventeenth centuries and conquered Egypt about 1730 B.C. They imposed on both countries a military ruling class which concentrated wealth and power in an aristocracy of chariot warriors. But they were not merely crude terrorists. They were expert metallurgists, skilled craftsmen in faience and inlaid bone and ivory, better potters and builders than their predecessors, patrons of surgery and mathematics. Expelled from Egypt about 1580 by Ahmose I, they retired into Syria, organized a federation of Semitic princes and were again defeated at Megiddo (Armageddon) in 1468 by Thutmose III. Thutmose fought continuously and successfully to break their power and reincorporate southern Syria in the Egyptian empire.

Egyptian administration of Syria aimed chiefly at preserving order and maintaining strong hold on the main highways, for which garrisons were used, and at exacting tribute handled by officials resident in key cities and by a network of travelling tax-collectors. The details of internal administration were left to native chieftains, who kept control over their own armed forces. Few Egyptians migrated to Syria, but many Syrian men and girls went to Egypt, taking with them religious ideas, artistic techniques and motifs, and such products as the tasselled lute, embroidered cloths and elegant vases.

One component of the Hyksos horde was the Hurrians (biblical Horites), a still unidentified people neither Semitic nor Indo-European in language. Under Indo-European kings they established, about 1500 B.C., a strong state called Mitanni east of the upper Euphrates, but after two centuries it was divided between the still stronger Hittites of Anatolia and the powerful Assyrians of Mesopotamia.

The Hittites were a mixture of Anatolian aborigines and Indo-European invaders who had overrun them about 2000 B.C. The facial type, represented by prominent nose and receding forehead and chin, was common to the aboriginal Hittites and the Hurrians. It still prevails in eastern Anatolia and among the Armenians and some Jews, and is sometimes erroneously considered Semitic. Hittites destroyed Aleppo about 1600 B.C., and plundered Babylon a few years later, but retired into Anatolia. Their main Syrian drive occurred in the fourteenth century, when Shubbiluliuma subdued and incorporated many Hyksos and Hurrians into his state. He succeeded in expelling the Egyptians, weakened by theological disputes, from their Syrian holdings, and established a stronghold at Carchemish on the Euphrates from which the Hittites dominated northern Syria. When the Hittite empire was overthrown around 1200 B.C. by invaders from the Aegean, petty native states arose in northern Syria, only to fall one by one to the expanding power of Assyria.

Mesopotamian cultural influence in Syria — whether material, like the plough and the wheel, or intellectual, like the measurement of time and of weights — had always surpassed Egyptian. Military incursions, however, from the east had been limited to occasional raids by such Babylonians as Sargon I and Naram-Sin. An Assyrian conquest in 1094 B.C. by Tiglath-pileser I proved to be premature, but Ashur-nasir-pal and his son Shalmaneser II in the ninth century did more permanent damage, which was consummated between 743 and 722 by Tiglath-pileser III and his son Shalmaneser V. Their successors Sargon II, Sennacherib, Esarhaddon and Ashur-bani-pal brought all Syria and Egypt into the Assyrian empire, which itself soon fell before the Chaldaeans (Neo-Babylonians).

As heirs of the Assyrians, the Chaldaeans claimed sway over Syria, but the Phoenician cities were restive. They on the whole preferred Egyptian suzerainty to Mesopotamian. Between 587 and 572 B.C. Nebuchadnezzar subdued these cities, extinguishing the last breath of Phoenician national life, though the Canaanite people kept their individuality

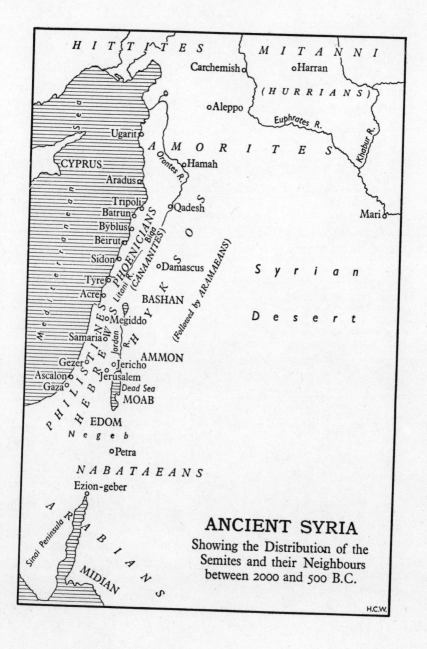

ANCIENT SYRIA

Showing the Distribution of the
Semites and their Neighbours
between 2000 and 500 B.C.

H.C.W.

down to Alexander's conquest in 333 B.C. None of the external invaders had made much of an ethnic impression on the Semitic population, but a new wave of Semitic invaders from Arabia — the Aramaeans and Israelites — had permanently affected the ethnic and cultural patterns of Syria.

The Aramaeans were originally Arabian nomads who had moved northward and settled along the middle Euphrates before 1500 B.C. There they developed a distinct nationality and language, and gradually spread eastward into Mesopotamia and westward throughout Syria. When the Hittites destroyed Mitanni about 1450 B.C., the Aramaeans filled the vacuum, concentrating around Harran in north-eastern Syria and near Carchemish on the Euphrates. They also found their way to Babylonia, with their close kinsmen and fellow-migrants the Chaldaeans. During the fourteenth and thirteenth centuries the Aramaeans multiplied and absorbed the remaining Amorites, Hurrians and Hittites of the Orontes valley. Mount Lebanon blocked this westward movement, and Hittite and Amorite communities continued to flourish there, while on the maritime plain the Canaanite settlements remained untouched. Damascus was peopled by Aramaeans before 1200 B.C. Gradually the newcomers assimilated the culture of the Amorites and Canaanites among whom they settled, but they retained their own language. Similarly in northern Syria they adopted Hittite and Assyrian cultural traits instead of originating a distinctive Aramaean culture.

By 1200 B.C. the Aramaean movement had been concluded, and they were settled in their new homes. The principal Aramaean states were one in north-eastern Syria which endured until wiped out by the Assyrians in the ninth century, a smaller version of this with its centre at Harran, and a south-western kingdom, with its capital first on the Litani and then at Damascus. This state expanded north and east until it encroached on Assyrian territory, and south at the expense of Israel, but did not challenge the Phoenicians on the coastal plain, contenting itself with a firm grip on the Syrian hinterland. One ruler of Damascus, Ben-Hadad, headed a Syrian coalition of Aramaeans, Israelites and Phoenicians which in 853 B.C. blocked an Assyrian invasion. Another, Hazael, repulsed Shalmaneser III twice, in 842 and 838, and brought a large part of Transjordan into his realm, exacting tribute from Israel and Judah. The end was thus delayed for another century, but in 732 Damascus fell, after a long siege, to Tiglath-pileser III. He had the trees of its orchards cut down and its inhabitants deported, ending Aramaean political hegemony for ever.

The peaceful penetration of Aramaean commerce and culture surpassed and survived Aramaean political and military achievements. This culture, which attained its height in the ninth and eighth centuries, is but little appreciated today, even in learned circles. No modern Syrians are conscious of their Aramaean ancestry and heritage, though many Lebanese emphasize their Phoenician origins. Aramaean merchants sent their caravans all over the Fertile Crescent, monopolizing the land trade of Syria as their Phoenician cousins and rivals monopolized the maritime trade, with Damascus as the port of the desert. The Aramaeans traded in purple from Phoenicia, in embroidered cloth, linen, jasper, copper, ebony and ivory.

Aramaean merchants were responsible for spreading their language rapidly and widely. By about 500 B.C. Aramaic, originally the speech of a Syrian mercantile community, had become not only the general language of commerce, culture and government throughout the entire Fertile Crescent, but also the vernacular of its people. Its triumph over its sisters, including Hebrew, was complete. It became the language of Jesus and his people. Nor was the penetration of Aramaic confined to the Semitic area. Under Darius the Great (521–486) it was made the official interprovincial language of the Persian government; this rendered it until Alexander's conquest the lingua franca of an empire extending 'from India to Ethiopia'. Such a triumph on the part of a language not backed up by imperial power has no parallel in history.

With the spread of Aramaic the Phoenician alphabet, which the Aramaeans were the first to adopt, also spread and passed on to other languages in Asia. The Hebrews got their alphabet from Aramaeans between the sixth and fourth centuries. The square characters in which Hebrew Bibles are now printed developed from the Aramaic script. The North Arabians received their alphabet, in which the Koran is written, from the Aramaic used by the Nabataeans. The Armenians, Persians and Indians acquired their alphabets likewise from Aramaean sources.

In the course of time the Aramaic language split into two groups, a western which included biblical Aramaic, Palmyrene, Nabataean and other dialects, and an eastern comprising Mandaic and Syriac. Syriac became, with local variations, the language of the churches of Syria, Lebanon, Palestine and Mesopotamia and was used from the third to the thirteenth centuries, when it was displaced by Arabic. It is still spoken in three villages of Anti-Lebanon, and is still used in the Maronite and other liturgies of the Syrian Christians.

The deity who received the largest measure of Aramaean worship was the storm-god Hadad, also called Rimmon (thunderer). A god of lightning and thunder, Hadad was beneficent when he sent rain which fructified the earth, maleficent when he sent floods. His consort, a goddess of generation, was worshipped under the name Atargatis, a typical Semitic earth-mother, often depicted veiled. Besides this divine couple the Aramaean pantheon comprised an assortment of minor deities, some local in character, others borrowed from neighbours. Chief among these were the sun god and moon god worshipped throughout the Semitic world.

The Hebrews were the fourth major Semitic people —
after the Amorites, Canaanites and Aramaeans — to settle
in Syria. In Amorite days the centre of gravity of Syrian
affairs was in the north, in the Syrian saddle; in Canaanite
times it shifted to the littoral; under the Aramaeans it lay
in the interior; with the Hebrews it moved to the south, to
Palestine. Hebrew entrance into Canaan, as the southern
part of Syria was then called, supposedly came in three ill-
defined movements. The first migration had its start in
Mesopotamia and was roughly contemporaneous with the
eighteenth-century movement which spread the Hyksos and
Hurrians over the eastern shore of the Mediterranean.
The second was connected with the fourteenth-century
Aramaeans. The third, about which much more is known,
was that from Egypt through Sinai and Transjordan under
Moses and Joshua in the late thirteenth century. Canaanites
formed the bulk of the population when the pioneers from
Mesopotamia, the Patriarchs, came. Amorites inhabited
the highlands, which were not thickly occupied by a
sedentary population, thus giving the newcomers an opportunity to settle. Smaller nationalities occupied out-of-the-
way places. With all these the new settlers intermarried.
The result was the Hebrew people, with a composite ethnic
origin consisting of Semitic, Hurrian, Hittite and other
elements.

Syria's power to absorb nomadic or quasi-nomadic intruders by encouraging them to become sedentary, and
inducing them to relinquish their peculiar source of power
— mobility — was once more illustrated in the case of the
Hebrews. Coming as wanderers, adventurers, mercenaries,
footloose soldiers, the future Hebrews gradually settled
among the older and more civilized population, learned
from them how to till the soil, build homes, practise the arts
of peace and, above all, how to read and write. More than
that, the Hebrews gave up their Aramaic dialect and adopted
the Canaanite one. In brief, the early Hebrews became

the heirs of the basic features of Canaanite material culture and the continuers of many Canaanite cults, practices and religious tenets.

The pre-Patriarchal history as sketched by the Hebrew chroniclers is clearly not history. Even from the Patriarchal narrative the kernel of historical fact is not easy to extract. The Abrahamic story may reflect the earliest migration; the Israelite may reflect the second; the Mosaic is definitely historical.

The real history of the Israelites as a people thus begins with the Exodus from Egypt, an event which took place probably between 1234 and 1215. The tribesmen lingered many years in the wilderness of Sinai and the Negeb. Their leader Moses married the daughter of a priest who worshipped Yahweh (Jehovah), a North Arabian desert deity, originally a moon god, whose abode was a tent and whose ritual comprised feasts and sacrifices.

After 1200 B.C. this mixed clan of desert-born nomads appeared from the south-east, the Transjordanian desert, intent upon the occupation of the fertile land. Their number could not have exceeded 7000, and they by-passed the petty kingdoms of Edom, Moab and Ammon. In Canaan (Palestine proper) they succeeded in taking Jericho and other towns, but the so-called Hebrew conquest was largely a slow and peaceful penetration. Having secured a foothold in the cultivated land, the newcomers were reinforced by intermarriage with older elements and by adhesion of their kinsmen who had remained in the land and never migrated to Egypt. As the land was acquired it was parcelled out among the eleven tribes, leaving the priestly tribe of Levi distributed among the others to minister to their religious needs. As a consequence Judah and Benjamin became domiciled in the hilly country around Jerusalem, and the remaining tribes were established in the more fertile plains to the north. The period of settlement lasted roughly a hundred years. It was followed by a long struggle with the Philistines, an Indo-European people from the Aegean who had seized the south Syrian coast and gave the whole country its permanent name, Palestine. From the coastal strip they worked their way inland, capturing many Canaanite towns and disarming the populace. The numerous punitive expeditions and severe exactions of successive Pharaohs had impoverished Syria and weakened its resistance to the onslaught of desert hordes as well as sea rovers. Neither Philistines nor Hebrews would have had such success in gaining a firm foothold in the land, had imperial Egypt still been able to exercise full control over it.

What gave the Philistines special advantage over their enemies was their superiority of armour, which depended upon knowledge of the smelting and use of iron for weapons of defence and offence. Prior to their advent, Hittites had made rare use of iron, but it did not become common in Syria until the arrival of the Philistines, who jealously guarded the secrets of its processing. It was not until the time of David in the tenth century that knowledge of the complicated process was acquired by the Hebrews, as well as by the Phoenicians, who learned to utilize iron in building ships. Thus the greatest Philistine contribution was the raising of Syrian culture from the bronze stage to that of iron. Beyond that and a few traces of material culture in the form of pottery, agricultural implements and iron adzes and chisels, the Philistines left hardly a relic by which they may be remembered. As a foreign community they had no guarantee of permanency except through continued replenishment of their blood by immigration, an impossibility under the then existing conditions. Towards the end of David's reign they tend to disappear as a colony. In due course they were Semitized and assimilated, leaving very little by which their language, religion, architecture and other aspects of their higher life could be determined.

Resistance to the Philistines led to the creation of the Hebrew monarchy, with which the history of the Hebrews as a nation begins. Uniquely among the ancient Semites, the nation developed an intense nationalist fervour, grounded in their exclusive monotheistic religion. Their subsequent history under the kings Saul, David and Solomon, and then in the divided kingdoms of Israel and Judah, is well known through its biblical connections, which have also given each detail exaggerated significance and fascination, but in the history of Syria it becomes increasingly alien and peripheral. Thus for details of the complex events in Palestine, and of the subsequent vicissitudes of the Jews, the reader should refer to any of several excellent narrative treatments. Here that history can only be sketched briefly in its wider Syrian context.

The first Hebrew monarch, anointed about 1020 B.C. by the religious leader Samuel, was Saul, a tall man of weak character and gloomy disposition. He struggled vainly against the Philistines, was defeated and wounded, and finally killed himself. His successor was David (about 1004–963 B.C.), the real founder of the monarchy. He threw off Philistine suzerainty and expanded his kingdom into the largest and most powerful native state that Palestine ever produced. He captured Jerusalem and made this stronghold his capital and a sanctuary of Yahweh worship. Under David, Hebrew commerce with Tyre prospered and literature throve, especially history and the religious poetry called psalms, many of which are ascribed to the king himself.

Under David's son Solomon (about 963–923 B.C.) the Hebrew monarchy engaged in extensive mining and mercantile enterprises and in lavish building, featuring a royal palace and a great temple of Lebanese cedar. Stories of Solomon's splendour and harem are true, those of his might and wisdom are not supported by the historical record. The compulsory labour and excessive expenditure required by his ostentatious public works created popular discontent which under his successor led to the division of the kingdom into the petty states of Israel and Judah. The northern Hebrews were agriculturalists whose religion was basically Canaanite, and who refused to pay heavy taxes for the glory of king and temple at Jerusalem, where Yahweh was worshipped by the southern Hebrews, who were largely pastoralists. The two kingdoms became rivals, at times enemies. Internal disintegration was hastened by frequent dynastic changes and by repeated revolts and intrigues in both states, compounded by intermittent invasions by more powerful neighbours.

Israel was conquered by the Assyrian Sargon II about 721, soon after the destruction of Damascus, and many of its young men were led off into captivity. They were replaced by tribes brought in by the Assyrians from Babylonia, Syria and Arabia. The newcomers mingled with the remaining Israelites to form the Samaritans, whose mixed ethnic origins and religious tenets led to constant clashes with the Jews.

Judah, although sacked about 920 B.C. by the Pharaoh Shishonk, survived Assyrian attacks, including a siege by Sennacherib in 701, but only by becoming a submissive vassal of mighty Nineveh, paying tribute regularly. After the Chaldaean conquest of Nineveh in 612, Judah vacillated between submission to the victors and defiant alliance with Egypt against them. Nebuchadnezzar's decisive triumph over Pharaoh Necho at Carchemish in 605 ended Judah's hopes, and Jerusalem fell in 597. Zedekiah, appointed king by Nebuchadnezzar, yielded to the chronic temptation and revolted, leading to the definitive fall of Jerusalem in 586, its utter destruction by the exasperated Assyrian, and the captivity of its leading inhabitants, estimated at 50,000. Almost every important town in Judah was laid waste and so remained for centuries. By 582 Nebuchadnezzar had completed the reconquest of Judah's neighbours with the exception of Tyre, which held out under siege until 572. All Syria was thenceforth secure in Chaldaean hands.

The culture of the Hebrews was almost entirely derived from their Canaanite precursors, whose very language and alphabet they adopted. From them they learned farming, with the accompanying fertility rites and rituals; Baal ever was a formidable rival of Yahweh among them. From them they borrowed all their ideas of religious art and architecture, of sacred and secular music, of parallelism in poetry. They copied Canaanite costumes and crafts, domestic utensils and burial customs, and every aspect of life, adding little of value even in improvements.

The sole contribution of the Hebrews to the culture of Syria and the world was, however, a stupendous one — the religious and ethical ideas embodied in the superb literary heritage of the Old Testament, which has been transmitted uninterruptedly as a living and dynamic force long after its contemporaneous literatures were lost or discarded as outmoded. The wisdom of Job and Ecclesiastes, the beauty of the Psalms and the Song of Songs, the uncompromising monotheism of Amos and Isaiah, the ethical nobility of Jeremiah and Hosea, the unprecedented objectivity of the anonymous historians who composed the books of Samuel and Kings, the narrative power of Ruth and Esther — all these are universally recognized. Their importance in cultural history rests on their absolute originality, for in each of the aspects mentioned they represented immense spiritual and intellectual advances over anything which preceded them, and, with only rare exceptions, have never been surpassed. During and after the collapse of Israel and Judah, this literature was preserved, culled, edited and commented upon by devoted scholars, surviving to rival the alphabet as Syria's gift to human progress.

The Chaldaean dominion over Syria, though catastrophic, was not enduring. Babylon fell to the Persians and Medes under Cyrus in 538 and any Jews who wished to return to Palestine were permitted to do so. The first group to return rebuilt the Temple at state expense by about 515, and was followed in the fifth century by other groups under Ezra and Nehemiah, who effected religious reforms and strove for ethnic purity. By this time Aramaic had replaced Hebrew as the vernacular and the official language of the Jews, though Hebrew remained the sacred tongue. The Jews who stayed in Babylon and resisted assimilation were the first members of what became known as the Diaspora.

The Persian capture of Babylon signalized more than the destruction of an empire. Then and there one era, the Semitic, ended; another era, the Indo-European, began. The days of Semitic empires were gone, not to return for more than a thousand years. And when they returned, they did so under the auspices of fresh representatives — the Arabians, who had played no important rôle in ancient international affairs. The Persians, who ushered in the Indo-European era, belonged to the Indo-Iranian branch of the family. In their mastery over the Semitic world they were succeeded by Macedonians, Romans and Byzantines, all of whom were Indo-Europeans. The petty states of Syria and Palestine now became part of a great empire, one of the largest of antiquity. Within a quarter of a century after its birth this empire was to comprise the whole civilized world from Egypt and the Ionian cities in Asia Minor to the Punjab in India and then to begin casting covetous eyes across the Hellespont into the only civilized part of Europe. The far-flung parts of the empire were brought together by better roads than had ever existed, by a uniform stamped coinage and by an official language, Aramaic. Syria, Palestine and Cyprus formed a trans-Euphrates satrapy or province, of which Damascus was the chief city.

The Persians used Phoenician ships in the conquest of Egypt by Cambyses (529–521) and in the attack on Greece under Xerxes (485–465). The Phoenicians evidently welcomed an opportunity to deal a blow to their ancient maritime rivals and furnished two hundred and seven ships. In digging the canal through the isthmus to avoid the storms around Mount Athos, Phoenician engineering skill showed its excellence. In the naval battle of Salamis (480) almost the entire fleet was destroyed. The Phoenician cities began to flourish again as centres of international trade. Aradus, Byblus, Sidon and Tyre were allowed local autonomy. In the fourth century these Phoenician city-states were federated with one another and a newly created city, Tripoli, was made the seat of the federal institutions. Originally consisting of three separate settlements for representatives of Tyre, Sidon and Aradus, the city of Tripoli coalesced into one about 359 B.C., serving as regional capital and meeting-place of the Phoenician common assembly.

A revolt at Sidon in 351 spread to the rest of Phoenicia, but Sidon was burned by the Persians and the other cities capitulated. Nevertheless, Persian power was clearly ebbing, while its cultural influence left little impress except for a tendency to dualism in religion. The whole Persian period is one of the most obscure in the entire history of Syria, but certainly its civilization continued to be broadly Semitic, increasingly modified by Greek influences, as manifested in silver coins and Attic sculpture and earthenware. In the seventh century Phoenicia was still influencing Greece; in the sixth there was a rough balance; in the fifth Phoenicia was definitely on the receiving end, with Greek trading settlements appearing in Syria. For at least a century before the Macedonian conquest the coastal cities were sprinkled with Greek merchants and craftsmen.

THE HELLENISTIC AGE

The gradual infiltration of Greek commercial and cultural influences into Syria was suddenly accelerated and intensified by its military conquest under the energetic and illustrious Macedonian known to us as Alexander the Great, and to his oriental subjects as Iskandar dhu-al-Qarnayn (the two-horned). After liberating the Greek cities of Asia Minor from Persian rule, his skilled and disciplined forces defeated the numerically superior Persian army at Issus in 333 B.C. To commemorate this decisive victory, the city of Alexandretta (Iskenderun, in the part of Syria now in Turkish hands) was founded near the site.

The Syrian satrapy lay defenceless before Alexander, who sent a cavalry detachment up the Orontes valley to occupy Damascus while he himself followed the coastal route and received the submission of Aradus, Byblus, Sidon and other ports. Only Tyre held out, but the Greeks built a wide mole out to the island stronghold and, after a seven-months' siege, captured it, hanging its leaders and selling about 30,000 of its inhabitants into slavery. After thus extinguishing the last spark of Phoenician spirit, Alexander repeated the lesson with the last of the Philistine cities, Gaza, overpowering its garrison after a heroic but futile resistance lasting two months. Its population, too, was sold into slavery, and enormous stores of the spices for which it was a celebrated depot were captured.

With Alexander's further conquests — in Egypt, where he founded Alexandria and accepted divine honours; in Mesopotamia, after crossing the Euphrates and founding al-Raqqah; in Persia, where the Achamaenid capitals of Susa and Persepolis were sacked; in Media, Parthia, Bactria and India, where his weary troops finally insisted on turning back — we are not concerned. He did not return to Syria due to his death at Babylon in 323, but his political and cultural legacy altered Syrian history for centuries to come. He had sought fervently to fuse Greek and oriental ideas and institutions, by intermarriage, by adopting local garb and customs, and — most importantly — by planting Greek colonies in existing or newly founded cities wherever he passed. These cities served the triple purpose of providing settlements for his discharged warriors, forming a chain of military posts on the lines of communication and creating centres for radiating Hellenic cultural influence. Greek soon became the language of learning, though Aramaean remained the language of commerce and both were used in political administration.

The hastily assembled far-flung Macedonian empire fell to pieces at the death of its founder. His generals scrambled for its choicest provinces, for which they waged bloody and protracted wars. Out of the chaos four generals emerged at the head of four states: Ptolemy in Egypt, Seleucus in the satrapy of Babylonia, Antigonus in Asia Minor and Antipater in Macedonia. Syria, including Palestine, at first fell to Antigonus, but in 312 B.C. Ptolemy — the shrewdest of the four — and Seleucus — the ablest — combined to defeat him at Gaza. The victors divided Syria between them, with Ptolemy receiving Palestine and Seleucus seizing northern and eastern Syria, to which he made good his claim by participating in another victory over Antigonus in 301. The year 312, however, is reckoned as marking the birth of the Syrian monarchy and as the starting-point of the Seleucid era, the standard calendar of which was a notable Seleucid achievement.

The boundary between the Ptolemaic and Seleucid territories fluctuated violently and constantly, as did the extent of the domains ruled from the newly established capital at Antioch on the lower Orontes. By 280 Seleucus I, surnamed Nicator (victor), had expanded his realm as far as the Oxus and the Indus, making it for a time much the most extensive and powerful of all the states which arose from the fragments of Alexander's ephemeral empire. While seeking to add Macedonia to his holdings, he was assassinated there in 280.

The most enduring accomplishment of Seleucus I, however, was not his territorial conquests, but the Greek cities he had founded in an effort to further the Hellenization policy projected by Alexander. These numbered over thirty, of which the most important inside Syria were the political and cultural capital Antioch, the military base and treasury at Apamea on the middle Orontes, and the port of Latakia (Laodicea). All sites for new cities were chosen with care, at strategic spots which were both readily accessible and yet easily defended. In many cases native hamlets or fortresses were transformed into Greco-Macedonian cities, both by Seleucus and his successors in the north, and by the Egyptian Ptolemies in the south. Old towns with Semitic names, which were recolonized and renamed, included Acre (Ptolemais), Beth-shean (Scythopolis), Hamah (Epiphania), Shayzar (Larissa) and Aleppo (Beroea). None of the new names survived, except Tripoli. In these recolonized cities the native element was allowed a larger place than in the new settlements, and in consequence the colonists themselves often went native, so that in due course these cities shed their thin veneer of Hellenism along with the Greek nomenclature and reasserted their Semitic character. Likewise most districts, mountains and rivers which were given Greek names eventually reverted to Semitic forms.

The new Greek city-colonies were laid out according to a preconceived plan characterized by straight streets intersecting at right angles, and were provided with forums, theatres, gymnasiums, baths and other institutions. In them the constitutional form of the Greek city-state was maintained with ample provision for the self-realization of the citizen as an integral part of the community. In all this the new settlements differed from the old Semitic ones, which were usually built around a fortress, a spring or a shrine as a nucleus, grew without plan and had no channels for a democratic way of life to find expression. The colonists were primarily Greek and Macedonian soldiers settled by royal decree. Wives were obtained partly from the native stock. Indigenous and alien civilians, attracted by opportunities to prosper, thronged to these settlements. In time half-breeds and natives who had put on the externals of Hellenism were added to the colonial population, which then came to comprise traders, artists, scholars and slaves. Syria now had more cities than ever before.

The empire built by Seleucus I was all but lost under his successors. Egyptian invasion, Parthian rebellion, Anatolian secession and other disasters sapped the strength of the Seleucid state, so that it had lost much of its territory and brilliance by 223 B.C., when Antiochus III became king and undertook to restore them. Antiochus first reconquered the Iranian territory as far as Bactria and India, and then in 198 defeated the Egyptian forces and recovered the amputated southern part of Syria. In this victory he used elephants, of which he had brought a fresh supply from India. By twenty years of incessant fighting Antiochus III had won back almost all that his predecessors had lost, and had earned the epithet the Great.

At this time an embassy from Rome appeared in his court to warn him to keep hands off Egypt. This is the first communication we hear of between Rome and Antioch; it marks a new era in ancient international affairs. It was then that Hannibal sought asylum in Syria and urged Antiochus to invade Italy. Antiochus was not fully conscious of the might of the new giant looming in the west. He ventured to strike a blow for Greece, where the Romans were penetrating, and there he met defeat at their hands at Thermopylae (191 B.C.). In the following year he suffered another defeat from the Romans near Magnesia, in western Asia Minor, and in 188 was forced to cede to them all his dominions beyond the Taurus and pay a heavy war indemnity. Asia Minor with its land trade routes and direct access to Greek civilization was permanently lost.

The ignominious peace and heavy tribute left Syria in a feeble condition, but by 169 B.C. Antiochus IV was strong enough to defeat the Egyptian army, capture Ptolemy VI and occupy lower Egypt. Only Alexandria refused to submit and was subjected to a siege. This was soon raised, however, under pressure from Rome, to whom Antiochus was still paying instalments of the war indemnity. The Syrian conqueror evacuated the land and returned home.

While Rome could circumscribe Antiochus's military activity, it certainly could not check his missionary activity as a champion of Hellenism. In this he was following the traditional policy of the Seleucid house, which considered Hellenism the common denominator on which all their subjects should meet. But Antiochus went too far. He proclaimed his own divinity, which was acceptable to most of his Syrian subjects, but not to some of the Jews. Although the rich and the aristocrats of Jerusalem had responded favourably to Hellenization, adopting the Greek language and customs and even garb, the fundamentalists and nationalists were united in their determined opposition to everything Greek, and especially to mongrelization of their rigid monotheism and defilement of their Temple.

In 168 B.C. a revolt broke out in Judaea under the leadership of one Judas, later called Maccabeus. At first the uprising was directed more against the upper class, who exploited the masses, than against the central government. Judas with his brothers organized guerrilla bands which operated in the hills and avoided pitched battles with the royal forces. At length Jerusalem was captured, the Temple was cleansed and the daily sacrifice was restored. Though of a religious character at the outset, the movement developed into a national revolt aimed at liberating the land. The clash was not only with the Syrian forces but also between nationalist fundamentalists who were unwavering in their devotion to Hebraism and adherents to the new culture who constituted the Hellenistic or Reform party. In both conflicts victory went to the Maccabean side. In 141 B.C. Judas's brother Simon was elected high priest and ruler, and Jewish independence was recognized by the Seleucid king, Demetrius II. A new Jewish commonwealth was born, lasting until the advent of the Romans eighty years later. The Maccabees forcibly Judaized the Aramaic-speaking pagan Arabs (Ituraeans) of Galilee and the Idumaeans of southern Judaea by offering them a choice between expulsion and circumcision. The latter was preferred by the majority.

The Jews were not the only nation to take advantage of Seleucid weakness. Parthia, Bactria and adjoining lands succeeded in reasserting their independence. Arab dynasties were established at Edessa, at Palmyra, at Homs and in the Biqa, reducing the incompetent successors of Antiochus IV from an imperial house to rulers of a local state in northern Syria. The entire century between his death in 164 and the Roman conquest in 64 B.C. presents a confused picture of native revolts, internal dissension, family quarrels and steady loss of territory.

Among the Arabians, the Nabataeans, established south of the Dead Sea at Petra, were now becoming a considerable power. They first appear early in the sixth pre-Christian century as nomadic tribes in the desert east of what is today Transjordan and was then the Aramaean states of Edom and Moab. In 400, while Syria was under Persian rule, they were still mostly nomads, living in tents, speaking Arabic, abhorring wine and uninterested in agriculture. In the following century they abandoned the pastoral way of life in favour of agriculture and trade, gradually evolving into a highly organized, culturally advanced, progressive and opulent society. Theirs was another case illustrating an ever-recurring theme of ancient Near Eastern history — the theme of herders becoming tillers and then traders in lands deficient in resources but favourably located for caravan commerce. In 312 B.C. they repulsed Antigonus's attacks against Petra which, as the only town between the Jordan and Hejaz with abundant pure water, they had developed into a strongly fortified caravan station at the junction of incense and spice routes. From Petra they extended their sway northward, rebuilding and resettling old Aramaean cities, erecting posts to guard the caravan routes to Gaza and Damascus, exploiting the mineral resources and using their skill in hydraulic engineering to irrigate and cultivate more of the desert margin than any other Arabian people before or after.

Little is heard of Nabataea in the third century while its settlers were developing their potentialities. Early in the second it emerged as a force to be reckoned with in Near Eastern politics, although it was for a time under Ptolemaic influence. In 169 B.C. a series of definitely known Nabataean kings commenced with Harithath I, who figured as an ally of the Maccabees against the Seleucid kings of Syria. Later the two houses became rivals. In 96 B.C. Harithath II rushed to the aid of Gaza, besieged by the Maccabean Alexander Jannaeus. A few years later the Nabataean king Obidath I defeated Jannaeus in a pivotal battle fought on the eastern shore of the Sea of Galilee and opened the way for the occupation of south-eastern Syria, now the Hawran plateau and Jabal al-Duruz. Taking advantage of the decline of their Seleucid and Ptolemaic neighbours, Obidath and his successor Harithath III continued to push the Arabian frontier northward until the Romans appeared on the scene.

This Harithath, whose enthusiastic response to Hellenistic civilization earned him the epithet Philhellene, was the real founder of Nabataean power and the first to strike Nabataean coinage. He repeatedly defeated the Judaean army and laid siege to Jerusalem. In response to an invitation from Damascus he installed himself in 85 B.C. as the master of that Seleucid city and of the rich plain dominated by it. The invitation was prompted by Damascene hatred for the Ituraean ruler of the Biqa, who had devastated the fields of Byblus and Beirut and aspired to the rule of all Syria. Twelve years later Harithath repulsed an attack by Pompey, the first direct Nabataean contact with Rome. The later history of Nabataea is linked with that of Roman Syria and belongs to the next chapter, but its main lines were already well established.

Arabic in speech, Aramaic in writing, Semitic in religion, Hellenistic in art and architecture, the Nabataean culture was synthetic, superficially Hellenic but basically Arabian, and so it remained. Petra, carved from the living multi-coloured sandstone in a unique application of art to nature, began to take on the aspect of a typically Hellenistic city, with a beautiful main street and several religious and public buildings. Inspired by Greek models, Nabataean artisans introduced a new type of pottery which stands out among the finest produced in southern Syria. Remains of cups, saucers, dishes, jugs and bowls are of amazing eggshell thinness and superior workmanship. The clay used is reddish buff, the designs usually stylized floral or leaf patterns. The prevalence of grapes and vine leaves in ceramic and architectural decoration is another indication that the earlier abstinence from wine was no longer practised.

With their proficiency in ceramics, architecture and hydraulic engineering the Nabataeans combined exceptional merchandising skill. Petran commerce penetrated as far as Italy and the Persian Gulf, and is even attested by Chinese records of traffic in raw silk. Myrrh, spices and frankincense from southern Arabia, rich silk fabrics from Damascus and Gaza, henna from Ascalon, glassware and purple from Sidon and Tyre and pearls from the Persian Gulf constituted the principal commodities. The native produce of Nabataea comprised gold, silver and sesame oil and probably asphalt and other remunerative minerals from the shores of the Dead Sea. Greek and Roman imports were brought in Attic jars, fragments of which can still be found around Petra. Nabataean forces protected the caravan routes and collected taxes on goods in transit. Presumably the merchants spoke not only Arabic and Aramaic but Greek and even Latin. A distinctive Nabataean script gradually differentiated itself from the Aramaic and eventually became in turn the source of the Arabic alphabet.

Nabataean religion was of the common Semitic type based on agricultural fertility rites. It preserved elements of the old worship associated with high places and standing stones. At the head of the pantheon stood the sun god Dushara, who was worshipped in the form of an unhewn black stone or obelisk. Associated with him was the moon goddess Allat, chief deity of Arabia. The Aramaean goddess Atargatis became the Nabataean goddess of grain, foliage, fruit and fish. Other deities also correspond to those of Syria and of Arabia. Serpent worship formed a part of this religion. As Hellenistic ways of thought gained favour, these old Semitic deities took on Greek guise, Dushara being equated with Dionysus. Further research would probably reveal a larger measure of Nabataean influence over infant Christianity and Islam than has generally been realized.

The delineation of Nabataean national character in Strabo and Diodorus is doubtless exaggerated but must be basically correct. The general picture is that of a sensible, acquisitive, orderly, democratic people absorbed in trade and agriculture. The society had few slaves and no paupers. The king was so close to his subjects that he often rendered an account of his kingship to the popular assembly.

While Jews and Arabs were troubling the southern and eastern frontiers of Seleucid Syria, the Phoenician ports were regaining their autonomy in the west and a new power was rising to the north. King Tigranes of Armenia overran

Mesopotamia, then under Parthian rule, and by 85 B.C. was attacking Cilicia and northern Syria. Worn out by civil wars and dynastic feuds, the Syrians were neither able nor eager to offer resistance, and even the Greek cities acquiesced in the new rule. In their southward drive the Armenians reached Acre and thus threatened both the Jewish kingdom and Egypt, where the Ptolemaic house was tottering, but in 69 B.C. the Romans forced their withdrawal from all Syria. Pompey's victories in Asia Minor over Mithradates of Pontus left Syria open to Roman occupation, ending the last throes of its once-glorious Seleucid period.

The Hellenistic civilization enjoyed a far longer span of life in Syria than did Greek political dominance, surviving for nearly a thousand years under Seleucids, Romans and Byzantines, and colouring the Arab civilization which replaced it in the seventh century of the Christian era. Hellenistic culture was synthetic and eclectic, in contrast to the pure Hellenic culture of Greece, and achieved supremacy not only in Syria but throughout south-western Asia and Egypt. Naturally different parts of Syria responded in differing measure to Hellenistic stimuli. In the north native deities were identified with Greek gods and rechristened, Baal becoming Zeus Olympus. A shrine south of Antioch was given the name of Daphne, the nymph beloved by Apollo and metamorphosed into a laurel tree. Pilgrims flocked from all over Syria to the sanctuary of Apollo there, making it a notorious centre of licentiousness. In fact, northern Syria became a second Macedonia, where the intrusive Greek element made itself thoroughly at home.

The Phoenician cities had already had contacts with the Greek world for several centuries and had no hesitancy in adopting the new synthesis. The Hellenism that developed in Phoenician Syria was more vigorous and productive than that of Aramaean Syria and exhibited none of the internal stresses which characterized contemporary Jewish society. Greek philosophy and literature were assiduously cultivated there, no less than in Greek cities such as Antioch. Farther south, Ascalon was a centre of Hellenistic culture, but most of the other coastal cities of Palestine stood desolate, ruined by the militant Maccabean Jews, who also chastised the pro-Hellenes in their own midst and in Samaria and Galilee.

Despite the general recognition of the superiority of Greek literature and civilization, the many educated Syrians who studied Greek and wrote in it produced little of lasting value. Aramaic persisted throughout as the vernacular of the people, who remained Semitic in their customs and manner of living. Basically they were no more Hellenized than modern Syrians were Frenchified. What the introduction of Greek thought did do was to disrupt the purely Semitic political and intellectual structure and to open the door for subsequent Romanizing influences. A thousand years had to pass before a reintegration was possible. Nor has Aramaic literature of Seleucid Syria left any remains, as indigenous literary activity apparently shrank to almost nothing, out of a sense of inferiority. Presumably some was written but did not survive. Certain Hebrew works would have met the same fate had they not found a Greek translator and been accepted among the Apocrypha. One of our main sources of knowledge of this era, 1 Maccabees, was evidently written between 105 and 63 B.C. and translated into Greek from a Hebrew original. Two Hebrew works of the Seleucid era worked their way into the canon: Ecclesiastes, written about 200 B.C. by an aristocratic Hellenized Jew, and Daniel, composed in the second pre-Christian century. Of the two, Ecclesiastes has much the closer affinity with Greek thought.

No part of the Seleucid empire developed into a real centre of artistic, literary or scientific creativeness. The kings were never munificent patrons of learning, though they established libraries in the capitals; Antioch had an outstanding one. Considering the improvement in communication and the spread of a common civilization with a common speech, learning would have flourished more had it received royal encouragement. Hellenistic Syria produced a couple of historian geographers, a few astronomers, a limited number of poets none of whom was of first rank, and a remarkable number of philosophers mainly of the Stoic school. Almost all belonged to the second or early first century before Christ. Stoicism from the outset established close connection with the Semitic conception of life and remained throughout its career congenial to the Semitized Greeks as well as to the Hellenized Semites. In its stress on brotherhood and a world state, virtue and ethical living, and in considering all that had to do with the body — strength and weakness, health and sickness, wealth and poverty — as a matter of indifference, this philosophy was in a sense a precursor of Christianity.

The political institutions of the Seleucid realm were a strange mixture of Greco-Macedonian and Syro-Persian elements, among which the latter predominated. At the head of the state stood the king with absolute power. In fact he was the state. All authority stemmed from him. He appointed and dismissed officials at his pleasure. His rule was personal and dynastic based on the right of conquest and succession. He was surrounded by a divine halo, a heritage from Alexander and the oriental monarchs. The divine descent of the founder of the house was proclaimed early in his career by an oracle and was generally accepted. The native Semitic population maintained an attitude which may best be described as passive acquiescence.

The régime of the palace, with its display of crimson and gold and the conspicuousness of its chamberlains and eunuchs, was more oriental than occidental. On state occasions the monarch wore on his head a diadem, symbol of his royalty. The signet ring also served as emblem of royalty. The monarch's dress remained the old national garb of Macedonia but glorified and made of purple cloth, with all its priestly and regal associations. Splendid banquets with lavish gifts and prodigal displays of wealth were, together with hunting and horsemanship, the chief recreation of the king and his court, comprised of the Macedonian nobility and the new official class.

The highest office was that of 'minister for affairs', a continuation of the Persian office of vizir. The hierarchy included the head of the royal chancery, the finance minister, the financial secretary, the quartermaster and the chief physician. In the provinces the officials were satraps, district governors, secretaries and overseers of taxes. The ministry of finance was an especially coveted office. In general, the Seleucids and Ptolemies were monogamous but kept mistresses. Members of both houses practised sister marriage, as the Pharaohs and Persian kings had done. Members of the royal family and of the official corps had a plethora of slaves. Hellenistic society everywhere was poor in machines, rich in slaves.

The Seleucid army, which in its early stages consisted of all the male Macedonians and Greeks in the realm, was influential in state affairs, with the cavalry ranking higher and receiving more pay than the infantry. Like the navy, the army was the king's, and provided a principal means by which men could rise to power. Its nucleus was the phalanx, armed with swords and twenty-one-foot-long spears, and protected by helmets and shields. The missile shooters consisted of archers, slingers and javelineers drawn from the non-Hellenic element of the population. The artillery of the Hellenistic kings, including catapults, opened a new chapter in the history of siegecraft and provoked a corresponding improvement in the art of city fortification. Persian and Kurdish bowmen and slingers, Median cavalry and Arabian archers mounted on dromedaries fought alongside Greeks and Syrians.

The camel and horse as instruments of warfare had been known in south-western Asia for centuries, but the elephant was a new feature of the Seleucid army and appears as an emblem on their coins. The Syrian kings alone could procure elephants from India, and kept about 500 in a training depot at Apamea. In battle an Indian mahout straddled the neck of the elephant, which carried a wooden tower with four fighting men. The animals were used not only against enemy elephants (the Ptolemies used elephants from Africa), but as a screen against cavalry and to break into fortified positions. In 163 B.C. the Romans sent a mission to destroy the war elephants of Syria, virtually ending the only period in history in which this animal played an important part in warfare outside India.

The same Roman mission which destroyed the war elephants was charged with burning the Seleucid fleet, which had been increased beyond the number allowed to Antiochus III in the treaty of 188. While the fleet played no decisive rôle in any of the recorded battles, yet it must have had enough nuisance value to necessitate inclusion in the treaty of a clause limiting the number of its units and confining its sphere of activity to Asiatic waters. A small part of it was evidently maintained in the Persian Gulf. On the whole, the function of the navy was to support the army and to protect military transports. It was no doubt manned mostly by Phoenicians. The ships were quinqueremes, having a single row of oars with five men to each oar. They could be used for ramming, a practice in which the Phoenicians excelled.

The unity of the Seleucid empire found expression in the uniformity of its military organization and in the administrative system of the provinces inherited in large part from the Persians. Of the local provincial government not much is known, but it is evident that the old governmental machinery was maintained. The administrative division kept its Persian name, satrapy, and was subdivided into districts for administrative purposes. The royal mint was, of course, at Antioch, but provincial mints existed at Tyre, Sidon, Aradus and other important cities. The towns were required to pay taxes and obey occasional royal ordinances, but were allowed to administer their own internal affairs and even to control neighbouring territories.

The native peasantry lived in villages that maintained their status and way of life unmindful of dynastic changes. The land they cultivated was mostly the king's or some landowner's and the tenants were bought and sold with it as serfs. In rural districts the Seleucids continued the practice customary in south-western Asia of collecting tithes, one-tenth of the harvest. From sporadic references it would seem that the tax was imposed not on the individual but on the community. A large part of it was paid in kind in the name of the city, people or tribe by the chief or high priest. Royal revenues were also derived from a poll tax and a tax on salt, while mines, quarries, forests and fisheries were probably owned and operated by the crown.

The trade of Syria on both the domestic and foreign levels was of great consequence to the kingdom and to its population. The Seleucid policy seems to have been first to attract to their country Arabian, Indian and Central Asian merchandise for local consumption and for transit, and secondly to promote Syrian commercial relations with the West, especially the Greco-Roman world. In bidding for transit trade Egypt was the rival of Syria. The unceasing military conflicts between Seleucids and Ptolemies, therefore, had economic as well as political bases.

During the period when southern Syria was a part of the Ptolemaic domain, the Seleucids received their chief supply of Arabian and Indian merchandise by way of the Persian Gulf. This merchandise consisted of myrrh, frankincense and other aromatics, which burned on every altar in the Hellenistic world. Cinnamon was another prized tropical product. These commodities were partly consumed in Syria and partly re-exported westward. Seleucid trade with the West followed land as well as sea routes and contributed no small share to the prosperity of Syria. It consisted of agricultural and industrial products of Syria as well as of goods in transit from lands east of it. An important component of this trade was the slave traffic, which was most active at this time, with the Seleucids more interested in it than the Ptolemies. War supplied the slave market with prisoners, and piracy supplied it with victims of kidnapping. Throughout the third and second centuries a steady flow of slaves moved from Syria and neighbouring lands into the cities of Greece. Slaves were in demand as domestic servants and as labourers in mines, construction and public works.

In this commercial renaissance of Seleucid Syria the Jews seem to have played no more conspicuous a part than in any earlier period. In the words of their historian and spokesman Josephus: 'We neither inhabit a maritime country nor delight in commerce, nor in such intercourse with other men as arises from it'.

In the later Hellenistic age Syria developed into an important agricultural-horticultural country. The upward curve began under the Ptolemies in the Biqa, Phoenicia and Palestine. Stimulated by greater demand, the traditional crops of barley and wheat, grapes and other fruits, wine and vegetables were increased by improved methods. A wider market for unguents for which native flowers were used was now created. The lively intercourse with neighbouring foreign lands resulted in the exchange of agricultural products and the introduction of new plants — Egyptian beans, lentils, mustard and gourds from Egypt; pistachio trees from Persia; apricot, peach and cherry trees from Persia by way, strangely enough, of Italy. Attempts to acclimatize aromatic and cinnamon shrubs were unsuccessful.

Under the Ptolemies the wine and oil industry became more lively. These two products, together with olives, bread and fish formed a substantial part of the diet of the people. In Hellenistic times the lumber industry was no less flourishing than in Pharaonic days. Treeless Egypt drew on the cedars of Lebanon, always a royal domain, and on the oaks of Bashan. The exploitation of Syria's and Lebanon's forests was the privilege of the sovereigns under the Seleucids as it was under the Persians, the Assyrians and the Phoenicians. The Sea of Galilee supplied scented bushes and Jericho had a monopoly of balsam.

The textile industry maintained its primacy. Syrian manufacturers continued to use the same skill and technique but varied the designs to suit the tastes of a varied clientele. The demand for woollen cloth and purple-dyed stuffs remained brisk. In pottery and glassware, a specialty of the Near East from time immemorial, Syria upheld its ancient reputation. Greek pottery, which subsequent to Alexander's conquest flooded the Near Eastern market, was soon imitated by Syrians and produced locally. Especially popular at first was black-glazed pottery, later superseded by a type of red ware with a fine brilliant glaze introduced in the second century. Sidon, near which excellent sand for use in glass was found, Tyre and other Phoenician cities continued to manufacture and export the best glass in the Hellenistic world. This glass was cast, as the epoch-making invention of glass-blowing did not occur until the Roman period. In the Hellenistic age clay tablets give way as writing material to parchment or papyrus rolls. Parchment was a monopoly of Pergamum (whence it got its name) in Asia Minor, while Alexandria supplied papyrus, although some was evidently grown locally in Syria.

The art of metalwork took long strides forward at this time. Silver and gold came from Nabataean Arabia; silver and iron from the Taurus mountains. Iron was also obtained locally in Palestine and Lebanon. For economic purposes this metal was undoubtedly the most valuable. The Ptolemies may also have exploited the copper and other minerals of the Lebanon range. In all the Hellenistic monarchies the coinage of money was promoted as an instrument for developing trade. Money as a medium of exchange gradually superseded the ancient system of barter. Uniform royal weights were also issued by the various governments.

With the increase of trade and its implementation with money and official weights, and with the improvement and progress of agriculture, Seleucid Syria enjoyed a period of comparative prosperity. The general standard of living was high, despite the political unrest and the constant raids and invasions. The population increased in size, until in the early Roman period it is estimated that five to six million people dwelt in Syria, of whom two million lived in Palestine.

ROMANS AND SEMITES

ALL geographical and traditional Syria was incorporated by Pompey in 64 B.C. into a single province, with Antioch as capital. Arab dynasts were allowed to remain, but their authority was restricted to their original domains and they paid annual tribute. The Nabataean king, however, kept Damascus for a lump sum of money. Judaea was left a subject state within the framework of the province of Syria, but the cities with a Greek constitution which the Jews had added to their domain were restored to their former status and granted internal freedom under provincial governors. Ten of these cities then formed a league known as Decapolis, of which all but Scythopolis lay east of the Jordan. Antioch, Gaza and other colony-cities were also given autonomy and placed under provincial governors.

The Syrian province was considered of such focal importance in the Asiatic possessions as to be put under the direct rule of a Roman proconsul with power to levy troops and engage in war. The first proconsul, Aulus Gabinius, further reduced the power of the Jewish monarchy by depriving the high priest of his royal rank, subjecting the people to heavy taxation and dividing the state into five small cantons, each under a council or Sanhedrin. He also rebuilt a number of Greco-Syrian cities which had been destroyed by the Maccabees, including Samaria, Scythopolis and Gaza. He was succeeded by the avaricious Crassus, who immediately upon his arrival in 54 B.C. made Syria a base of military operations against Parthia, whose wealth was considered inexhaustible. With the successive elimination of Pontus and Armenia and the acquisition of Syria, Rome had come into direct contact with Parthia. In his second campaign in

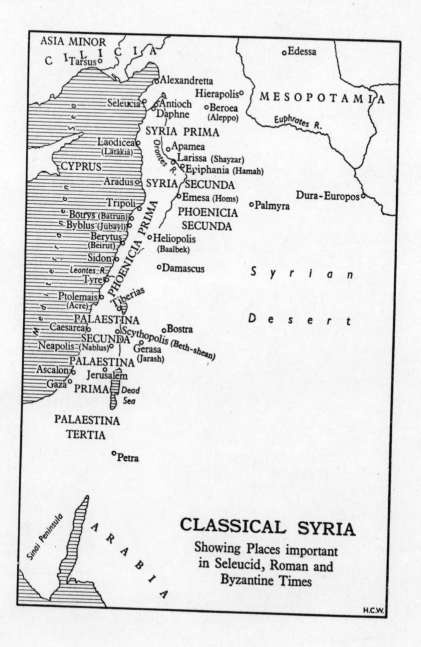

ASIA MINOR

CILICIA

Tarsus

Edessa

MESOPOTAMIA

Alexandretta

Hierapolis

Seleucia

Antioch
Daphne

Beroea
(Aleppo)

Euphrates R.

SYRIA PRIMA

Laodicea
(Latākiā)

Apamea

Larissa (Shayzar)

Epiphania (Hamah)

CYPRUS

Aradus

SYRIA SECUNDA

Emesa (Homs)

Dura-Europos

Tripoli

Palmyra

Bōtrys (Batrun)

Byblus (Jūbayl)

PHOENICIA
SECUNDA

Berytus
(Beirut)

Heliopolis
(Baalbek)

Sidon

Leontes R.

S y r i a n

Tyre

Ptolemais
(Acre)

Tiberias

Damascus

PHOENICIA PRIMA

D e s e r t

PALAESTINA

Caesarea

Scythopolis

Bostra

SECUNDA

(Beth-shean)

Neapolis (Nablus)

Gerasa
(Jarash)

PALAESTINA

Ascalon

Jerusalem

Gaza

PRIMA

Dead
Sea

PALAESTINA
TERTIA

Petra

CLASSICAL SYRIA

Showing Places important
in Seleucid, Roman and
Byzantine Times

Sinai Peninsula

ARABIA

H.C.W.

the spring of 53 Crassus was betrayed by his Arab ally and was slain in battle in the Syrian Desert south of Harran; his army was cut to pieces.

Crassus' able treasurer and successor, Cassius, realized that this crushing defeat put all Syria in jeopardy and hastened to prepare for the coming invasion, which did not materialize until the year 51. At the head of two legions the proconsul took his stand in Antioch ready to offer determined resistance. Sensing a lengthy siege, the Parthians retired along the Orontes and ultimately withdrew from all Syria. The incursion, however, left its effect in the resurgence of several local dynasts, many of whom favoured the Parthians.

With civil war raging in Rome and the whole realm in a condition of unrest and instability, Syria rapidly reverted to the confused anarchy in which Pompey had found it as a result of the ineffectiveness of the later Seleucids. Arab chiefs in the north and east, Nabataeans and Jews in the south, robbers in Lebanon and Cilicia and pirates along the Phoenician coast disdained the power of distant Rome. Trade, already disrupted by the successive Armenian and Parthian invasions, came to a virtual standstill. A brief visit by Julius Caesar in 47 B.C. and four years under the irresponsible Mark Antony (40–36) brought no improvement. A major Parthian incursion dislodged the Romans from the entire province with the exception of Tyre; they regained control only slowly and with difficulty.

During Mark Antony's tenure the Maccabean family was replaced by that of Herod, a nominal Jew of Idumaean origin who established himself as king at Jerusalem in 37 B.C. and maintained power until his death thirty-three years later. Herod promoted Roman as against national interests and succeeded, where the Seleucids had failed, in forcibly making of Judaea a passable imitation of a Hellenistic realm. He mercilessly crushed all opposition to his despotic rule and left a pacified kingdom to his sons, but in A.D. 6 it was restored to the direct rule of Roman governors.

Meanwhile a rising Roman general, Octavian, had vanquished Mark Antony and Cleopatra at the naval battle of Actium (31 B.C.), had passed through Syria and been welcomed by provincials desperately longing for a stable government and had received from the Roman senate the rank of emperor and the title Augustus Caesar. During Augustus's imperial rule Syria was fully incorporated into the Roman provincial system, under which native communities suffered but little restriction in the exercise of their autonomy. They retained their own religion, language and customs. The Romans took upon themselves the responsibility for their protection, afforded by garrison legions of Italian troops. In lieu of military service tribute was exacted from the native population. The Roman governors, who exercised general supervision over provincial affairs, were normally appointed for short periods and received no pay, but made themselves wealthy by farming out taxes and other oppressive methods.

By the time Augustus became emperor, the Romans and their subject peoples had virtually harmonized the Greek and Latin civilizations. Greek remained the cultural language of the eastern provinces and Aramaean the vernacular, but Latin became the official language of administration. The Greeks were weak on the political and organizational side, which was exactly where the Romans were strong. The Romans were rather poor in the artistic and philosophic field, where the Greeks were rich. Thus did Hellenism, strengthened and enriched under the Roman aegis, continue its sway over Syria. Under Roman protection the land remained secure from 'barbarian' peril; Syrian Greek city life, with its characteristic political forms, round of festivities, amusements and intellectual exercise, moved on as before. Such local dynasties as were suffered by the mighty Romans to persist — in Judaea, Petra, Palmyra and elsewhere — had by this time all acquired a strong Hellenistic tinge.

As a frontier province bordering on Parthia, the only serious rival and formidable foe of Rome, Syria was constituted an imperial province of which the emperor himself was the titular proconsul. As such it was placed under a legate, always of consular rank, whose term of office lasted from three to five years. Its governorship, with that of Gaul, was the most honourable and highly prized that the empire could confer. Syria in the east, like Gaul in the west, was a central seat of military control. The governor was assisted by an adequate staff among whom the procurators stood high as collectors of state revenue. The collection was made either directly or through tax farming. Under the legate's control was a strong military force of four legions, consisting in the early empire almost entirely of Italian troops. The legate of Syria was responsible for the security of Roman possessions throughout south-western Asia.

The local communities lived under a variety of governments. The Greco-Macedonian colonies kept their own magistrates under whom were a senate and a popular assembly. The Phoenician city-states likewise retained their traditional oligarchical systems, and the Aramaean communities of the interior continued in control of their internal affairs as before. The Arabs of Homs and the Biqa were ruled by their own princes, while on the desert frontier, where the nomadic or semi-nomadic way of life was still the rule, the tribe was the social unit and the patriarchal form of administration was maintained. In Judaea the high priest, no longer a king, acted as head of the community and was nominated by the Jewish aristocracy. Throughout Rome displayed a remarkable flexibility in its dealings with these diverse communities and their leaders.

Behind this diversity of organization and control was a measure of ethnic and cultural similarity far beyond anything that had prevailed before. All Syrians were by this time fully Semitized and were mingling and hence becoming more and more homogeneous. Phoenicians and Aramaeans, Arabs and Jews, Macedonians and Greeks — all could be found in any city of Syria, where ancient antagonisms consequently faded away. From this mingling the Romans kept somewhat aloof, unmindful of the culture of the provincials whom they ruled. They planted few colonies, of which the most important were a settlement of veterans at Beirut and another at Baalbek, both destined to become vital centres of Roman culture. But inevitably the chief Roman interest in Syria was to use it as a base against Parthia and to exploit its resources. The Syrians manifested but little interest in the Roman military campaigns except when their own safety was threatened.

The performance of Roman administration in such a province as Syria, which had a civilization as high as the Roman though differing in character, was not as successful or brilliant as in such half-civilized provinces as Spain or Gaul. In Syria the Greek settlements, Phoenician cities and Judaean towns, with their developed social, intellectual and economic life and their schools of art, philosophy and literature, found but little to borrow from Rome. To them Latin literature remained of no interest. But the Arabs, whether speaking Arabic or — like the Ituraeans, Idumaeans and Nabataeans — Aramaic, responded differently. Among them, east of Anti-Lebanon and of settled Transjordan, Roman colonies were set up, each starting with a nucleus of Italian settlers around which others were grouped, and developing into special communities.

After reducing insurgent Petra in A.D. 105 Trajan annexed the regions east and south of the Dead Sea and incorporated them into the empire as the province of Arabia. With Syria as the focus of Roman power in the Near East, Roman administration established a chain of posts along the fringe of the desert to protect the more settled and civilized areas. The forts were often garrisoned with auxiliaries recruited from friendly tribes. The transversal road from east to west, connecting the cities of the Tigris and Euphrates with those of the Mediterranean and passing through Palmyra, cut across this territory, bisecting the caravan route from Arabia to Damascus. Political security and the improvement in communications promoted a tendency towards settled life on the part of nomadic or semi-nomadic communities. Urbanization was a cardinal point in Roman policy.

In brief, it may be claimed that the chief service which Roman administration rendered the Syrian province was immunity from civil disturbances and protection against external enemies. Incidentally it opened up a wider market, a world market before it. In the first century of imperial rule Syrian recovery from the depression into which it had sunk as a result of foreign and civil wars was rapid. The province found itself an integral part of an empire that stretched from the Atlantic and the North Sea to the Euphrates and from the Rhine and the Danube to the Sahara. Under the shelter of imperial arms order and peace prevailed; security from brigandage and piracy was established. Parthian and Arabian incursions were checked. Strategic passes, like the Cilician, were well guarded. A network of well-drained roads, an outstanding achievement of administrative and engineering skill, knit all parts of the empire into a relatively compact unit. Augustus instituted a postal service which brought the central government into closer contact with its provincial agents. Trade was stimulated. The curve of prosperity tended upward again. After A.D. 70 the entire Roman state enjoyed a long period of immunity from serious civil disturbances. From A.D. 96 to 180 it was fortunate in having an unbroken succession of worthy emperors beginning with Nerva and ending with Marcus Aurelius. Under them Roman Syria attained its widest extent and greatest prosperity.

The sense of security, the extension of the road system

and the creation of a new world trade stimulated economic production beyond anything hitherto known. Prosperity was reflected in a higher standard of living and the appearance of new towns. The increased population of greater Syria must in the second century have reached the all-time high of 7,000,000. The whole Orontes valley, today partly desert, must have been intensely cultivated, as Roman engineering skill lifted the river water and distributed it to the fields, where improved ploughs helped produce better crops. Even Transjordan, now mostly desert, abounded in grain and grapes, as well as date palms and olive trees. The fertility of the Hawran plateau became proverbial. From a country of shepherds it was transformed into one of cities and villages. The entire region was dependent on the use of reservoirs in which the irregular but sometimes heavy rainfall was collected. The degree of prosperity attained by this region under the Romans was never again approached even under the Umayyad caliphs.

Syrian gardening was a pleasant feature of ancient Roman civilization. It goes back to early Semitic beginnings which grew out of the widespread fruit, flower and herb cultivation dependent solely upon summer irrigation. Given an impetus under Persian rule, Semitic gardening technique was perfected under the Romans. It was applied not only on a private but also on a public scale, as exemplified in the sacred grove of Daphne. The flowery retreats which attended the Mediterranean civilization and were represented in Antioch, Damascus and Jerusalem became a prototype of the pleasure gardens that spread as far as Moorish Granada. Even today water is still handled as an artistic motif in the flowing jets emitting a veil-like spray in the courtyards of Damascus.

All aspects of Syrian agriculture and all districts prospered. Grain constituted the principal nourishment. In addition to the staple cereals rice, which requires artificial irrigation, was cultivated spasmodically along the coast.

The commonest adjunct to cereal food was a leaf vegetable. Meat was not in regular demand except among the rich. Of the legumes lentils, beans, kidney beans, chick-peas, vetch and lupin were widely cultivated. Onions, leeks and garlic were relished by the poor. Of the spices coriander, mustard, anise, cumin, ginger and mint flourished in Syria, as did mushrooms, cabbage and radishes. Non-food plants included henna, lilies and papyrus, as well as flax, cotton and hemp for use in making cloth.

The production of dyes in the textile manufacturing districts of Sidon and Tyre seems to have continued under the Romans. Phoenician purple was held everywhere in high esteem. Syria was, with Egypt, the main source of linen goods for the empire, and among the best sources of leather, for tanning which sumac leaves were used, as they are today. All industry was hand production which, lacking machinery and the experimental outlook, remained virtually static. Other Syrian exports included medicinal and aromatic plants, as well as wines popular throughout the whole ancient world. Mineral products comprised asphalt from the Dead Sea region, cinnabar and orpiment for painting, amber, alabaster from Damascus and gypsum. Stone and chalk quarries existed near Antioch. Copper was mined in several localities, largely by slaves under government supervision. Sidon was especially noted for its bronze and its glass, including the newly invented blown-glass vessels.

Commerce provided the main source of wealth. The richest cities of the Roman Near East were such commercial centres as Petra, Palmyra and the Phoenician coast towns. By and large the traders were natives of Syria, though Italians and Greeks competed briefly. Commerce remained as individualistic as industry, with even partnerships rare. Trade in slaves continued to flourish. Insolvent debtors forfeited their persons to their creditors, and professional slave traders seized unwary adults, kidnapped infants and bought unwanted ones. Incense and spices from southern Arabia and India, perfumes and drugs, oils and unguents all passed through Syria by caravan, leaving prosperity in their wake.. Syrian imports were less romantic — pottery, papyrus and dried fish exceeding silk, jewels and spices in quantity if not in value.

The general aspect of country life in Roman Syria did not radically differ from the earlier pattern. The land was studded with thousands of villages inhabited mostly by peasants living on the produce of the vineyards or farms. No traces of serfdom can be found among these villages; nor is there record of the presence of public slaves doing menial labour. Little or no money was spent for education, public health or charity. With the peasants lived village specialists — carpenters, blacksmiths, shoemakers and shopkeepers. These villages were as little affected by the Romanizing process as they had been by the Hellenizing process. The villagers, especially those far removed from urban centres, tenaciously clung to their traditional ways of life. Ancient rites and customs persisted unchanged.

Above the peasantry stood the native aristocracy, owners of large land-holdings or flocks of sheep and goats. The members of this class were also leaders in religious affairs. The caravan cities, coastal towns and Greco-Roman colonies housed the rich merchants and industrialists as well as the government officials. The majority of this leisure class devoted themselves to sports, amusements and social functions. The climatic conditions and traditional concepts of life, however, made for temperate habits; and the sense of family loyalty, a most precious element in the legacy of the patriarchal age, never lost its hold upon the people. It is still a living force there.

In the Hellenized or Romanized cities and in the coastal towns amusements were those of the ordinary Greco-Roman type — wrestling, chariot racing, musical competition and theatrical performances. Dromedary racing was popular in the districts bordering the desert. Hunting was the favourite sport of the well-to-do, with bears, antelopes, gazelles and wild boars as the quarry. The combination of gymnasium and hot bath, which emerged under the Seleucids, continued to attract patrons. Syrians soon became noted as entertainers — actors, ballet dancers, flute players, circus performers, buffoons, wrestlers and jockeys. Troupes of these entertainers toured the provinces, and were available for hire for banquets and festal occasions.

Antioch and its suburb Daphne were particularly notorious for luxurious and dissolute living and for the magnificence of their public structures and private villas, as well as for the abundant fresh water so precious in that dry land. Since Seleucid days Daphne had been the scene of the greatest celebration of games in Syria. A wealthy Antiochene senator under Augustus willed his fortune to the establishment of a thirty-day Daphnean festival comprising dances, dramatic performances, chariot races, athletic and gladiatorial contests. Women participated in some of these performances, and the festival — and Daphne itself — became proverbial for licentiousness.

Proud, turbulent and satirical, the Antiochenes were noted for their mastery of the art of ridicule. They evidently could not forget that theirs was once a royal city, and stood ready to side with any pretender whom the Syrian army put up. With the emperors who sojourned in their city they invariably quarrelled. Hadrian withdrew from the city the right of coinage, Marcus Aurelius the right of assembly; Septimius Severus transferred the primacy of Syria to Latakia. Emperors bestowed titles and rights upon a city as a reward for good behaviour; they withdrew these privileges as a punishment for disloyalty. In A.D. 115 the city suffered one of the most violent earthquakes on record, and in 260 it was captured and burned by the Persian shah Shapur I, but it recovered from both catastrophes in short order.

Other prosperous cities of Roman Syria included the

Seleucid colonies of Latakia and Apamea and the cities under native aristocracies such as Homs, Damascus, Edessa and Palmyra. Each of the latter group was the centre of a petty state, among which that of Palmyra became formidable. This caravan city had grown up around a spring in the Syrian Desert, a natural stopping-place for trade between Seleucid and Roman Syria to the west and Parthian Mesopotamia to the east. Its isolated location in the heart of the desert put it beyond the easy reach of Roman legions and of Parthian cavalry, and its Arab politicians shrewdly exploited its strategic situation between the two great rivals, keeping the balance of power and profiting by neutrality. By playing one adversary against the other, they maintained the independence of their city as a buffer state.

Palmyrene chiefs secured safe-conducts for passing caravans from desert sheikhs; guides led those caravans through the barren region; mounted archers protected them against bedouin raids; and the city imposed heavy duty on each article of merchandise as it passed through its gates. The commodities comprised some of the necessities and many of the luxuries of the classical world. They did not differ much from those which had passed through Petra: wool, purple, silk, glassware, perfumes, aromatics, olive oil, dried figs, nuts, cheese and wine. The greater part of the Mediterranean trade with Persia, India and China was then handled by Palmyrenes. Industry and even agriculture flourished alongside commerce. The result was the growth of Palmyra into one of the richest cities of the Near East.

Gradually its mud huts were replaced by limestone houses. Wide streets were laid out, with the main one leading to the sanctuary of Bel. The streets were lined with colonnades, and the city assumed the aspect of a prosperous Greco-Roman town. It was not easy for the desert city to preserve full sovereignty in face of the growing ascendancy of the empire on its west. By the start of the Christian era Palmyra must have acknowledged the suzerainty of Rome, but it maintained its independence. Trajan incorporated it in the province he created in 106, and its dependent cities such as Dura-Europos also became vassals of Rome. As such Palmyra and its satellites entered upon a fresh period of prosperity lasting for over a century and a half. Roman roads connected Palmyra with Damascus, capital of inland Syria, and with the cities of the Euphrates.

It was not until the late third century that Palmyra began to play a conspicuous part in international affairs. By then a new and energetic Persian dynasty had replaced the old Parthian. This was the Sasanid, which lasted from A.D. 227 to the rise of Islam. In 260 the Sasanid army under Shapur I defeated the Roman legions near Edessa and captured the emperor Valerian. Udaynath of Palmyra rushed to his rescue with a mixed army of Syrians and Arabs, defeated the Persians and pursued them to the walls of Persepolis, but was unable to liberate Valerian, who died in captivity. Udaynath's loyalty to the new emperor Gallienus was rewarded in 262 by recognition as imperial commander over the eastern part of the empire. The empire was then in a feeble and confused state, with the whole barbarian world falling upon it in Europe as well as Asia. In the zenith of his success Udaynath was murdered together with his heir under mysterious circumstances. Of hardy and athletic physique, he had excelled in those pastimes and virtues prized highly by Arabs. His munificence manifested itself in elaborate and spectacular banquets, in patronizing religious festivals and in gifts of oil for public baths.

As a historical figure, however, he was eclipsed by his ambitious and beautiful widow Zenobia. Under her the Palmyrene state attained the proportions of a real empire, extending over Syria, part of Asia Minor, northern Arabia and even lower Egypt, where in 270 her army established a garrison at Alexandria. In 271 she declared Palmyra's full independence. Rome's reaction was swift and effective. The emperor Aurelian reduced the Palmyrene garrisons in Asia Minor and then proceeded against Syria. Antioch, which was pro-Roman, offered little opposition; Homs, whose people harboured jealousy because of the primacy claimed by Palmyra, was occupied after some resistance. Zenobia and her outmanœuvred heavy cavalry retired to Palmyra, which Aurelian besieged. Zenobia fled but was overtaken, and Palmyra had no choice but to surrender. The conqueror despoiled it of its rich fabrics and precious ornaments, some of which were taken to embellish the new sun temple at Rome. The populace was punished only to the extent of the imposition of a fine and a Roman governor with a body of archers. As he was returning to Rome, Aurelian heard of a fresh uprising in Palmyra resulting in the murder of his governor and the overpowering of his garrison. He rushed back, took the city by surprise, destroyed it and put its inhabitants to the sword. Zenobia was taken to Rome where, in gold chains, she was made to grace the triumphal entry of Aurelian into his capital (274). Palmyra fell into insignificance and obscurity; as its people relaxed their grip on the desert, the desert overcame them. The remains of its colonnade and triumphal arch stand today as the most imposing sight in the desert, attracting lovers of antiquity from all over the world.

The Palmyrene was a peculiar culture, a blend of Syrian, Greek and Persian elements. The original inhabitants were doubtless Arabian tribes who adopted in their speech and writing the prevalent Aramaic tongue. The bulk of the population remained Arab though mixed with Aramaeans. Native inscriptions do not date earlier than 9 B.C., when the city was on its way to becoming a prosperous caravan centre. The only known Palmyrene of high intellectual calibre was the pagan philosopher Longinus, teacher of Porphyry, adviser of Zenobia and one of Aurelian's victims.

Romans and Semites

The frescoes of Palmyra and of Dura are significant in the history of art. They help bridge the gap between the ancient Semitic art of Assyro-Babylonia and Phoenicia and early Christian art. Through them may be traced the beginnings of oriental influences over Greco-Roman paintings, thus preparing the way for the advent of Byzantine art. The Palmyrene pantheon comprised an assortment of deities from Syria, Arabia, Babylonia and Persia. Chief among these was Bel, a cosmic god of Babylonian origin who was accompanied by solar and lunar deities.

In addition to such Arab cities as Palmyra and Damascus — less important in Roman times than it had formerly been and would again be — and such Greek cities as Antioch and Latakia, northern Syria had two important Roman cities: Beirut and Baalbek. Of the maritime cities Beirut was the only one important for reasons other than the commercial and industrial activity which characterized and enriched Sidon and Tyre. As a Roman veterans' colony and a garrison town it became an isle of Romanism in a sea of Hellenism. Jewish kings eager to ingratiate themselves with Roman emperors by bestowing gifts on the colonies made it the recipient of many material favours, featuring a sumptuous theatre for musical and dramatic performances and a lavish amphitheatre for gladiatorial combats and circus games. The city was more justifiably distinguished, however, as the seat of the most renowned provincial school of Roman law, remaining throughout the Roman period a Mecca for the best legal minds of the eastern provinces.

Baalbek (Heliopolis), like Beirut, was both a veterans' colony and a garrison town, but was less Roman and more Semitic. The fame of this city rested on its great temple, which housed a gold statue of Hadad, a Semitic deity called by the Romans Jupiter Heliopolitanus, and a smaller temple honouring his consort Atargatis. The ruins of these temples, the smaller of which is the best preserved and most richly ornamented ancient building in all Syria, surpass any others bequeathed from Roman days, not excluding those at Rome itself. The whole temple complex, still visible at a great distance, rests on an artificial terrace formed by a huge understructure of vaults. Aside from the huge size of the stone blocks in the walls and the colossal magnitude of the pillars, it is the wealth of detail in ornamentation and the figure work in the friezes that constitute the most impressive feature of the surviving structures.

Cities of a variety of types were scattered throughout southern Syria. There were the old Philistine cities along the coast — Gaza, Ascalon, Jaffa and Acre —, all of which by this time had become Hellenized. There were Herodian foundations such as Tiberias and Caesarea, a few Roman colonies like Nablus (Neapolis), the league of 'ten cities' (Decapolis) in the interior, and of course Jerusalem; but none of them had the importance at this time that the northern and central cities did.

Still farther south, Petra was flourishing under the early emperors. The most beautiful façade and the impressive theatre belong to this period, as do other picturesque structures of the incredible 'rose-red city, half as old as time'. Politically, the Nabataeans promptly accepted the rôle of ally to Rome. Their kingdom attained its height under the long and prosperous rule of Harithath IV (9 B.C.–A.D. 40), who continued the process of Romanization. His realm included southern Palestine and Transjordan, south-eastern Syria and northern Arabia, where Nabataean caravans utilized well-policed wadi routes to by-pass Decapolis and bring Arabian goods to the markets of Syria. After this king a gradual decline set in, and not much is known of the last rulers of Nabataea. Damascus passed into Roman hands, probably under Nero, and other outlying holdings went the same way. Just what happened in that fateful year 105–106 which resulted in the overthrow of this border Syro-Arab state and its annexation by imperial Rome is not determined. Rome had already absorbed all the petty kingdoms of Syria and Palestine and was getting ready to cross swords with Parthia. Nabataea was brought into the empire as part of the province of Arabia, trade routes shifted, and Petra was relegated to the limbo of history until rediscovered as a modern tourist attraction.

The cultural remains of Roman Syria, from Baalbek to Petra, are indeed largely architectural; the other visual arts marked time, while hardly any Syrian contribution to Latin literature is worth mention, save possibly that of the philologist Probus of Beirut (fl. A.D. 60). Probus produced critical versions of Vergil and Horace. The sole noteworthy addition to Greek literature was the work of the Jewish historian Josephus, our principal authority for the history of Syria under the early empire. In the field of geography a significant contribution was made by Marinus of Tyre, the first to substitute maps mathematically drawn according to latitude and longitude for those based merely on itineraries. He thus was the founder of scientific geography and precursor of Ptolemy. A northern Syrian, Lucian of Samosata, composed an important source work on the religion of Roman Syria, *The Syrian Goddess*, and the first dialogues between the dead, an oft-imitated satirical device.

In the domain of philosophy, particularly of the Neo-Platonic type, Syrian thinkers rendered no mean contribution. This was in line with Seleucid tradition, but now Sidon and Tyre were outstripped by Apamea, where Numenius founded Neo-Platonism (though the credit usually goes to Plotinus). Numenius's fame was surpassed by that of Porphyry, who edited Plotinus's works and was himself the most learned and prolific of the Neo-Platonists. Most of his works, including a treatise against Christians, were publicly burned in 448, long after his death in 305.

As Apamea made its mark in philosophy, Beirut made its in jurisprudence, thanks to the school of Roman civil law which flourished there from the early third to the mid-sixth century. Beirut was a creative intellectual centre, more

Roman than Greek, successfully attracting a galaxy of brilliant students and professors who made of the academy a university and spread its fame far and wide. Legal training was then a prerequisite for holding a government office. Two names shed lustre on the academy and have been immortalized in the Code of Justinian: Papinian, whose legal erudition guided by intellectual honesty and integrity of character made him a model jurist, and Ulpian, extracts from whose perspicuous writings form about one-third of Justinian's *Digest*. Through the copious extracts from their writings both jurists exercised abiding influence on the systems of Europe.

Certain pieces of Syrian literature, written in barbarous Greek in the early Roman imperial period, however, have had a more enduring and far-reaching influence than all the Greek and Latin classics put together. These were, of course, the Gospels and other early Christian writings.

With the details of the life and teachings of Jesus of Nazareth, a son of a Jewish carpenter, who according to Tacitus 'had undergone the death penalty in the reign of Tiberius', this history cannot properly concern itself. That some of his followers took pains to record the teachings and doings of their master, producing the Gospels, is a minor footnote to literary history, though it proved to be of immeasurable import to all subsequent history, political, social and intellectual. No extraordinary event reported of Jesus' life — virgin birth, astral association, miracle performance, crucifixion, descent to the underworld, reappearance, exaltation to heaven — lacks its parallel in earlier Near Eastern religious mythology. Hardly a teaching of his was not anticipated by Hebrew prophets or other early Semitic teachers. Even his emphasis on love of God and of man and on the relation between faith and ethical living were not unprecedented, though no precursor expressed himself so memorably, or so wholeheartedly practised what he taught.

Romans and Semites

The unique original contribution of primitive Syrian Christianity lay in its message, universal rather than provincial or national, spiritual instead of ritualistic and ceremonial, unselfish and other-worldly as opposed to this-worldly, full of hope for the poor and the weary, the outcast and, above all, the sinful who would repent and seek redemption. Unlike heathen religions, it touched the inmost springs of conduct and conviction. Thus the new faith, buttressed by the dogmatic certainty and missionary zeal of its early adherents, was evidently able to satisfy spiritual and social demands which enlightened people everywhere must have been making — unsuccessfully — on their traditional religions. Slowly but surely it spread throughout the empire, developing effective institutions and techniques, converting Jews and pagans and inevitably attracting official opposition and sporadic persecution.

Through the efforts of Paul and the early Christian Fathers, many of whom — Ignatius, Justin Martyr, Origen and others — had Syrian connections, Christianity was so Hellenized as to make it palatable to Greeks and Romans, and was provided with a plethora of doctrine and a host of martyrs. It outdistanced all its competitors including the state cult of emperor-worship, the ancient mystery religions and their youngest and most popular rival Mithraism, the Gnostic sects and the local fertility deities, which in Syria meant chiefly Hadad and Atargatis. Early in the fourth century under Constantine it was adopted as the official religion of the Roman state. In this development the church at Antioch had been the headquarters from which Paul and other early missionaries had set out and to which they had reported if they returned. After the destruction of Jerusalem by Titus in A.D. 70 it became the capital of Christendom, exercising a limited jurisdiction over other sees, and bishops met there frequently in councils. Antioch also gave its name to a school of theology which flourished in the late Roman and early Byzantine eras, stressing the human and historical aspects of Christianity against the emotional and mystical.

From apostolic times both Greek and Aramaic were used in Christian worship. After Antioch's rise to a position of leadership in the Greek-speaking part of Syria, Edessa began to rise to a corresponding position in the Aramaic (Syriac)-speaking world. This city was the earliest seat of Christianity in Mesopotamia and the cradle of Syriac literature, which began there probably late in the second century with Syriac versions of the Bible.

The penetration of Christianity into the farthest parts of the Roman empire and its final triumph over all Greco-Roman cults and oriental rivals was but one phase of the Syrianizing process that was going on, the religious phase. The other phases were economic, social and political. Meanwhile, Romanizing processes were operating in the opposite direction. Romanization decreased as distance from Rome increased. In Syria there were too few Italian residents to act as foci for Latin culture. Those were mostly government officials who collected taxes, decided important lawsuits, attended games and festivals but continued to be treated as outsiders. But from the outset the emperors bestowed on native residents of such colonies as Beirut and Baalbek Roman citizenship, which gave them a favoured position among the provincials. By grant or treaty other cities which were not colonies received citizenship or special privileges. Tarsus was among these, enabling Paul to claim Roman citizenship and 'appeal unto Caesar'. 'Divide and rule' was a standard Roman political technique applied to prevent the different cities or communities from clubbing together against Rome. In 212 Caracalla bestowed full Roman citizenship on practically all free residents of the provinces, Syria included. Rome was thus well on the way to solving the knotty problem of moulding a cluster of different nationalities into a single entity, moderately uniform in culture, economically prosperous and politically loyal.

Of the numerous Syrian communities the Jewish was the least responsive to Romanizing stimuli. The aristocracy was already Hellenized. The Sadducees, who represented the aristocratic party and monopolized the offices, received support from Rome. The Pharisees, who represented the commonalty, adhered to strict orthodoxy and aimed at liberation. Because of the strict monotheism of their religion the Jews had been treated since Pompey's days as a privileged community. Under the emperors they were exempt from military service and the obligation of the imperial cult. They were not required to participate in the sacrificial worship of the Roman ruler. As they maintained their policy of exclusiveness and isolationism, they nourished their national feeling. This led to clashes which broadened into national rebellion in A.D. 66–70 under Nero and in 132–134 under Hadrian. These two rebellions resulted in the final breach between Jews and Christians and in enduring disaster to the Jewish society. It was after the first that Titus destroyed Jerusalem and burned the Temple. More than a million Jews are estimated to have perished then, many of them in the amphitheatre battling one another or wild beasts. Judaea as a political state ceased to exist, and the Jews became a stateless, homeless people. Judaism decayed with its adherents, as its narrow national basis and certain features of its ritual rendered it unacceptable to other peoples. One last spark of life appeared in 132, when the Jewish banner of revolt was unfurled by a mysterious leader, Simon Bar Kokba. But Hadrian crushed the rebellion and turned Jerusalem into a Roman colony called Aelia Capitolina. More than half a million more Jews reportedly died in this futile uprising.

Syrian influence at Rome penetrated to the throne when the purple fell to Septimius Severus (A.D. 193–211), a Punic-speaking African general whose wife was a remarkable Syrian lady named Julia Domna, daughter of a priest of Elagabal at Homs. She is described as having great beauty, intellectual power and political and literary ability, and as collaborating with her husband in the conduct of state affairs. After his death in battle she attempted to wield control over her sons Caracalla and Geta, who succeeded their father as co-emperors. But in 212 Caracalla had Geta murdered in his mother's arms in her own apartment; Julia herself received a wound in her hand trying to shield her son. She stood by, helpless, as Caracalla continued his blood-stained career, killing some twenty thousand persons including the jurist Papinian. She was put in charge of his correspondence and the state papers. Her *salon* included Papinian's successor Ulpian, the Greek physician Galen, the Roman historian Dio Cassius and other notable thinkers. After Caracalla's death in 217 she committed suicide, not from grief but because she could not face retirement to private life.

The Syrian dynasty did not end, however, for the imperial power was soon captured by her younger and abler sister Julia Maesa for her grandsons Elagabalus (218–222) and Alexander Severus (222–235). Elagabalus was a priest of the Baal of Homs, whose sacred black stone accompanied him to Rome, and whose worship became for a few years supreme in the empire. Alexander, at his accession a lad of thirteen under his mother's control, was the last and best of this Syrian dynasty. He sent the black stone back to Homs, forbade the worship of himself while alive, put down court luxury, lightened taxes, raised the standard of the coinage and encouraged art and science. After recovering Mesopotamia from the Persians, he was killed in a mutiny in 235. Another Syrian, called Philip the Arab, was enthroned in 244, presided in 248 at the ceremonies commemorating the thousandth birthday of Rome and fell victim to a mutiny in 249, ending Syrian influence at court. His coins depict the great temple of Heliopolis.

Syrian economic penetration in the Latin provinces was manifested by the number of commercial settlements which, especially in the second and third centuries, sprang up along all the coasts of the Mediterranean and inland on the trade routes. The islands of Delos and Sicily, the ports of Naples and Ostia, the cities of Lyons and Arles were especially favoured. Syrian ships once again dotted the sea and the old Phoenician energy, adaptability, love of lucrative trade and ability to make bargains and close large and small deals were reactivated.

As importers Syrian merchants monopolized a great deal of the trade of the Latin provinces with the Levant; as bankers they had no rivals. Wines, spices, grain, glassware, fabrics and jewellery were their chief commodities. Wherever Syrian merchants settled, there they established their temples. As carriers of the Christian religion these merchants and Syriac-speaking colonists, soldiers and slaves were no less enthusiastic than as carriers of pagan cults. Their influence on its development in the West was manifest in the direction of asceticism, monasticism and a more emotional form of worship. Devotion to the cross and its adoption as a religious emblem were other Christian elements introduced by Syrians into Europe. In Rome their colony was strong enough to furnish the church with a number of popes, two of whom achieved canonization.

During the third century, while Syrian religious and economic influences were penetrating Latin as well as Greek provinces, all was not well with the empire. Its cultural homogeneity was being fragmented by resurgent provincial patriotisms. Its prosperity was being wrecked by exorbitant taxes unjustly apportioned. Its security was being undermined by protracted civil wars and repeated foreign invasions. Its tottering intellectual and spiritual pillars were subjected to the onslaught of new waves of Christian ideas. A new culture and state, the Byzantine, were emerging to replace those of Rome.

BYZANTINES AND ARABS

On May 11, 330, the emperor Constantine dedicated as the new capital of the Roman empire the city of Constantinople, located on the site of ancient Byzantium on the European side of the Bosporus. Its strategic position, relatively secure against the barbarian bands which had made Rome untenable, gave the city economic and military advantages that made it a natural centre about which the eastern provinces could readily cluster. The shift itself indicates a recognition of the preponderance those provinces possessed in wealth and natural resources. The major civilized antagonist of the empire, Persia, lay to the east. The centre of gravity in world affairs was returning eastward after four centuries' sojourn in Italy.

Prior to his foundation of a new capital for the state Constantine gave recognition to a new official religion. Whether his own conversion to Christianity about 312 was one of convenience or of conviction is of no historical consequence. The fact remains that at his command this once persecuted and obscure cult now became the official religion of the empire. As Greece had conquered the minds of the Romans, Syria now conquered their souls. By this time the most influential men in the empire had become followers of Christ, though the majority of the population, including Constantine's foes, were still pagan. Discipline, organization, wealth and enthusiasm were on the side of the minority, to which the emperor now added the power of the state. In 325 he convened an ecumenical council of all the bishops of the empire at Nicaea, the first congress of its kind. In it Arianism was condemned and the Christian faith was definitely codified in what became the Nicene Creed. All but one of the successors of Constantine professed the Christian faith.

These two events in the reign of Constantine — the transference of the capital from Rome to Constantinople and the official recognition of Christianity — mark out that reign as one of the most significant in the long history of the Roman state. Christian in doctrine, Greek in language, eclectic in culture, the new empire inaugurated by Constantine was to endure, with many vicissitudes, for about eleven centuries and a quarter. From the seventh century on it served as a bulwark against Islam. Finally, in 1453, it succumbed under the onrush of the new champions of that religion, the Ottoman Turks.

For a few years after the establishment of Constantinople the external and theoretical unity of the empire was maintained. In practice, however, the two halves of the empire were frequently separated and ruled by different emperors. The final division came in 395 when Theodosius died and his sons Honorius and Arcadius succeeded, the former ruling over the western portion and the latter over the eastern. At last, in 476, Rome fell to Germanic invaders.

Byzantine Syria presents a different picture from Roman Syria. It was, on the whole, a Christian land. In fact this is the only period in which Syria has been a fully Christian country. Sandwiched in between the pagan Roman and the Arab Moslem, the Byzantine period was therefore unique in Syrian annals. At the end of the fourth century the province was divided into seven districts, with their capitals at Antioch, Apamea, Tyre, Homs, Caesarea, Scythopolis and Petra. The first two were still called Syria, the next two Phoenicia (though including inland cities which had never belonged to either Phoenicia or Lebanon) and the last three Palaestina, including the former province of Arabia.

Not only was the country Christian but the age was an ecclesiastical age. The church was its greatest institution;

97

saints were its most revered heroes. From the fourth to the
sixth centuries monks, nuns, anchorites, priests and bishops
flourished as never before or since. Churches, chapels,
basilicas and monasteries — all with a new style of architecture featuring domes, bell towers and prominent cruci-
fixes — dotted the land. Hermit caves were excavated or
enlarged. Pillars were erected on which curious ascetics
called Stylites lived and died. Pilgrimage boomed. Vows
and prayers at tombs of saints became standard remedies
for ill health and misfortune. Monasticism was a favoured
way of life. Its ideals of celibacy, poverty and obedience
held wide appeal. The decline of population, the waning
of prosperity and the civil disturbances that marked the late
Roman and early Byzantine decades had led to a widespread
loss of confidence in secular institutions. Christianity presented something supernatural and ultramundane, including
a belief in spiritual values worth renouncing this world for
and dying for.

Linguistically the church in Syria had developed along
two lines : Greek on the coast and in the Hellenized cities,
Syriac in the interior. The Syriac-using church had had its
start as early as the second century. With the spread of
Christianity in the third century Syriac had asserted itself
against Greek. In the Byzantine period revulsion from
Greek and reversion to Aramaic signalized the new awakening among Syrians. The revived interest in the ancient
Semitic tongue was an index of a revival of national consciousness as well as a reaction against paganism. Always
polyglots, Syrians interested in the bar studied Latin ;
those addicted to philosophy took up Greek ; but the rest,
especially those outside of cosmopolitan centres, stuck to the
native tongue. The Syriac literature extant is almost entirely
Christian, but comprises also handbooks of science and
philosophy translated from Greek. Its first great centre,
away from the Greek-speaking cities, was Edessa, the Athens
of the Aramaic world, where Syriac had first been used for

literary purposes, in versions of the Bible.

Opposition to Christian thought as represented by Constantinople and Antioch resulted in schisms, 'heresies' from the orthodox viewpoint. As in the case of language these schisms were to a certain extent an expression of national awakening. After a submergence of centuries under a wave of Greek culture the Syrian spirit was at last asserting itself. The alienation of the people from their Byzantine rulers was due to ideological as well as to political and economic causes. The Byzantines were more autocratic in their rule than the Romans had been and more oppressive in their taxation. They disarmed the natives and had little regard for their feelings. Even in matters religious they displayed less tolerance than their pagan predecessors.

Theological controversy was the breath of life among the intelligentsia of the fourth and fifth centuries. It centred on the nature of Christ and kindred topics which no longer agitate Christian minds. The result was innumerable heresies and schools of thought, some of which reflect the exercise of Aristotelian logic and the application of Neo-Platonic principles. Meanwhile, cults akin to Zoroastrianism and to Buddhism were appearing amidst Christian communities. The patriarch John Chrysostom (d. 407) refers to a group in Antioch who believed in transmigration of souls and wore yellow robes. Most dangerous among the new religions spreading westward was Manichaeism, which combined Christian, Buddhist and Zoroastrian tenets in one syncretistic system. Its vigorous dualism and other 'errors' aroused the Syrian Fathers as no other 'errors' did.

Several protagonists of the so-called heresies were of Syrian nativity or education. The series began with the fourth-century Arius, whose system was condemned in the Council of Nicaea but retained great importance, both theological and political. As a reaction against Arianism, with its emphasis on the humanity of Christ and its implied denial of his divinity, Apollinaris of Latakia affirmed that while Christ had a true human body and soul, the Logos or Word occupied in him the place of the spirit, which is the highest part of man. Apollinarism links Arianism and Nestorianism by opposing the one and paving the way for the other.

Nestorius was born in eastern Cilicia and lived in a monastery near Antioch. In 428 he was elevated to the bishopric of Constantinople, but three years later his position was condemned by the Council of Ephesus. The objectionable view he held was that in Jesus a divine person (the Logos) and a human person were joined in perfect harmony of action but not in the unity of a single individual. Nestorius had many followers who constitute the real Nestorians. The so-called Nestorians of Persia, more properly the Church of the East, came later. Cut off from the Roman empire, its adherents evolved their local doctrines and ritual which still survive. Although some of its writers have used decidedly Nestorian language, the liturgical and synodical vocabulary of the church as a whole is remarkably free from it. This is the church which in later times had sufficient vitality to send missionaries as far as India and China.

Next to Nestorianism, Monophysitism was the greatest schism the oriental church suffered. Strictly the Monophysites were those who did not accept the doctrine of the two natures (divine and human) in the one person of Jesus, formulated by the Council of Chalcedon (451). In the late fifth and early sixth centuries Monophysitism won to its doctrine the major part of northern Syria and fell heir to Apollinarism in the south. The Monophysite church in Syria was organized by Jacob Baradaeus, who was ordained bishop of Edessa about 543 and died in 578. In consequence the Syrian Monophysites came to be called Jacobites. The western part of the Syrian church thus became entirely separated from the eastern. From Syria the Monophysite doctrine spread into Armenia to the north and Egypt to the south. Armenians and Copts to this day adhere to the Monophysite theology. In Syria and Mesopotamia the number of its adherents has been on the decrease ever since Islam became the dominant power in those lands.

Another offshoot of the ancient Syrian church was the Maronite, named after its patron saint, an ascetic monk who lived east of Antioch, where he died in 410. Maron's disciples erected a monastery on the Orontes in his memory. In the early sixth century, after clashing with their Jacobite neighbours, they sought and found in northern Lebanon a safer refuge. Thence they spread to become the largest and most influential sect in Lebanon.

Even aside from the struggle against heresy and schism, confusion marked the intellectual life of Byzantine Syria in its early period. Polemics between Christian and non-Christian Greek and Latin writers were carried on for years after Constantine's profession of the Christian faith. Neo-Platonism was far from dead, though its great century had been the third. Church Fathers were inching their way to the front as leaders of thought. Sophists and rhetoricians were retreating though not quite disappearing.

The writings of a fourth-century Syrian rhetorician named Libanius, who was educated at Antioch and Athens and taught at Constantinople, give a vivid picture of the times and places in which he lived. They also open before us a small window through which we may gain a glimpse of the educational methods of the day. At Antioch courses extended over the winter and spring months; summer was taken up with festive activities. Classes began early and lasted till noon. Some students were as young as sixteen. Higher education was in the hands of rhetoricians, who were elected in the cities by the local senate, in the small towns by the communities at large. The rhetors taught, declaimed by way of example and were responsible for discipline. For their services they received pay from the cities and the students. Greek classics formed the core of the curriculum.

Latin was patronized only by those intent upon a government career. Logic was emphasized. Aristotle enjoyed a renaissance consequent upon his rediscovery by Porphyry.

Due to the productive efforts of such pagan authors as Libanius, Antioch became the intellectual capital of northern Syria. Among the eminent Christians educated there was his pupil, the brilliant John Chrysostom, whose eloquent preaching was marked by a denunciation of laxity in morals and luxury in living. The rich were condemned for acquiring their riches by violence, deceit, monopoly and usury and for their attitude of indifference to the sufferings of the poor. His was a social message in an age of ecclesiasticism and theology. So celebrated did he become as a preacher that in 398 he was chosen patriarch of Constantinople, where he sold for the benefit of the needy the treasures collected by his predecessor and uncompromisingly insisted on moral and social reform. He was twice banished and died on his way to exile near the Caucasus. Altogether he was one of the most eloquent preachers and most remarkable teachers of Christian ethics that the church has ever produced.

Two distinguished historians were born at Caesarea in Palestine, Eusebius and Procopius. Eusebius (264–about 349) became bishop of his native city and at the Council of Nicaea delivered an opening address condemning the heresiarch Arius, but his enduring reputation rests on his *Ecclesiastical History*, in which he narrates in detail the rise of Christianity and its relation to the empire. Procopius provided a valuable contemporary account of the eventful reign of Justinian (527–565).

Several Christian notables not of Syrian nativity are associated with southern Syria. Outstanding among them was Jerome (345–420), whose ascetic temperament led him to a monastery in Bethlehem and thence to five years of solitary life among the hermits of the Syrian Desert. His translation of the Bible into Latin, called the Vulgate, has ever since been the standard version for services in the Roman Catholic church.

Early Christian art had been chiefly indebted to the mediocre Jewish art, just as the primitive churches had been merely elongated rooms modelled on Jewish synagogues. In freeing themselves from the limitations of this naïve and rigidly restricted source, Christian artists in Syria and else-where drew increasingly upon pagan Hellenistic formulas. These were modified from time to time and place to place until in the fourth and fifth centuries there emerged a standardized Byzantine style, within which there was ample scope for individual talents to find expression. In archi-tecture, painting, sculpture and other fields of visual ex-pression, this new style aimed resolutely at realism, and this paved the way for Christian medieval art as well as for Moslem art.

It is probable that artistic craftsmen from Syria were summoned to embellish the new capital, Ravenna, to which Honorius (395–423) removed his court to escape the dangers of the Germanic invasions. They remained there to teach their craft to native artists, introducing mosaic techniques and Syrian decorative motifs. In the fifth century Ravenna became the artistic capital of northern Italy. Its school of art and architecture has been termed half-Syrian; the city itself could also be thus characterized. Venice, too, was an outpost of eastern culture on Italian soil.

Although some Syriac-speaking emigrants were artists and many were soldiers, monks or slaves, the majority were merchants and other men of affairs. The division of the empire and the fragmentation of its Syrian province do not seem to have affected the domestic and foreign trade rela-tions of Syria adversely. In the Byzantine period as in the earlier one Mediterranean trade was almost entirely in Syrian and Greek hands. Syriac-speaking merchants con-tinued traversing the entire Roman world in the fourth century, prompted by their love of lucrative trade and defying all dangers. They had flourishing settlements at Rome, Naples and Venice in Italy, Marseilles, Bordeaux and Paris in France, Carthage and the Spanish and Sicilian ports. They imported wines from Ascalon and Gaza, purple from Caesarea, woven fabrics from Tyre and Beirut, pistachio nuts and sword blades from Damascus and embroidered stuffs from several towns. Embroidery was especially in demand for ecclesiastical use. An old commodity which now assumed new importance was silk, the entire trade being in Syrian hands. Imported from China through Arabia, the silk was dyed and rewoven in Phoenicia. Both dyeing and silk-trading soon became monopolies of the Byzantine state. From Arabia and India, Syria continued to import spices and other tropical products. In exchange Syria exported to these lands — as well as to China — glass, enamels and fine textiles.

As it was in the Roman period, Beirut remained the only city of the Phoenician coast famous for intellectual rather than commercial and industrial activity. It still housed the academy of law, a science more assiduously cultivated than any other in the Byzantine era. This institution reached its greatest development in the fifth century, when it attracted some of the finest young minds in the Byzantine empire. The curriculum included science, geometry, rhetoric, Greek and Latin. It covered four years, but Justinian added a fifth year. Some students diverted themselves at horse races and theatres or by drinking and gambling, while others were passionately addicted to theological disputation, asceticism and occultism. Earthquakes between 551 and 555 and a disastrous fire in 560 brought the university to a tragic end.

Throughout the Byzantine period, the aggressive Sasanid dynasty of Persia posed a constant threat to the Syrian province. One incursion between 527 and 532 was checked by Justinian's able general Belisarius. Procopius of Caesarea, the historian of this war, accompanied Belisarius as an adviser. In 540 the Persians appeared again under Chosroes I. At

the head of 30,000 men this energetic monarch descended
on Syria, exacting 2000 pounds of silver from Hierapolis
as the price of immunity. He demanded double this sum
from Aleppo, and set fire to the city when it failed to raise
the amount specified.

From Aleppo Chosroes proceeded to Antioch, which was
weakly garrisoned, as most of Justinian's army was in Europe
attempting to reassemble the ancient Roman empire. A
last-minute reinforcement of 6000 soldiers from the district
of Homs proved no match for the Persian invader. The city
was sacked. Its cathedral was stripped of its gold and silver
treasures and of its splendid marbles. The whole town was
completely destroyed. Its inhabitants were carried away as
captives. The career of the city as an intellectual centre
thus after eight centuries came to an end. In its last days
Antioch was a prominent Christian city, ranking with Constantinople and Alexandria as a patriarchal see. The
economic and human consequences of the Persian sack,
following catastrophic earthquakes in 526 and 528, were
permanently disastrous.

From Antioch Chosroes moved on to Apamea, another
flourishing Christian centre. Its church claimed the possession of a piece of the true cross, which was reverently
preserved in a jewelled casket and displayed annually as
the whole population worshipped. This casket, together
with all the gold and silver in the town, was taken by the
invader, but the relic itself was spared, being devoid of value
to him. The natives ascribed the deliverance of their city
from destruction to the efficacy of the holy relic.

In 542 a truce was concluded and thereafter renewed
several times until 562, when a fifty-year treaty was signed
binding Justinian to pay tribute to the 'great king' and to
refrain from any religious propaganda in Persian territory.
In the early seventh century hostilities were renewed by
Chosroes II, who swept over Syria from 611 to 614, carrying
plunder and destruction wherever he passed. He pillaged

Damascus and decimated its people by murder and captivity. In Jerusalem he left the Church of the Holy Sepulchre in ruins, and carried its treasures — including the bulk of the true cross — off as booty. The Byzantine emperor Heraclius, after six years of war with several reverses, in 628 succeeded in recovering the battered Syrian province, in 629 restored the cross to Jerusalem and was hailed as the deliverer of Christendom and the restorer of the unity of the empire.

One of the tactics used by both Greeks and Persians in this prolonged and mutually exhausting warfare was the maintaining of subsidized Arab kingdoms as allies and buffer states along the northern borders of Arabia. Against the Persian puppet monarchy — the Lakhmids of al-Hirah on the Euphrates — the Byzantines backed the Ghassanids, a South Arabian tribe which had settled in the Hawran plateau in the third century and been converted to Christianity in the fourth. Its history is obscure, as Arabic chronicles are contradictory and vague, while Byzantine authors record only contacts with Constantinople. Only the last few monarchs, whose reigns cover the century preceding the birth of Islam, are fairly well known.

First and greatest among these was al-Harith ibn-Jabalah, who makes his debut in 528 battling against the Lakhmids. In recognition of his services the emperor Justinian in the following year appointed al-Harith lord over all the Arab tribes of Syria. Loyal to the Byzantine crown, al-Harith continued his struggles against the Lakhmids, contributed to the suppression of the Samaritan rebellion and fought in the Byzantine army under Belisarius in Mesopotamia. He killed his Lakhmid rival in a decisive battle (554), and in 563 visited Justinian's court, where the imposing bedouin sheikh made a profound impression on the courtiers. While in Constantinople al-Harith secured the appointment of Jacob Baradaeus of Edessa as prelate of the Syrian Monophysite Church. During his and his son's reigns the new doctrine spread all over Syria.

Al-Harith was succeeded about 569 by his son al-Mundhir. The son followed in the footsteps of the father. He promoted the cause of Monophysitism and battled against the Lakhmid vassals of Persia. His zeal for the rite considered unorthodox by Byzantium, however, alienated him from Justin, who even suspected his political loyalty. The emperor therefore tried to dispose of him by treachery, but he survived to receive a crown from a later emperor and burn the Lakhmid capital in 580. Two years later he was apprehended and sent with his wife and three children to Constantinople and thence to Sicily. The annual subsidy from Byzantium was cut off and all friendly relations were terminated.

Under the leadership of al-Numan, al-Mundhir's eldest son, several raids were directed from the desert against Roman Syria. About 584 he was himself tricked and carried to Constantinople. The Ghassanid nation was thereby broken up. The kingdom was split into several sections, each with a princeling of its own. Some princes allied themselves with Persia; others maintained their independence; still others remained on the side of Byzantium. At this point the Greek chroniclers lose all interest in the subject; the Arab chronicles remain confused. Anarchy prevailed until Persia conquered Syria in 611–614. When Heraclius regained Syria in 628, he may have restored the old dynasty, as at the time of the Moslem conquest the tribes of the former state of Ghassan were reported fighting on the Byzantine side.

The glowing splendour of the court of the Ghassanid kings has been immortalized in the anthologies of several pre-Islamic poets who found in its princes munificent patrons. Their military prowess, lavish hospitality and fabulous generosity were effusively extolled, but rested in fact on a flourishing economy. Like their Nabataean predecessors, they transmitted vital elements of Syrian culture to their kinsmen in Arabia, making possible the germination of Islam.

MOSLEM CONQUEST

Two episodes of late classical times surpass all others in significance: the migration of the Teutonic tribes which resulted in the destruction of the western part of the Roman empire and the eruption of the Moslem Arabian tribes which annihilated the empire of the Persians and stripped the Byzantine of its fairest provinces. Of the two the Arabian episode was the more phenomenal. At the time of its occurrence Persia and Byzantium were the only world powers; the Arabians were known merely as a hopelessly fragmented desert people whose only importance outside their own uninviting peninsula was as unreliable allies of the two great antagonists and as middlemen in the spice and incense trade.

Their unification, the indispensable prelude to their triumphal emergence, was accomplished in the brief span of ten years (622–632) by the Meccan prophet Muhammad, founder of the Islamic faith and father of the Arabian nation. During Muhammad's lifetime little was heard of him in Syria, despite a few attacks on border towns south and east of the Dead Sea. The first of these, in 629, seemed to the natives to be merely another of the frequent bedouin raids to which they were all too accustomed. In perspective, however, it was the opening skirmish in a struggle that was not to cease until Byzantium itself had surrendered and the name of Muhammad had replaced that of Christ on its cathedrals.

In the following year a few of these border settlements submitted to the Moslem columns. Their people were granted security and the right to retain their property and profess their religion on condition that they paid an annual tribute. These terms, formulated by Muhammad himself, set the pattern followed by his successors in treating with conquered populations. The prevailing notion that Moslems offered Christians only a choice between conversion to Islam and death by the sword has no basis in fact; they much preferred to hold such peoples under their rule and collect tribute, which normally ceased once the conquered accepted Islam.

By 633, the year after Muhammad's death, the dissident Arabian tribes had been subdued and the whole peninsula north of the Empty Quarter had been consolidated and unified under the leadership of one man, the first caliph abu-Bakr (632–634). The momentum acquired in these internal wars had to seek new outlets, especially since the new religion had supposedly converted its adherents into one brotherhood. The martial spirit of the tribes, to whom raids had been a sort of national sport from time immemorial, was not weakened by Islam; on the contrary it was redirected and intensified.

Viewed in its proper perspective, the Islamic expansion was the last in the long series of migrations which took the surplus Semitic population from the barren peninsula to the bordering fertile regions and the more abundant life they offered. The Islamic movement, however, did possess one distinctive feature — religious impulse. Combined with the economic, this made the movement irresistible and carried it far beyond the confines of any preceding one. Islam provided a battle-cry, serving as a cohesive agency cementing tribes never united before. But while the desire to spread the new faith or to attain paradise may have motivated some of the bedouin warriors, the desire for the comforts and luxuries of settled life in the Fertile Crescent was the driving force in the case of many more of them.

Several considerations directed this martial energy Syriaward. The Arabian tribes domiciled there were expected to collaborate with their invading kinsmen, as the annual subsidies which for years they had been receiving from Heraclius for guarding the frontiers had recently been suspended as an economy measure. The forts along that southern border had also been neglected and stripped of their garrisons to enable concentration in the north in face of the Persian danger. This does not mean, however, that this invasion or the simultaneous attack on Mesopotamia were the result of purposeful planning. They were surely designed as casual raids for booty, with no thought of permanent conquest, though this was the outcome to which the logic of events inexorably led.

In 633 one column invaded Syria by the coastal route, two followed the inland caravan route north, and one under Khalid ibn-al-Walid penetrated Mesopotamia. Each detachment was approximately 3000 strong at first, but reinforcements more than doubled this strength as they moved north. Two engagements sufficed to clear southern Palestine of Byzantine troops, and fruitful raiding followed. The emperor Heraclius organized a fresh army at Homs and dispatched it under his brother Theodorus, while abu-Bakr ordered Khalid and his column to join their co-religionists in Syria. This Khalid did by an epic eighteen-day march across the desert, appearing with dramatic suddenness directly in the rear of the improvised Byzantine army. He defeated the Christian Ghassanid forces and pressed through Transjordan to Palestine, where the four reunited detachments won a major victory in July 634.

All Palestine now lay open before the invader. For six months random raids were launched in all directions. Another Byzantine army was routed and sought refuge behind the walls of Damascus. Khalid pursued it, isolated the city for six months and in September 635 gained possession of it through treachery. With the fall of the metropolis, total victory was assured. Baalbek and Homs were occupied in 635, and Aleppo, Antioch, Hamah and others early in 636. Only Jerusalem, Caesarea and a few ports held out in expectation of aid from Heraclius.

Heraclius did not intend to disappoint them. He mustered from the vicinity of Antioch and Aleppo an army of some fifty thousand, mostly Armenian and Arab mercenaries, and again put it under the command of his brother Theodorus. Realizing the numerical superiority of this army, the Arabian generals immediately abandoned Homs, Damascus and other cities to concentrate about 2500 men on the Yarmuk river east of Lake Tiberias. After a period of skirmishing, the desert tribesmen on August 20, 636, forced a showdown during a dust storm which gave them a decisive advantage. Before the Moslem onslaught the Armenian and Syro-Arab mercenaries could not hold their own. Some were slaughtered then and there; others were driven relentlessly into the river; still others deserted and were caught and annihilated on the other side. Theodorus was one of the victims. The fate of Syria was sealed, as even Heraclius reluctantly admitted.

Damascus and the other cities previously occupied now received the conqueror with open arms. 'We like your rule and justice', declared the natives of Homs, 'far better than the state of tyranny and oppression under which we have been living.' Farther north Aleppo and Antioch were soon reduced. Only the Taurus mountains, natural boundary of Syria, finally halted the uninterrupted advance of Arabian arms. Along the coast Acre, Tyre, Sidon, Beirut, Byblus and Tripoli were taken. Jerusalem held out until 638 and Caesarea, reinforced and supplied by sea, until 640. In seven years (633–640) the entire country was subdued.

This easy conquest of a strategic province of the Byzantine empire is not difficult to explain. The military structure of that empire had been as effectively undermined by the Persian incursions of the early seventh century as the spiritual unity of its society had been disrupted by the Monophysite schism of the middle fifth. Last-minute efforts to effect a religious compromise only made matters worse. The bulk of the Syrians held on to their church. To them it was more than a religious institution; it was an expression of a sub-merged, semi-articulate feeling of nationality.

At no time after Alexander's conquest did the people of Syria, as a people, lose their national character, their native tongue or their Semitic religion and identify themselves wholeheartedly with the Greco-Roman way of life. At its thickest Hellenistic culture was only skin-deep, affecting a crust of intelligentsia in urban settlements. The bulk of the population must throughout that millennium have considered their rulers aliens. The alienation between rulers and ruled was no doubt aggravated by misrule and high taxation. To the masses of seventh-century Syria the Moslem Arabians must have appeared closer ethnically, linguistically and perhaps religiously than the hated Byzantine masters.

Once conquered, Syria became the base for Arab armies fanning out in every direction. Between 639 and 646 Mesopotamia was subjugated, and Persia lay open to attack. Between 640 and 646 Egypt was subdued and the way cleared to North Africa and Spain. From northern Syria, Anatolia was vulnerable to devastating incursions which were mounted intermittently for almost a century. All these conquests, however, belong to the category of systematic campaigning rather than the casual raiding to which the seizure of Syria belonged. But it was this first victory which gave the nascent power of Islam prestige before the world and confidence in itself.

In historical significance the Moslem conquests of the seventh century rank with those of Alexander as the principal landmarks in the political and cultural history of the Near East. For a thousand years after Alexander's conquest the civilized life of Syria and its neighbouring lands was oriented westward, across the sea; now the orientation turned eastward, across the desert. Links with Rome and Byzantium were severed; new ones with Mecca and Medina were forged. Strictly the latest orientation was a reversion to an old type, for the Arab Moslem civilization did not introduce many original elements. It was rather a revivification of the ancient Semitic culture. Thus viewed, Hellenism becomes an intrusive phenomenon between two cognate layers.

In about a decade the Moslem conquests changed the face of the Near East; in about a century they changed the face of the civilized world. Far from being peripheral or ephemeral, they proved to be a decisive factor in the evolution of medieval society. The Mediterranean became a Moslem lake, and sea trade routes were severed. This, coupled with the Arab occupation of the eastern, western and southern shores, replaced the late classical world with a new world, that of the Middle Ages.

Meanwhile in Syria the Arabians had awakened after the intoxication of the great victory to find themselves confronted with a new and colossal problem for which they were ill prepared, the administration of their new domain. In their past experience there was nothing on which they could draw. Clearly the laws of their primitive Medinese society were not adequate and those of their new Islamic society were not applicable, as the conquered people were not yet Moslems.

Umar, who had succeeded abu-Bakr as caliph in 634, was the first to address himself to this task. Details of his enactments are obscured by later interpolations, but certain principles are clear. First among these was the policy requiring that Arabian Moslems in conquered lands should constitute a sort of religio-military aristocracy, keeping their blood pure and unmixed, living aloof and abstaining from holding or cultivating any landed property. The conquered peoples were given a new status, that of second-class citizens under a covenanted obligation to pay a tribute which comprised both land tax and poll tax, but they were entitled to protection and were exempt from military duty.

Only a Moslem could draw his sword in defence of the land of Islam. Thus the principle of inequality between victor and vanquished was established as a permanent basis of policy.

Another principle said to have been enunciated by Umar was that movable property and prisoners won as booty belonged to the warriors as before, but that the land belonged to the Moslem community. Those who cultivated it had to continue paying land tax even after adopting Islam. This and other tax legislation traditionally ascribed to the initiative of Umar clearly resulted from years of experience. The first caliphs and provincial governors could not have devised and imposed a system of taxation and of finance administration; it was easier for them to continue with minor modifications the system of Byzantine provincial government already established in Syria. In the Moslem empire tribute varied from place to place according to the nature of the soil and the previously prevailing system. Poll tax was an index of lower status and was exacted in a lump sum. It was generally four dinars for the well-to-do, two for the middle class and one for the poor. Women, children, beggars, the aged and the diseased were exempt except when they had independent income.

Umar in 639 divided Syria for administrative purposes into four military districts — Damascus, Homs, Jordan (including Galilee) and Palestine — corresponding to the Byzantine provinces at the time of the conquest. A military camp south of Damascus served as the temporary capital; other military camps were set up in each district. To these camps Arabian soldiers, soon to become the new citizenry of the conquered province, brought their families; many of their wives or concubines were no doubt captured native women. As warriors and defenders they enjoyed rights and privileges which later immigrants from Arabia could not enjoy. At their head stood the commander-in-chief and governor-general, who combined in his person all the executive, judiciary and military functions. The governmental framework of the Byzantine system was preserved; even the local officials who did not withdraw from the country at the time of conquest were left in their positions. Obviously the Arabians had no trained personnel to replace such officials. Besides, their paramount interests were to keep the captured province under control and to collect the taxes due from its people. In its primitive phases Arabian provincial government was military in form, financial in aim and flexible in method.

In 639 a terrible plague spread havoc among the troops. Some 20,000 of them are said to have perished, including the governor-general and his successor Yazid. Umar thereupon (640) appointed Yazid's brother Muawiyah governor. For twenty years Muawiyah was to dominate Syria; for twenty more he would dominate the world of Islam as the first of the Umayyad family of caliphs. The policies he initiated as governor and pursued as caliph earned for him a permanent and prominent niche in the Arab hall of fame. He made the starting-point of his policy the cultivation of his new Syrian subjects, who were still Christians, as well as the Arab tribes, such as the Ghassanids, who had been domiciled in the country since pre-Islamic days and were Christianized. Many of these tribes were of South Arabian origin as opposed to the new emigrants, who were North Arabians. For wife Muawiyah chose a Jacobite Christian girl of the Kalb, a South Arabian tribe. His personal physician, his court poet and his financial controller were likewise Christians. Arab chronicles stress the sense of loyalty which the Syrians cherished toward their new chief consequent upon his enlightened and tolerant policy.

Muawiyah proceeded to organize the province on a stable basis. The raw material which constituted the Arab army he now whipped into the first ordered, disciplined military force in Islam. Its archaic tribal organization, a relic of patriarchal days, was abolished. There was no interference from Medina, especially since the new caliph Uthman, who succeeded Umar in 644, was a relative of Muawiyah, both being members of the aristocratic Umayyad branch of the Quraysh. Muhammad belonged to another clan of the same tribe. The army was kept in fit condition by semi-annual raids into the 'land of the Romans' — Asia Minor.

For the defence of a province bordering on the sea, Muawiyah realized that a body of disciplined, loyal troops did not suffice. In Acre he found fully equipped Byzantine shipyards which he developed into an arsenal second only to that of Alexandria. The new Moslem fleet, doubtless manned by Greco-Syrians with a long seafaring tradition, took Cyprus in 649 despite the reluctance of desert-reared caliphs to approve of expeditions across the alien sea. Rhodes was pillaged in 654 and in the following year the long-supreme Byzantine navy was virtually annihilated by the simple expedient of tying each Arab ship to an enemy vessel and converting the engagement into a hand-to-hand conflict.

Muawiyah, however, could not take full advantage of these exploits by his admirals and generals. Domestic disturbances leading to civil war were convulsing the Moslem world. In 656 Uthman was murdered by rebellious partisans of Ali, first cousin of Muhammad and husband of his only surviving daughter Fatimah. These partisans (Shiah) insisted that Ali was the divinely designated and therefore the only legitimate successor, and that his descendants were entitled to the caliphate by hereditary right. After some deliberation he was proclaimed caliph.

The caliphate of Ali was beset with trouble from beginning to end. The first problem was how to dispose of two rival claimants, Talhah and al-Zubayr, who with their followers in Hejaz and Iraq refused to recognize his succession. Both men were defeated and killed in a battle near Basra in December 656. Ali established himself in his new capital al-Kufah as the seemingly undisputed caliph. A second civil war, however, was not far off.

The usual oath of fealty was accorded the new caliph by every provincial governor except Muawiyah. The well-entrenched governor of Syria and kinsman of Uthman now came out as the avenger of the martyred caliph. Dramatically Muawiyah exhibited in the Damascus mosque the blood-stained shirt of Uthman and the fingers chopped from the hands of his wife as she tried to defend him. Carefully keeping his own interests under cover, Muawiyah publicly confronted Ali with this dilemma : punish the assassins or accept the position of an accomplice. Punishing the culprits was something Ali neither would nor could do. But the basic conflict transcended personalities. The fundamental question at issue was whether Iraq or Syria, Kufah or Damascus, should head the Islamic world. Medina clearly was out of the race. The far-flung conquests had shifted the centre of gravity to the north and relegated the former capital to a marginal position.

The army of Iraq led by Ali and that of Syria under Muawiyah met south of the Euphrates in July 657 for what should have been the decisive battle. Ali's forces were on the point of achieving complete victory after three days of bloody fighting when suddenly their foes lifted lances to which were fastened manuscripts of the Koran. This gesture was interpreted as meaning an appeal from the decision of arms to the decision of the Koran — whatever that might mean. Hostilities ceased. Ali, pious and simple-hearted, accepted Muawiyah's proposal to arbitrate and thus spare Moslem blood. The arbitration which ensued in January 659 has been embellished by legend, but apparently both principals were deposed, depriving Ali of a real office and Muawiyah only of a tenuous claim which he had not yet even dared publicly assert.

Two years later Ali was assassinated by a personal enemy and hastily interred outside Kufah at Najaf, where his shrine has become the greatest centre of pilgrimage in Shiite Islam. Deficient in the traits that make a politician, he was rich in those that, from the Arab point of view, constitute a perfect man. Eloquent in speech, sage in counsel, valiant in battle, true to his friends, magnanimous to his foes, he was raised by tradition to the position of paragon of Moslem chivalry. Proverbs, verses and anecdotes unnumbered have clustered around his name and even his sword. The youth movement in Islam, which developed later along lines parallel to those of the medieval orders of chivalry, took Ali for its model. Many dervish fraternities have likewise considered him their ideal exemplar and patron. To most of his partisans he has remained through the ages infallible; to the extremists among them he even became the incarnation of the deity.

THE GLORY THAT WAS DAMASCUS

EARLY in 661 Muawiyah was proclaimed caliph at Jerusalem, but it was Damascus that he chose as his capital,
thus inaugurating its most glorious epoch. His first problem
was to pacify the empire and consolidate his control over
rebellious provinces. Hejaz was naturally lukewarm in its
loyalty to Muawiyah, as the Moslems of Mecca and Medina
never forgot that the Umayyads were late believers and
that their belief was one of convenience rather than conviction. But for the time being the cradle of Islam gave no
serious trouble. Syria was loyal to its former governor and
Egypt was firmly held.

Iraq, however, immediately and openly declared for
al-Hasan, elder son of Ali and Fatimah. To its people he
was the only legitimate successor of his assassinated father.
In the course of a swift campaign Muawiyah secured from
al-Hasan a definite renunciation of all claims, in return for
a generous subsidy to be paid him for life. He retired to
an existence of ease and luxury in Medina and died eight
years later after having married and divorced at least a
hundred wives. His death may have been caused by
tuberculosis or by poisoning connected with some harem
intrigue, but his followers blamed it on the caliph and considered al-Hasan 'lord of all the martyrs'. At his death,
his claims passed to his brother al-Husayn, who did not
dare assert them during the lifetime of Muawiyah.

After disposing of the Alid threat, Muawiyah brought
Iraq to heel by naming a series of capable and heavy-handed
governors who transplanted 50,000 troublesome Arabians
and bedouins to eastern Persia and took other drastic
measures to subject the turbulent province. With the

territory of Islam temporarily pacified, Muawiyah's extra-ordinary energies sought new outlets in military campaigns by land and sea, thus resuming the course of Moslem expansion which had been interrupted by the two civil wars.

Eastward these campaigns resulted in completing the subjugation of Khurasan (663–671), crossing the Oxus and raiding Bukhara in Turkestan (674). Merv, Balkh, Herat and other cities which were to develop into brilliant centres of Islamic culture were captured. The army returned to Iraq laden with booty from the Turkish tribes of Trans-oxiana. They thus established the first contact between Arabs and Turks, destined to play a major rôle in later Islamic affairs.

To the west the city of Kairawan was established in Tunisia as a base for military operations against the Berbers. It was built partly with material taken from the ruins of Carthage. As the Berbers were Islamized, they were pressed into the Arab army and utilized in chasing the Byzantines out of Algeria. Brilliant as it was, this campaign, like that in Central Asia, was of no lasting significance, because it was not followed up by occupation. Here, as in Transoxiana, the work had to be done over again.

During the Umayyad period, as in the early Abbasid, the frontier between Arab and Byzantine lands was formed by the great ranges of the Taurus and Anti-Taurus. As the two hostile states stood face to face across this line, they first sought to keep each other off by turning the intervening stretch of land into a desolate terrain. Muawiyah con-tributed to the creation of this unclaimed waste zone. Later Umayyads pursued a different policy, aiming at establishing a footing there by rebuilding as fortresses abandoned or destroyed towns and building new ones. Thus grew a cordon of Moslem fortifications stretching from Tarsus in Cilicia to Malatya on the upper Euphrates. These fortresses were strategically situated at the inter-sections of military roads or the entrances of narrow passes.

The Glory that was Damascus

As the city commanding the southern entrance of the celebrated pass across the Taurus known as the Cilician Gates, Tarsus served as a base for major military campaigns against the territory of the Greeks. In Muawiyah's time and later a major campaign was undertaken every summer and a minor one every winter as a matter of routine. The objective, as in the case of the traditional bedouin raids, was booty, though the dim spectacle of Byzantium may have beckoned from the distance. At no time did Arabs establish a firm foothold in Asia Minor. Their main military energy followed the line of least resistance and was directed eastward and westward. The Taurus and Anti-Taurus blocked their northward expansion permanently. No part of Asia Minor ever became Arabic-speaking, and its basic population was never Semitic.

The recurring raids into Asia Minor did at last reach the capital, in 668, only thirty-six years after Muhammad's death. The army wintered at Chalcedon (the Asiatic suburb of Constantinople), where it suffered severely from want of provisions and from disease. Muawiyah sent his pleasure-loving son Yazid with reinforcements early in 669, and the capital was besieged, doubtless with naval support. The siege was raised that summer, and the army withdrew with its booty. Again in 674 the Arabs reached the Straits, occupying the peninsula of Cyzicus, which projects from Asia Minor into the Sea of Marmara. For six years this spot served as a naval base for a Moslem fleet, as winter headquarters for the invading army and as a base for spring and summer attacks. The city was reportedly saved by the use of Greek fire, a newly invented highly combustible compound which would burn even on or under water. The inventor was a Syrian refugee from Damascus named Callinicus. This was perhaps the first time this 'secret weapon' was used. The Byzantines kept its formula unrevealed for several centuries, after which the Arabs acquired it; but it has since been lost. Greek accounts dilate on the disastrous

121

effects of this fire on enemy ships. What was left of the Arab fleet was wrecked on the return journey, occasioned by the death of Muawiyah in 680.

To this period also belong several naval attacks on islands in the Aegean and eastern Mediterranean waters. Cyprus was already securely in the Moslem fold. Rhodes was temporarily occupied in 672 and Crete in 674. Sicily was attacked first about 664 and repeatedly thereafter. The Arab fleet was an imitation of the Byzantine and was manned mostly by Syrians. The galley, with a minimum of twenty-five seats on each of the two lower decks, was the fighting unit. Each seat held two rowers; the hundred or more rowers in each ship were armed. Those who specialized in fighting took up their positions on the upper deck.

These campaigns, colossal as they were, did not make the commander-in-chief neglect domestic affairs. The financial administration of the state was left in capable and experienced Christian hands. All provincial expenses were met from local income, principally tribute from subject peoples; only the balance went to the caliphal treasury. Such was the revenue that Muawiyah could double the pay of the soldiers, strengthen the Syrian frontier fortresses against the northern enemy, undertake projects of agriculture and irrigation in Hejaz and appease rival factions through subsidies. In Syria he instituted a bureau of registry, a state chancery charged with preserving a copy of each official document dispatched and a postal service. He maintained a standing army of 60,000 at a yearly cost of 60 million dirhems.

Throughout his undertakings, peaceful or military, he was sustained by the unwavering loyalty of his Syrian subjects, natives and Arabian immigrants. The Syro-Arabs were mostly of South Arabian origin and had been Christianized. His wife, his physician and his court poet were Christians. Maronites and Jacobites brought their religious disputes before him. In Edessa he reportedly rebuilt a Christian church that had been demolished by an earthquake. By such acts of tolerance and magnanimity Muawiyah fastened his hold upon the hearts of the Syrians and firmly established the hegemony of their country in the Moslem empire.

Perhaps his most prominent talent was the political finesse which made him unerring in doing the right thing at the right time. This supreme statesmanship he defined in these words: 'I apply not my sword, where my lash suffices; nor my lash, where my tongue is enough. And even if there be but one hair binding me to my fellow men, I do not let it break. When they pull, I loosen; and if they loosen, I pull.' The letter he sent to al-Hasan inducing him to abdicate further illustrates this trait: 'I admit that because of your blood relationship you are more entitled to this high office than myself. And if I were sure of your greater ability to fulfil the duties involved, I would un-hesitatingly swear allegiance to you. Now, then, ask what you will.' Enclosed was a blank already signed by Muawiyah. This ability made his personal relations with his contemporaries frank and friendly, even when they were Alids or other opponents.

In the autumn of 679, six months before his death at the age of eighty, Muawiyah nominated his son Yazid as his successor, an unprecedented procedure in Islam. Yazid had been brought up by his mother partly in the desert around Palmyra, where her Christian tribe roamed. In the capital he also associated with Christians. In the desert the youth-ful prince became habituated to the chase, rough riding and hard life; in the city, to wine-bibbing and verse-making. The desert from this time on became the open-air school in which the young royal princes of the dynasty acquired manly virtues and pure Arabic — unadulterated with Aramaicisms — and incidentally escaped the recurring city plagues. That the caliph had had the nomination of his son in mind for some time may be inferred from his sending him as early as

669 against Constantinople, where Yazid's success served to dispel any doubts that the puritans might have entertained regarding his qualifications. And now Muawiyah, after being sure of the capital, summoned deputations from the provinces and took from them the oath of allegiance to his favourite son. Unsympathetic Iraqis were cajoled, coerced or bribed.

This master-stroke was a landmark in Islamic history. It introduced the hereditary principle, which was followed thereafter by the leading Moslem dynasties. It established a precedent enabling the reigning caliph to proclaim as his successor him among his sons or kinsmen whom he considered competent and to exact for him an anticipatory oath of allegiance. The designation of a crown prince tended to promote stability and continuity and to discourage ambitious aspirants to the throne.

Despite his unparalleled contributions to the cause of Arabism and Islam, Muawiyah was no favourite with the Arab Moslem historians. Nor were his 'tyrannical' lieutenants. The explanation is not difficult to find. Most of those writers were Shiites or Iraqis or Medinese and thus anti-Umayyad. As historians they reflected the puritanical attitude which resented the fact that he was the man who secularized Islam and transformed the theocratic caliphate into a temporal sovereignty. He is blamed for several innovations abhorrent to pious conservatives. The fact remains that such was the example of energy, tolerance and astuteness he set before his successors that while many of them tried to emulate it few came near succeeding.

As long as the rule of powerful Muawiyah lasted, no Alids dared dispute his authority in an overt act; but the accession of the frivolous Yazid was an invitation to secession or rebellion. In response to urgent and reiterated appeals from Iraqis, al-Husayn, younger son of Ali and Fatimah, now declared himself the legitimate caliph. At the head of a weak escort of devoted followers and relatives, including his harem, al-Husayn, who had hitherto resisted the solicitations of his Iraqi partisans and lived in retirement in Medina, set out from Mecca for Kufah. The governor, forewarned, posted patrols one of which, 4000 strong, intercepted al-Husayn at Kerbela and demanded his surrender. He refused and was killed, as were his band of 200. The day of his death (Muharram 10) has become a day of mourning in Shiah Islam. An annual passion play portrays his 'heroic' resistance and tragic martyrdom. His tomb in Kerbela is considered by Shiites the holiest place in the world, a pilgrimage to which is more meritorious than one to Mecca.

The elimination of al-Husayn did not end the struggle for the caliphate. Abdullah ibn-al-Zubayr, a son of the man who had fruitlessly disputed the title with Ali, was now proclaimed caliph in Hejaz. Quick to act, Yazid dispatched against the Medinese dissidents a disciplinary force in which many Christian Syrians served. This force defeated ibn-al-Zubayr, who took refuge in Mecca. The Syrians attacked its traditionally inviolable soil, burning the Kabah and splitting into three pieces the Black Stone, a pre-Islamic fetish considered the holiest relic of Islam. Yazid's death late in 683 led to the suspension of operations.

Yazid was followed by his son Muawiyah II, a weak and sickly youth whose reign lasted only three months. His successor was an elderly cousin, Marwan I, whose South Arabian troops in 684 inflicted a crushing defeat on the North Arabian supporters of ibn-al-Zubayr. This claimant had now been proclaimed caliph not only in his home Hejaz but in Iraq, South Arabia and even parts of Syria. This victory ended the third civil war in Islam, but the anti-caliphate of ibn-al-Zubayr continued until Marwan's son and successor Abd-al-Malik sent against it his iron-handed general al-Hajjaj with 20,000 men. For six and a half months in 692 he besieged Mecca, finally killing ibn-al-Zubayr and sending his head to Damascus. With his death the last champion of primitive Islam passed away. Uthman was avenged. The new Syrian, secular, political orientation was secure. Mecca and Medina took back seats, and the history of Arabia came to deal more with the effect of the outer world on the peninsula and less with the effect of the peninsula on the outer world. The mother 'island' had spent itself.

Abd-al-Malik committed to al-Hajjaj the government of Hejaz. This he held for a couple of years in the course of which he pacified not only that region but Yemen and other parts of Arabia. In 694 he was called to an even more difficult task, that of subduing Iraq, a seething cauldron of discontent. Zubayrites and Kharijites, as well as Shiites and other Alids, kept it in turmoil.

No sooner had al-Hajjaj received his appointment than he set out from Medina with a small mounted escort, crossed the desert by forced marches and arrived at Kufah disguised and unannounced. It was early dawn, time of prayer. Accompanied by only twelve cameleers and with his bow on his shoulder and sword at his side, he entered the mosque, removed the heavy turban which veiled his stern features and delivered a fiery oration which began, 'O people of Kufah. Certain am I that I see heads ripe for cutting, and verily I am the man to do it.' This former teacher who had taken up the warrior's sword was as good as his word. No neck proved too high for him to reach, no head too strong to crush. His task was to establish the ascendancy of the state over all elements within its framework — cost what it may. This he did. Human lives to the number of 120,000 are said to have been sacrificed by him; 50,000 men and 30,000 women were found held in prison at his death. These undoubtedly exaggerated figures with the equally exaggerated reports about his tyranny, bloodthirstiness, gluttony and impiety indicate that what the historians — mostly Shiites or Sunnites of the Abbasid régime — have left us is a caricature rather than a portrayal of the man.

Al-Hajjaj had to his credit several constructive achieve-

ments. He had old canals dug and new ones opened. He
built a new capital — Wasit — midway between Kufah
and Basrah. He introduced regulations to reform currency,
taxes and measures. He is credited, perhaps wrongly, with
introducing orthographical signs into the Koran to indicate
vowel sounds and to distinguish between similar-appearing
consonants in order to prevent incorrect reading of the
sacred text. Justifiable or not, the repressive measures he
took restored order in Kufah and Basrah, hotbeds of discontent and opposition. The state authority was likewise
firmly established along the eastern coast of Arabia, including
hitherto independent Oman. His viceroyalty also embraced
Persia, where his forces practically eliminated the most
dangerous Kharijite sect and even penetrated into India.
His success depended upon the faithful support of his Syrian
troops, in whom his confidence — like his loyalty to the
Umayyad house — knew no bounds.

During the reigns of Abd-al-Malik (685–705) and his
four sons the Umayyad dynasty in Damascus reached the
meridian of its power and glory. The Islamic empire
attained its greatest expansion, from the shores of the
Atlantic and the Pyrenees to the Indus and the confines of
China — an extent greater than that of the Roman empire
at its height. At no time before or after did the Arabs
control so large a territory. It was during this period that
the definitive subjugation of Transoxiana, the reconquest
and pacification of North Africa and the acquisition of the
Iberian peninsula were accomplished. To this era also
belong the Arabicization of the state administration, the
introduction of the first purely Arab coinage, the development of a system of postal service and the erection of such
architectural monuments as the Dome of the Rock in
Jerusalem, the holiest sanctuary in Islam after those of
Mecca and Medina.

Syria's severance from the Byzantine empire consider-
ably reduced its maritime trade, but that was somewhat

compensated for by new markets opened by the acquisition of Persia and Central Asia. Commercial vessels plied the Persian Gulf and Indian Ocean as far as Ceylon, as well as the Mediterranean. Abd-al-Malik founded a shipyard at Tunis, while his son Hisham transferred the main naval yard from Acre to Tyre. Commerce, especially by land, flourished, as did Syrian agriculture, despite the greed of the exchequer. Prosperity spread.

It was under Abd-al-Malik that hostilities with the Byzantines were renewed. While ibn-al-Zubayr was contesting the caliphate, Abd-al-Malik paid tribute to the 'tyrant of the Romans' and to his Christian allies the Mardaites, an obscure highland people who had spread from the Taurus and Amanus ranges into the fastnesses of Lebanon and occupied its chief strategic points as far as Palestine. Mount Lebanon then must have been very sparsely populated and thickly wooded; only the part bordering on the maritime plain was fairly settled. Around these Mardaites as nucleus, fugitives and malcontents gathered. In northern Lebanon they were fused with the Maronites. They furnished scouts and irregular troops to the Byzantines and constituted a thorn in the side of the Arabs, to whom mountain warfare was never palatable. Like his predecessor Muawiyah I, Abd-al-Malik found it expedient to buy them off rather than suffer their marauds or divert his military strength from conquest abroad to policing Syria. With his internal foes thus bribed to remain quiet, he was able to resume periodic attacks on the Greeks of Asia Minor and defeat them in battle. The Maronites themselves in 694 routed a Byzantine army which attempted to end their autonomy. Armenia, which had been overrun while Muawiyah was governor of Syria but had taken advantage of ibn-al-Zubayr's debacle to revolt, was again reduced under Abd-al-Malik.

North Africa too had to be reconquered at this time. Both Berber resistance and Byzantine authority were ended in a series of land campaigns with naval support. Under Musa ibn-Nusayr, son of a Syrian Christian captured by Khalid ibn-al-Walid, it was divorced from Egypt and made a separate province held directly under the caliph at Damascus. Musa extended its boundaries westward as far as Tangier and brought the Berbers permanently into the fold of Islam and into the advancing Moslem armies. The subjugation of North Africa as far as the Atlantic opened the way for the conquest of Spain in subsequent reigns.

Under Abd-al-Malik the administration of the expanding empire was strengthened. Arabic began to replace Greek and Persian as the official language of the government bureaus. Thus in the couse of a millennium three written languages succeeded each other in Syria : Aramaic, Greek and Arabic. With the change of language went a change in coinage. At first the Byzantine coinage found current in Syria at the time of conquest was left undisturbed. Next occasional koranic superscriptions were stamped on the coins. A number of gold and silver pieces were struck in imitation of Byzantine and Persian types, and some copper pieces were issued on which the portrait of the king holding a cross was replaced by that of the caliph brandishing a sword. But it was not until 695, under Abd-al-Malik, that the first purely Arabic dinars and dirhems were struck.

It was this caliph, moreover, who developed a regular postal service designed primarily to meet the needs of government officials and their correspondence. In this he built on the foundation laid by his great predecessor Muawiyah I. Abd-al-Malik promoted the service through a well-organized system knitting together the various parts of his far-flung empire. To this end relays of horses were used between Damascus and the provincial capitals. Postmasters were installed, charged among other duties with the task of keeping the caliph posted on all important happenings in their respective territories.

Other changes in this period involved taxes and fiscal

matters. In theory the only tax incumbent on a Moslem, no matter what his nationality might be, was the alms tax, but in practice only the Moslem of Arabian origin usually enjoyed this privilege. Taking advantage of the theory, new converts to Islam, particularly from Iraq, began under the Umayyads to desert their farms and villages and head for the cities with the hope of enlisting in the Arab army. From the standpoint of the treasury the movement constituted a double loss, for at conversion the taxes were supposedly reduced and upon joining the army a special subsidy was due. As a measure of remedy al-Hajjaj ordered such men restored to their farms and reimposed the high tribute originally paid, the equivalent of the land tax and poll tax. This policy restored the revenues but caused widespread resentment among converts.

Abd-al-Malik was succeeded by his son al-Walid I (705–715). The new caliph resolved to put an end to the effrontery of the Mardaites, and put his brother Maslamah in charge of a punitive operation. Maslamah attacked the troublesome people in their own headquarters and demolished their capital. Some perished, others migrated to Anatolia, and of those who remained some joined the Syrian army and fought under the banner of Islam.

It was the generals of al-Hajjaj who brought about the final reduction of the regions now called Turkestan, Afghanistan, Baluchistan and the Punjab. Qutaybah ibn-Muslim, governor of Khurasan under the viceroy, within a decade after his appointment in 704 reduced Balkh, Bukhara and Samarkand and extended nominal Moslem rule as far as the Jaxartes. Meanwhile, a column of 6000 Syrian troops reduced Sind (the lower valley and delta of the Indus) and in 713 took Multan in the southern Punjab and reached the foot of the Himalaya range. Multan was the seat of a great Buddhist shrine from which enormous plunder was secured. It became the capital of Arab India and the outpost of Islam there.

The Glory that was Damascus

At the opposite extreme of the empire, an Arab-Berber army crossed the Strait of Gibraltar in 710 in a raid for plunder. Encouraged by its success and by dynastic trouble in the Visigothic kingdom of Spain, Musa ibn-Nusayr in 711 dispatched his freedman Tariq with 7000 men, most of whom were, like him, Berbers. They met 25,000 Visigoths and — aided by treachery of disgruntled nobles — routed them. This turned out to be a decisive victory. The march of Moslem arms throughout the peninsula went on unchecked. Tariq with the bulk of the army headed toward the capital Toledo. On his way he sent detachments against neighbouring towns. Seville, a strongly fortified city, was by-passed. Cordova, future resplendent capital of Moslem Spain, fell through treachery. Malaga offered no resistance. Toledo was betrayed by Jewish residents. In less than six months the Berber raider found himself master of half of Spain.

Musa did not relish the idea of having all the honour and booty go to his lieutenant. He arrived in Spain in 712 with an army of 10,000 Arabians and Syrians, attacking the towns avoided by Tariq. Near Toledo he caught up with his former slave, whom he whipped and chained for refusing to obey a halt order early in the campaign. The triumphal march was then resumed. Soon Saragossa in the north was reached and occupied. The highlands of Aragon, Leon and Galicia would have come next but for an order from al-Walid in distant Damascus. The caliph charged his viceroy with the same offence for which the viceroy had disciplined his subordinate — acting independently of his superior.

Musa left his son in command and slowly made his way overland toward Syria. His princely train comprised, besides his staff, 400 of the Visigothic royalty and aristocracy, wearing their crowns and girdled with gold belts, followed by a long retinue of slaves and captives loaded with treasures of booty. The triumphal passage through North Africa and southern Syria was extolled by Arab chroniclers. At Tiberias

Musa received orders from Sulayman, brother and heir of the sick caliph, to delay his arrival at the capital so that it might synchronize with his accession to the caliphal throne. Evidently Musa ignored the orders. In February 715 he made his impressive entry into Damascus and was received by the caliph with great dignity and pomp in the courtyard of the newly and magnificently built Umayyad Mosque, adjoining the caliphal palace. If any single episode can exemplify the zenith of Umayyad glory, it is this memorable day on which such booty was displayed and such numbers of Western princes and fair-haired European captives were seen offering homage to the commander of the believers. Nevertheless Sulayman disciplined Musa and humiliated him. After making him stand until exhausted in the sun, he dismissed him from office and confiscated his property. Musa met the same fate that many a successful general and administrator in Islam met. The conqueror of Africa and Spain was last heard of begging for sustenance in a remote village of Hejaz.

Spain was now incorporated in the Syrian empire. Musa's successors carried on the work of rounding out the conquered territory in the east and north. Half a dozen years after the landing of the first Arab troops on Spanish soil, their successors stood facing the towering and mighty Pyrenees. Such seemingly unprecedented conquest would not have been possible but for internal weakness and dissension. The population of the country was Spanish-Roman; the rulers were Teutonic Visigoths (West Goths) who had occupied the land in the early fifth century. They ruled as absolute, often despotic, monarchs. For years they professed Arian Christianity and did not adopt Catholicism, the denomination of their subjects, until the latter part of the following century. The lowest stratum of the society was held in serfdom and slavery and, with the persecuted Jews, contributed to the facility with which the conquest was achieved.

The Glory that was Damascus

Al-Walid had pressed the offensive against Byzantium, taking Tyana, the strongest fortress in Cappadocia, and preparing a great expedition against Constantinople itself. No sooner had Sulayman (715–717) succeeded his brother than he undertook to expedite the departure of this expedition under Maslamah, supported by a fleet. Constantinople was blockaded by land and sea in the late summer of 716. Of all the Arab attacks on the capital this was unquestionably the most threatening and the best recorded. The besiegers used naphtha and siege artillery. But the defending emperor, Leo the Isaurian, was a capable and vigorous soldier of humble Syrian origin from Marash. He was probably born a subject of the caliph and knew Arabic as perfectly as Greek. While the besieged were hard pressed, the besiegers were equally harassed. Pestilence, Greek fire, scarcity of provisions and attacks from Bulgars wrought havoc among them. The rigours of an unusually severe winter added their share. Yet Maslamah stubbornly persisted. Neither such hardships nor the death of the caliph seemed to deter him. But the order of the new caliph, Umar ibn-Abd-al-Aziz (717–720), he had to heed. The army withdrew in a pitiful state. The fleet, or what was left of it, was wrecked by a tempest on its way back. The Syrian-born emperor was hailed as the saviour of Christian Europe from Moslem Arabs.

The new caliph, Umar II, was in several respects unique among the Umayyads. His piety, frugality and simplicity contrasted sharply with the luxurious worldliness of his cousins. His ideal was to follow in the footsteps of his maternal grandfather, the second orthodox caliph, whose namesake he was. During his brief reign the theologians had their day. Hence the saintly reputation he acquired in Moslem history. Umar abolished the practice introduced by Muawiyah of cursing Ali from the pulpit at the Friday prayers. He introduced fiscal reforms which failed of survival because they lowered the revenue collected from

133

converts, as Berbers, Persians and others flocked to Islam for the pecuniary privileges that accrued. His unworldly but well-intentioned enactment nevertheless substantially contributed toward the treatment as equals of Arab and non-Arab Moslems and the ultimate fusion of the sons of conquerors and conquered.

Yazid II (720–724), a son of Abd-al-Malik, was a frivolous misfit who spent most of his time with his two favourite singing girls. When one of them choked on a grape which he had playfully tossed into her mouth, the passionate young caliph fretted himself to death. He was succeeded by still another brother, Hisham (724–743), rightly considered by Arab historians the last statesman of the house of Umayyah. Hisham's governors had to re-conquer the territory in Central Asia overrun by Qutaybah, extending his sway as far as Kashgar. This city constituted the limit of Arab expansion eastward. The Umayyad army was modelled on the Byzantine, and in outfit and armour the Arab warrior was hard to distinguish from his Greek counterpart. The cavalry used plain, rounded saddles like the ones still in fashion in the Near East. The heavy artillery comprised ballista, mangonel and battering-ram. Such heavy engines, together with the baggage, were trans-ported on camels behind the army.

The Arabs and Berbers in Spain had started crossing the Pyrenees to raid the convents and churches of France, with varying success. Narbonne had been captured in 720 and was later converted into a huge citadel with an arsenal, but an assault on Toulouse in 721 failed. In 732 a full-scale invasion commenced with a victory over the duke of Aquitaine and the storming of Bordeaux. Between Tours and Poitiers the French under Charles Martel turned back the invaders at what proved to be the high-water mark of Moslem conquest in western Europe. Despite this set-back, Arab raids in other directions continued. In 734 Avignon was captured; nine years later Lyons was pillaged.

These were the last accessions made under the Umayyad caliphs.

In 732, when Arab expansion was checked at the Loire just a century after the death of Muhammad, the Umayyad caliphs ruled an empire extending from the Bay of Biscay to the Indus and the confines of China and from the Aral Sea to the cataracts of the Nile. The capital of this huge domain was Damascus, the oldest living city, set like a pearl in an emerald girdle of gardens watered by snow-fed brooks. The city overlooked a plain stretching south-westward to that venerable patriarch of Lebanon crests, Mount Hermon, called by the Arabs al-Jabal al-Shaykh (the grey-haired peak), because of its turban of perpetual snow. In the centre of the city stood the Umayyad Mosque, a gem of architecture that still attracts lovers of beauty. Near by lay the green-domed palace where the caliph held his formal audiences, flanked by his relatives, with courtiers, poets and petitioners ranged behind.

Caliphal life in Damascus was fully regal in contrast with that of Medina, which had been on the whole simple and patriarchal. Relations with the Umayyad caliphs began to be regulated by protocol. Ceremonial clothes with the name of the caliph and religious sentences embroidered on their borders came into use. The evenings of the caliph were set apart for entertainment and social intercourse. Muawiyah I enjoyed listening to tales and drinking rose sherbet, but his successors preferred stronger beverages and livelier amusements. Yazid I and Hisham's successor al-Walid II were confirmed drunkards, and the frivolous diversions of Yazid II have already been noted. Debauched parties were held in the desert palaces, far from censorious eyes. Several caliphs and courtiers engaged in more innocent pastimes such as hunting, dicing and horse-racing. Polo was introduced from Persia probably toward the end of the Umayyad period. Cock-fights were not infrequent. The chase was always popular, at first with saluki dogs, later with cheetahs. Al-Walid I was one of the first caliphs to institute and patronize public horse-races.

The harem of the caliphal household apparently enjoyed a relatively large measure of freedom. They undoubtedly appeared veiled in public, veiling being an ancient Semitic custom sanctioned by the Koran. The harem system, with its concomitant auxiliary of eunuchs, was not fully instituted until after the death of Hisham.

The city of Damascus cannot have changed much in character and tone of life since its Umayyad days. Then, as now, in its narrow covered streets the Damascene with his baggy trousers, heavy turban and red pointed shoes rubbed shoulders with the sun-tanned bedouin in his flowing gown surmounted by a head shawl encircled by a band. A few women, all veiled, crossed the streets; others stole glimpses through the latticed windows of their homes overlooking the bazaars and public squares. There was no right or left rule of way, no part of the passage reserved for riders or pedestrians. Amidst the confused crowd an aristocrat might be seen on horseback cloaked in a silk robe and armed with a sword. The screaming voices of sherbet sellers and sweet-meat vendors competed with the incessant tramp of passers-by and of donkeys and camels laden with the varied products of the desert and the town. The entire city atmosphere was charged with all kinds of smell. The demand on eye, ear and nose must have been overwhelming.

As in Homs, Aleppo and other towns the Arabians lived in separate quarters of their own according to their tribal affiliations. The door of the house usually opened from the street into a courtyard in which an orange or citron tree flourished beside a large basin with a flowing jet emitting intermittently a veil-like spray. It was the Umayyads who, to their eternal glory, supplied Damascus with a water system unexcelled in its day and still functioning. The luxurious gardens outside of Damascus, al-Ghutah, owe their very existence to the Barada river, which rushes from the north to fling tassels of silver streams across the plain. Its canals spread freshness and fertility throughout the city. About sixty remaining public baths, some with mosaics and decorated tiles, testify to the richness and distribution of its water supply.

LIFE UNDER THE UMAYYADS

THE population of the Umayyad empire was divided into four social classes. At the top stood the ruling Moslems, headed by the caliphal family and the aristocracy of Arabian conquerors. Few Arabians were interested in agriculture, so the newcomers mostly congregated in cities. Lebanon was naturally avoided. The mountain does not seem to have received an influx of Arabians till the ninth and succeeding centuries. In other places with fertile soil and spring water, however, some doubtless did establish agricultural villages on easily defended sites. In Syria, as elsewhere, they remained a small minority; but Arabian tribal traits such as family solidarity, exaltation of individual prowess, hospitality and emphasis on the personal touch in all human relations spread to other peoples and are still manifest and highly prized throughout Syria.

The Arab concentration in cities was so marked that Arabic by Hisham's time had become the urban language. As the country folk came to these cities to sell their products or practise their crafts, they acquired the new tongue without necessarily forsaking the old one. The indigenous intellectuals also found it convenient to acquire Arabic in order to qualify for government posts.

Next below the Arabian Moslems stood the Neo-Moslems. These were native Syrians who, from conviction or calculation, had professed Islam and were thereby in theory, though not in practice, admitted to the full rights of Islamic citizenship. Such converts usually attached themselves as clients to some Arabian tribe and became members thereof. These neophytes formed a lower stratum of Moslem society, a status which they bitterly resented. Some of them expressed their dissatisfaction by espousing the dissident Shiite or the Kharijite cause, while others became fanatical exponents of militant orthodox Islam. Other converts were naturally the first members of the Moslem society to devote themselves to learned studies and the fine arts. They mediated their old traditions and culture to their new co-religionists. As they demonstrated their superiority in the intellectual field, they began to contest with them political leadership. And as they intermarried with them they diluted the Arabian stock and ultimately made the term Arab applicable to all Arabic-speaking Moslems regardless of ethnic origin.

Damascus and other cities may by the late Umayyad era have presented the aspect of Moslem towns, but the other places, more particularly the mountain regions, preserved their native features and ancient culture pattern. The number of country people who readily accepted the new faith must have been fewer than those who accepted the new language, mainly because the Umayyad caliphs, with the exception of the pious Umar II, did not favour conversion, especially from among owners of arable land. The total number of Moslems in Syria about 732 could not have exceeded 200,000 out of an estimated population of 3,500,000.

The third class consisted of members of tolerated sects which professed revealed religions — Christians, Jews and Sabians — with whom the Moslems had entered into a covenant relationship. The tolerated status was granted to Christians and Jews by Muhammad himself and was accorded to the Sabians (and the pseudo-Sabians of Harran) on the assumption that they were monotheists. It was later extended to the fire-worshipping Zoroastrians, the heathen Berbers and others. In Arabia proper, however, because of a statement ascribed to Muhammad, no non-Moslems were tolerated except the small Jewish community in Yemen. This recognition of tolerated sects was predicated on disarming their devotees and exacting tribute from them in return for Moslem protection. Not being members of the dominant religious community they held an inferior position socially and politically. In matters of civil and criminal judicial procedure they were left under their own spiritual heads unless a Moslem was involved. Moslem law was considered too sacred to be applicable to non-Moslems.

In Syria Christians and Jews were generally well treated until the reign of Umar II, the first caliph to impose humiliating restrictions on them. He issued regulations excluding Christians from public offices, forbidding their wearing turbans and requiring them to cut their forelocks, don distinctive clothes with girdles of leather, ride without saddles, erect no places of worship and pray in subdued voices. The penalty for a Moslem's killing of a Christian, he further decreed, was only a fine, and a Christian's testimony against a Moslem was not acceptable in court. It may be assumed that such legislation was enacted in response to popular demand. In administration, business and industry the Arabian Moslems, still predominantly illiterate, could offer no competition to the indigenous Christians. The Jews, who were fewer than Christians and often held meaner jobs, were evidently included under some of these restrictions and excluded from government posts.

At the bottom of the social ladder stood the slaves. Slavery, an ancient Semitic institution, was accepted by Islam but modified by legislation to ameliorate the condition of the slave. Canon law forbade a Moslem to enslave a co-religionist, but did not guarantee liberty to an alien slave on adopting Islam. In early Islam, slaves were recruited by purchase, kidnapping, raiding and from unransomed prisoners of war, including women and children. Soon the slave trade became brisk and lucrative in all Moslem lands. East and Central Africa supplied black slaves, Turkestan yellow ones, the Near East and south-eastern Europe white ones. The institution was self-perpetuating, as most children of slave mothers were also slaves. Only the children borne to her master by a slave concubine were considered free by right, but the liberation of a slave has always been looked upon as praiseworthy.

In the melting-pot process which resulted in the amalgamation of Arabians and non-Arabians, slaves, no doubt, played a significant rôle. This was true of the royalty as well as the commonalty, for the mothers of the last three Umayyad caliphs were slaves. Yazid III was the son of al-Walid I and a captured Persian princess, but his brother Ibrahim was the son of an obscure concubine, perhaps a Greek. The mother of Ibrahim's successor, Marwan II, was a Kurdish slave. According to one report she was already pregnant with Marwan when his father acquired her, which would make the last Umayyad not an Umayyad at all.

As Syrians, Iraqis, Persians, Copts and Berbers joined the band-wagon of Islam and intermarried with Arabians, the gap between Arabians and non-Arabians was bridged. The follower of Muhammad, no matter what his original nationality might have been, would now adopt the Arabic tongue and pass for an Arab. The Arabians themselves brought no science, no art, no tradition of learning, no heritage of culture from the desert. The religious and linguistic elements were the only two novel cultural elements they introduced. In everything else they found themselves dependent upon their subjects. In Syria and the other conquered lands they sat as pupils at the feet of the conquered. What Greece was to the Romans Syria was to the Arabians. When, therefore, we speak of Arab medicine or philosophy or mathematics, what we mean is the learning that was enshrined in Arabic books written by men who were themselves Syrians, Persians, Iraqis, Egyptians or Arabians — Christians, Jews or Moslems — and who drew their material from Greek, Aramaic, Persian and other sources.

Intellectual life in the Umayyad period was not on a high level. In fact the whole period was one of incubation. The frequency of its civil and foreign wars and the instability of its economic and social conditions militated against the possibility of high intellectual attainment. But in it the seeds were sown to come into full bloom in the Abbasid caliphate. The study of Arabic grammar was one of the first disciplines cultivated in this period. It was necessitated by the linguistic needs of Neo-Moslems eager to learn the Koran, hold government positions and push ahead with the conquering class. Arabic grammar went through a process of slow, long development and bears striking marks of the influence of Greek logic and Sanskrit linguistics.

The twin sciences of lexicography and philology arose as a result of the study of the Koran and the necessity of expounding it. The same is true of the most characteristically Moslem literary activity, the science of tradition (*hadith*). The Koran and tradition lay at the foundation of theology and jurisprudence, both based on Islamic law. Roman law too was adapted and applied to contractual transactions and state monopolies such as coinage, official seals and papyrus for documents. The Arabs followed the Byzantine precedent in considering it the state duty to protect its citizens against forgery, counterfeit, contraband and other abuses connected with these commodities, and in administering heavy punishments. But we know of no book on Roman law translated into Arabic.

The judges of the Umayyad period were usually appointed by provincial governors from among scholars learned in the Koran and Islamic tradition. Their jurisdiction was limited to Moslem citizens ; non-Moslems were allowed autonomy under their own religious heads, especially in personal matters relating to marriage, divorce and inheritance. Besides judging cases these officials administered pious foundations (*waqfs*) and the property of imbeciles and orphans.

History-writing developed from interest in Islamic tradition, and hence was one of the earliest disciplines cultivated by Arab Moslems. The stimuli for historical research were provided by the interest of the believers in collecting old stories about Muhammad and his companions, the necessity of ascertaining the genealogical relationship of each Moslem Arab in order to determine the amount of state stipend to be received and the desire of the early caliphs to scan the proceedings of kings and rulers before them.

Public speaking in its varied forms attained in the Umayyad epoch heights unsurpassed in later times. It was employed for sermons, for military exhortations and for patriotic addresses. The fiery orations of al-Hajjaj are among the chief literary treasures of the period. Early official correspondence must have been brief, concise and to the point. It was not till the days of the last Umayyads that the flowery style was introduced. Its ornate, excessively polite phraseology betrays Persian patterns. Persian literary influence may also be detected in the many early wise sayings and proverbs.

The strenuous period of conquest and expansion had produced no poet in a nation that had a long tradition of poetry. But with the accession of the worldly Umayyads, poets throve. Satirical verse, love lyrics, odes in praise of wine, fulsome panegyrics, political rhymes, anthologies of pre-Islamic poetry and other productions were turned out in great quantities, but quality remained high. The closeness of Umayyad poetry to Islam and to pre-Islamic poetry endowed it with purity of style, strength of expression and natural dignity that raised it to the position of a model for generations to come. Its techniques and motifs set the pattern and provided the mould into which the Arabic poet's individual feeling and composition has since been cast. His inability since then to dissociate himself from his literary heritage and create original masterpieces has been evident.

Arab science was based on the Greek and had its start with medicine. Moslem regard for medical science is echoed in a tradition ascribed to Muhammad : 'Science is twofold : that which relates to religion and that which relates to the body'. Medical treatises and other works were translated from Greek, Syriac and Coptic into Arabic, and segregation of persons afflicted with leprosy, blindness and other chronic diseases was instituted and special treatment provided. Umar II is said to have transferred the schools of medicine from Alexandria, where the Greek tradition flourished, to Antioch and Harran.

The Umayyad period also saw the beginnings of several movements of a religious and philosophical nature. Theological speculation provoked by contacts with Christianity led to the rationalist Mutazilite school, while reaction against the harsh predestination of Islam motivated the Qadarite doctrine of free will. Muawiyah II and Yazid III subscribed to the Qadarite doctrine. Chief among the Christian protagonists who induced these speculations was St. John of Damascus (675–about 749), a Syrian who wrote in Greek but no doubt spoke Aramaic at home and also knew Arabic. He was a boon companion of the court and a government councillor before retiring to a life of asceticism and devotion. Besides debating theology with Moslems, he wrote dialogues which emphasize the divinity of Christ and the freedom of human will. He defended the use of images and ritual and composed many hymns. As theologian, orator, apologist, polemicist and father of Byzantine art and music, St. John stands out as an ornament of the church under the caliphate.

Other movements which weakened the universal Moslem orthodoxy included the tolerant Murjiites, who suspended judgment of sinners and tended to justify the secularism of the Umayyad caliphs, and the intolerant Kharijites, who aimed at maintaining the primitive democratic principles of puritanical Islam. In pursuit of their aim the Kharijites caused rivers of blood to flow in the first three centuries of Islam. They opposed the prerogative conferred on the Quraysh that the caliph should be one of their number, forbade the cult of saints with its attendant local pilgrimages and prohibited Sufi fraternities.

More important than all these were the Shiites, partisans of Ali and his descendants. The orthodox Sunnite view considers the caliph the secular head of the Moslem community, the leader of the believers and the protector of the faith, but bestows no spiritual authority on him. In opposition to that the Shiite view confines the imamate to the family of Ali and makes the imam not only the sole legitimate head of the Moslem society but also the spiritual and religious leader whose authority is derived from a divine ordinance. Extremist Shiites went so far as to consider the imam the incarnation of the deity. Shiism germinated most successfully in Iraq, but Syria and Lebanon still contain nearly a quarter million, fragmented into several minor sects and heterodoxies. Like a magnet Shiism attracted to itself all sorts of nonconformists and malcontents — economic, social, political and religious.

No sooner had the awe inspired by Islam worn off than male and female professional singers and musicians began to make their appearance. In the Umayyad era Mecca and, more particularly, Medina became a nursery of song and a conservatory of music. They attracted gifted artists from outside and supplied the Damascus court with an ever-increasing stream of talent. The second Umayyad caliph, Yazid I, himself a composer, introduced singing and musical instruments into the court. Other Umayyads — except the austere and puritanical Umar II — followed suit. So widespread was the cultivation of musical art under the Umayyads that it provided their rivals, the Abbasid party, with an effective argument in their propaganda aimed at undermining the house of the 'ungodly usurpers'.

Moslem hostility towards representational art does not manifest itself in Umayyad times. The caliphs had Christian painters decorate their palaces with mural frescoes and mosaics which combine Nabataean, Syrian, Byzantine and Sasanid motifs. They depict royal enemies of the Arabs, hunting scenes, nude dancers, musicians and merrymakers. The fringes of the Syrian Desert, especially in its southern part, are strewn with remains of palaces and hunting lodges either erected by Umayyad architects on Byzantine and Persian patterns or restored by them. Some no doubt were originally Roman fortresses. Many caliphal residences evidently had walled gardens in which wild game was kept for hunting.

For fully half a century after the conquest of Syria Moslems worshipped in converted churches and erected no special mosques. In Damascus they divided not the church itself, as tradition states, but the sacred enclosure. All Damascene worshippers entered through the same gate; the Christians turned left and the Moslems right. The principal mosques of Hamah, Homs and Aleppo were originally Christian places of worship. First among the mosques built in Syria was the Dome of the Rock in Jerusalem, erected in 691 by Abd-al-Malik. His purpose may have been to divert the current of Syrian pilgrimage from Mecca, then in an anti-caliph's hands, and to outshine the Church of the Holy Sepulchre and Christian cathedrals of Syria. To this end Abd-al-Malik employed native architects and artisans trained in the Byzantine school. The bronze doors, decorated with incrustation in silver — a distinguished achievement of Byzantine artists — are among the oldest dated ones of their kind. Tiles and mosaics were lavishly used in the original structure and later in its renovation. East of this edifice stands an elegant small cupola called the Dome of the Chain, which served as a treasure house for the Rock.

Next in chronology and importance was the Umayyad Mosque of Damascus. It was not until 705 that al-Walid I seized the Cathedral of St. John the Baptist and converted it into this mosque, one of the sublimest places of worship in the world. Persian, Indian, Greek and Syrian craftsmen laboured for seven years to create its multicoloured mosaics and its murals of gold and precious stones. Rare marbles adorn its upper walls and ceiling. On its north side stands the oldest purely Moslem minaret in existence, while the two on the south side stand on earlier church towers. The indigenous Syrian type of minaret, a plain square structure, is clearly descended from the watch or church tower. The slender, tapering, round style, reminiscent of classical Roman columns, was a later adoption by the Turks, who introduced it into Syria as exemplified at Homs.

Al-Walid I, greatest among Umayyad builders, was also responsible for rebuilding the mosque of Medina, enlarging and beautifying that of Mecca and erecting in Syria a number of schools, hospitals and places of worship. In his reign, peaceful and opulent, whenever people in Damascus got together — according to Arab historians — fine buildings formed the chief topic of conversation.

In the palaces and mosques left by the Umayyads the harmonization of Arabian, Persian, Syrian and Greek elements is accomplished and the resultant synthesis called Moslem art makes its debut. The Arabian element is endless repetition of small units to which one could add or from which he could subtract without materially affecting the whole. The columns of the Cordova mosque illustrate the point. The motif suggests the monotony of the desert, the seemingly endless rows of trunks of date palms in an oasis or the legs of a caravan of camels. The Persians contributed delicacy, elegance, multicolour. In Umayyad Syria the ancient Semitic and the intruding Greek elements and motifs were reconciled and pressed into the permanent service of Islam.

Hisham's four successors were incompetent even if not dissolute and degenerate. Corruption was widespread. The eunuch system, inherited from Byzantium and Persia, was now assuming large proportions and facilitating the harem institution. Increased wealth brought in its wake a superabundance of slaves, and both resulted in general indulgence in luxurious living. Nor was the moral turpitude limited to high classes. The vices of civilization, including wine, women and song, had evidently seized upon the sons of the desert and were now beginning to sap their vitality.

Disturbances in the provinces, dissatisfaction among the South Arabians, who formed the bulk of the Arab population of Syria and who had steadfastly supported the Umayyad dynasty, and family feuds led to the murder of al-Walid II, the death of his cousin Yazid III and the abdication of Yazid's brother Ibrahim — all within the year 744. A distant cousin, Marwan II, was installed as caliph, but anarchy was on the march throughout the whole domain. An Umayyad claimant arose in Syria, a Kharijite one rebelled in Iraq and leaders in Khurasan refused to acknowledge the caliph's authority. Marwan moved his seat of government to Harran, where he could rely upon North Arabian support and deal more effectively with his two worst enemies — the Alids and the Abbasids.

To the Shiites the Umayyads were but ungodly usurpers who had perpetrated an unforgivable, unforgettable wrong against Ali and his descendants. As the focus of popular sympathy, their camp gradually became the rallying point of the dissatisfied, politically, socially and economically. The Iraqis nurtured a grudge against the Syrians for depriving them of the seat of the caliphate. Sunnite pietists joined the band of critics who charged the house of Umayyah with worldliness, secularism and indifference to koranic law. The Abbasids likewise took advantage of the general chaotic condition to press their own claim to the throne, based on the nearness of their kinship to Muhammad as compared with the Umayyads'.

Another factor that entered into the situation was the discontent felt by non-Arabian Moslems in general and Persian Moslems in particular because of the treatment accorded them by Arabian Moslems. Far from being granted the equality promised by Islam, these neophytes were actually reduced to inferior status, and sometimes were not even granted exemption from the capitation tax. The resentment reached its height in Persia, whose more ancient and venerable culture was acknowledged even by the Arabians. The soil of Khurasan in the north-east proved especially fertile for the germination of Shiite doctrine, but decisive leadership was furnished by the Abbasid claimant, abu-al-Abbas Abdullah, a master of propaganda.

Actual revolt began in Khurasan in 747 under the Abbasid agent abu-Muslim, a freedman of obscure origin. At the head of an army of South Arabians he seized Merv and other Persian cities while Marwan was kept busy by a rebellion in Syria and a Kharijite revolt in Iraq. Kufah fell in 749, and abu-al-Abbas was proclaimed caliph. A final decisive battle in January 750 was won by the Abbasids, and Marwan fled to Egypt. Of the towns of Syria, only Damascus put up the semblance of a fight. A few days of siege were enough to reduce the proud capital. Marwan was captured and killed, as were almost all survivors of the Umayyad house except a grandson of Hisham named Abd-al-Rahman.

After an odyssey of some five years, fraught with danger, Abd-al-Rahman reached Spain and established himself in 756 as the undisputed master of the peninsula. For capital he chose Cordova, which blossomed into the seat of a new kingdom and a brilliant culture. Abd-al-Rahman endeavoured to fashion his state after that of Damascus. He inaugurated an enlightened, beneficent régime, which on the whole conducted itself in the best tradition of its Damascene predecessors. Fourteen years before his arrival a Syrian army of twenty-seven thousand sent by Hisham had established itself in military fiefs throughout the principal districts of south-eastern Spain. Climatic and other physical similarities helped to make the newcomers feel at home. As the Syrians conquered the land, Syrian songs, poetry and art conquered the people of the land. From Spain and Portugal several of these cultural elements were later introduced into the New World. Arab geographers began to refer to Spain as a Syrian province, but meanwhile Syria itself had been reduced to an Abbasid province.

ABBASID PROVINCE

WITH the Umayyad fall the hegemony of Syria in the world of Islam ended and the glory of the country passed away. The Abbasids made Iraq their headquarters and Kufah their first capital. The Syrians awoke to the humiliating and infuriating realization that the Islamic centre of gravity had left their land and shifted eastward. As a last resort they set their hopes on an expected descendant of Muawiyah I to appear like a Messiah and deliver them from their victorious Iraqi rivals. A surviving Umayyad named Ziyad did assemble 40,000 men from Homs and Palmyra, but this revolt, like those of Marwan's ex-generals in Qinnasrin and Hawran, accomplished nothing.

Meanwhile abu-al-Abbas was busy consolidating his newly acquired domain. In the inaugural address delivered at Kufah he had assumed the appellation al-Saffah (blood-shedder), which proved to be no idle boast. The incoming dynasty chose to depend more than the outgoing on the use of force in the execution of its plans. For the first time the leathern bag ready to receive the head of the executioner's victim found a place near the imperial throne. The new caliph surrounded himself with theologians and legists, giving the infant state an atmosphere of theocracy as opposed to the secular character of its predecessor. On ceremonial occasions he hastened to don the mantle of his distant cousin, Muhammad. The well-geared propaganda machine which had worked to undermine public confidence in the old régime was now busy entrenching the usurpers in public esteem. They proclaimed that if the Abbasid caliphate were ever destroyed, the entire universe would be disorganized. Anti-Umayyad, pro-Abbasid hadiths were fabricated wholesale. Even Umayyad names were effaced from inscriptions on buildings, and the tombs of every Umayyad caliph except Muawiyah I and Umar II were violated and their corpses desecrated.

The most significant difference between this and the preceding caliphate, however, lay in the fact that the Abbasid was oriented Persia-ward. Persian protocol pervaded the court, Persian ideas dominated the political scene and Persian women prevailed in the royal harem. It was an empire of Neo-Moslems in which the Arabs formed but one of the component parts. The Iraqis felt relieved from Syrian tutelage. The Shiites felt avenged. Persians found high posts in the government open to them; they introduced and occupied a new office, the vizirate, highest after the caliphate. Khurasanians flocked to man the caliphal bodyguard. The Arabian aristocracy was eclipsed.

The first governor of Abbasid Syria was the caliph's uncle Abdullah, who had won the decisive battle over Marwan II. When al-Saffah died in 754, Abdullah disputed the caliphate with al-Mansur, brother of the deceased caliph. His claim rested on the huge disciplined army which he had assembled presumably for use against the Byzantines. He did not trust the Khurasanian troops, so had 17,000 of them butchered before moving eastward with the rest of his men, mostly Syrians. He was met and defeated by abu-Muslim, the virtually independent governor of Khurasan and idol of his people. So successful was he in suppressing all personal and official enemies that al-Mansur's suspicions were aroused, and he had the general to whom he owed so much treacherously put to death.

The caliphate founded by al-Saffah and al-Mansur was the longest-lived and the most celebrated of caliphates. All the thirty-five caliphs who succeeded al-Mansur (754-775) were his lineal descendants. As a site for his capital al-Mansur chose a Christian village on the west bank of the Tigris, Baghdad. The city was built in 762 and officially named Dar al-Salam (abode of peace). It soon fell heir to the power and prestige of its predecessors in the area — Babylon and Ctesiphon — and has lived in legend and in history as the peerless symbol of the glory of Abbasid Islam and the scene of *The Thousand and One Nights*.

With the removal of the capital to distant Baghdad the hereditary Byzantine enemy ceased to be of major concern. Nevertheless, al-Mansur and his successors strengthened the border fortresses of Syria and fortified the seaports of Lebanon. In 759 a band of Christians in Lebanon, resentful of harsh conditions and intolerable exactions and encouraged by the presence of a Byzantine fleet in the waters of Tripoli, burst forth from their mountain stronghold al-Munaytirah and plundered several villages in the Biqa. They were ambushed by Abbasid cavalry and cut down. In retaliation the governor uprooted the mountain villagers, many of whom had taken no part in the revolt, and had them dispersed all over Syria. This was the first of many such desperate uprisings, all repressed with similar ruthlessness.

Next on al-Mansur's list of victims were the Alids, who had helped overthrow the Umayyads on the naïve assumption that the Abbasids were fighting their battles but were now disillusioned. The Alids persisted in claiming for their imams the sole right to preside over the destinies of Islam, thus reducing the caliphs to the position of usurpers. Their movement again went underground but never missed an opportunity to rise in open revolt. A rebellion in 762 headed by two great-grandsons of al-Hasan was ruthlessly crushed and the brothers were promptly executed.

Despite these set-backs the Syrians continued to express their opposition by word and deed. A rejoinder by one of them to al-Mansur's remark that the people were lucky to escape the plague in his days typifies the then prevailing sentiment: 'God is too good to subject us to pestilence and your rule at the same time.' They never did wholly reconcile themselves to the loss of Syria's privileged position, nor to their exclusion from government offices. In the case of the Christians the situation was aggravated by unfair extortion and increased taxation. Al-Mansur's son and successor al-Mahdi (775–785) forced 5000 Tanukh Arabians around Aleppo to adopt Islam and had their churches demolished. After the brief reign of al-Mahdi's elder son al-Hadi, the caliphate passed to his younger son Harun al-Rashid (786–809), extolled in Moslem legend but a harsh master to Syrian Christians and Moslems alike.

In 782, while still a prince, Harun had led his forces as as far as Byzantium and exacted from the regent Irene a heavy tribute. As caliph he conducted from his favourite residence al-Raqqah in northern Syria a series of raids into the land of the Romans. Dissension between North Arabians (Qays) and South Arabians (Yaman) split Syria in his time, with official favour accorded to the Qaysites in the bitter strife. For two years the district of Damascus was the scene of relentless warfare, but in 795 Harun entrusted a punitive expedition to a Barmakid general who completely disarmed both factions. The Barmakids, a Persian vizirial family exalted by al-Mansur, achieved such distinction and displayed such generosity in the use of their immense wealth that by 803 Harun was no longer able to tolerate their prestige; he annihilated them and confiscated their property.

Harun re-enacted some of the anti-Christian and anti-Jewish measures introduced by Umar II. In 807 he ordered all churches erected since the Moslem conquest demolished. He also decreed that members of tolerated sects should wear the prescribed garb. But evidently much of this legislation was not enforced. His death led to a struggle for the throne between his sons al-Amin (809–813) and al-Mamun (813–833); the accompanying convulsions had repercussions in Syria. Syrian troops deserted wholesale, or followed an Umayyad pretender who held Homs and Damascus briefly.

But al-Mamun's victory was followed by a relatively peaceful reign. In Egypt the Copts, after expressing their individuality by several risings against their Moslem overlords, were themselves converted to Islam.

In 829 al-Mamun visited Syria and made a fresh survey of its lands with a view to increasing the revenue from it. Four years later he visited Damascus to test the judges there and enforce his decree that any judge who did not subscribe to the Mutazilite view of the creation of the Koran could not hold office. Several of his predecessors had visited Syria on their way to the pilgrimage or to battle against the Byzantines. They were all kept fully informed by their governors and postmasters, who doubled as chiefs of secret police.

Another brother, al-Mutasim (833–842), succeeded al-Mamun and moved the capital to Samarra. It was he who, in 838, led a victorious expedition against Amorium, the last incursion into Anatolia before a long period of peace on Syria's northern border. Palestine was the scene of a major revolt during his reign. In 840 a Yemenite Arab who always wore a veil in public raised the white Umayyad banner and attracted a large but undisciplined following among the peasants. A thousand Abbasid troops readily took him captive and dispersed his men.

The quiet which prevailed under al-Mutasim's son al-Wathiq was shattered under his brother al-Mutawakkil (847–861). In 850 and 854 he revived the discriminatory legislation against members of tolerated sects and supplemented it by new features which were the most stringent ever issued against the minorities. Christians and Jews were enjoined to affix wooden images of devils to their houses, level their graves even with the ground, wear outer garments of yellow and ride only on mules and asses with wooden saddles marked by two pomegranate-like balls on the cantle. Violent outbreaks took place in Damascus (854) and Homs (855), with both Christians and Moslems participating. The people of Damascus killed their Abbasid governor and were subsequently put to the sword for three consecutive days by a Turkish general sent by the caliph at the head of a band of seven thousand horse and three thousand foot, who also plundered the whole city. The Homs revolt was likewise repressed after vigorous resistance. The leaders were decapitated or flogged to death and then crucified at the city gate; all churches, with the exception of one which was added to the great mosque, were demolished; all Christians banished from the tumultuous city.

Incredible as it may seem, in 858 al-Mutawakkil transferred the caliphal residence to Damascus, possibly to escape the arrogant domination of his praetorian guard, consisting mostly of turbulent, undisciplined Turks, originally mercenaries and slaves taken into the service by his predecessor. The humid climate of the city, its violent wind and abundant fleas drove the capricious caliph out in thirty-eight days.

Thus far Syria seems to have maintained its general Christian character, but now the situation began perceptibly to change. It may be assumed that after al-Mutawakkil's enactments many Christian families in Syria emigrated or accepted Islam. The converts were actuated mainly by the desire to escape the humiliating disabilities and tribute and to acquire social prestige or political influence. The theological conquest thus followed the military by over two centuries. No Moslem could embrace Christianity or Judaism without risking his life.

The slowest and last victory — after the political and the religious — was the linguistic. Here the subject peoples of Syria and other lands offered the greatest measure of resistance. They showed themselves more ready to give up political and even religious loyalties than linguistic ones. Literary Arabic won its victory before the spoken did. Syrian scholars under caliphal patronage began to compose in Arabic long before Syrian peasants adopted the new tongue. The oldest dated Christian manuscript in Arabic that has come down to us was composed by abu-Qurrah

(d. 820) and copied in 877. By the early thirteenth century, toward the end of the Abbasid era, the victory of Arabic as the medium of everyday communication was virtually complete. Linguistic islands remained, occupied by non-Moslems: Jacobites, Nestorians and Maronites. In Lebanon the native Syriac lingered until the late seventeenth century, and indeed is still spoken in three villages in Anti-Lebanon and still used in the Maronite and other liturgies of the Syrian churches.

In general, however, the entire Semitic world was Arabicized under the Abbasids. Aram, as the native name for Syria, was replaced by al-Sham, 'the left', because it lay to the left of the Kabah in Mecca, in contrast to Yemen, which lay to its right. For the first time the consciousness of unity engendered by the use of a common tongue and — with important exceptions, especially in Lebanon — the profession of a common faith prevailed. Syriac did not disappear without leaving an indelible imprint on Syrian Arabic in morphology, phonetics and vocabulary. It is primarily this imprint that distinguishes the Syrian–Lebanese dialect from those of neighbouring lands.

More than any other one people the Syriac-speaking Christians contributed to that general awakening and intellectual renaissance centred in Abbasid Baghdad which is considered the chief glory of classical Islam. Between 750 and 850 the Arab world was the scene of one of the most spectacular and momentous movements in the history of thought. The movement was marked by translations into Arabic from Persian, Greek and Syriac. The Arabian Moslem brought with him no art, science or philosophy and hardly any literature; but he demonstrated keen intellectual curiosity, a voracious appetite for learning and a variety of latent talents. In the Fertile Crescent he fell heir to Hellenistic science and lore, unquestionably the most precious intellectual treasure then extant. Within a few decades after Baghdad was founded (762), the Arabic-reading public found at its disposal the major philosophical works of Aristotle and the Neo-Platonic commentators, the chief medical writings of Hippocrates and Galen, the main mathematical compositions of Euclid and the geographical masterpiece of Ptolemy. In all this the Syriac-speakers were the mediators. The Arabians knew no Greek, but the Syrians had been in touch with Greek for over a millennium. For two centuries before the appearance of Islam, Syrian scholars had been translating Greek works into Syriac. The same people who had opened the treasures of Greek science and philosophy to the Persians now busied themselves in making them available to all who could read Arabic.

All branches of learning shared in this activity. The clergy translated Aristotelian logic and Neo-Platonic philosophy for their bearing on theological controversies, as before the Moslem conquest they had put the Septuagint and the Gospels into Syriac at Edessa. Besides philosophy and theology, medicine and astronomy, viewed from the astrological standpoint, attracted Syrian attention. Many of the distinguished professors at the Jundi-Shapur academy of medicine and philosophy were Christians using Syriac as a medium of instruction. The dean of the academy, Jurjis ibn-Bakhtishu, was summoned by al-Mansur in 765 to give medical advice; he became the founder of a family of physicians which for six or seven generations almost monopolized the entire court medical practice.

A Christian named Yuhanna ibn-Masawayh supposedly translated for al-Rashid several manuscripts, mainly medical, which the caliph had brought back from raids into Asia Minor. Yuhanna's pupil Hunayn ibn-Ishaq (809–873) stands out as one of the foremost translators of the age. He translated most of the works of Aristotle and Galen into Syriac, which his son and nephew then rendered into Arabic. Hunayn is also said to have translated Hippocrates' medical treatises and Plato's *Republic*. The Syrians were indifferent to Greek poetry and drama and so were the Arabians.

Translations of Homer's *Iliad* and *Odyssey* by a Maronite astrologer did not survive.

Not only Christian but pagan Syrians made a major contribution to Arab intellectual life. These were the star-worshippers of Harran, incorrectly called Sabians. They had interested themselves in astronomy and allied sciences from time immemorial. As lovers of Hellenistic science they stood on a par with their Christian compatriots. Outstanding among their scholars was Thabit ibn-Qurrah (d. 901). He and his disciples are credited with translating the bulk of Greek astronomical and mathematical works, including those of Ptolemy and Archimedes.

Clearly the bulk of Syriac literature consisted of translations and commentaries and was lacking in originality and creativeness. Only in the field of ascetic mysticism did they produce, both before the Moslem conquest and in Abbasid times, original contributions, strikingly parallel to Sufi material. A Jacobite bishop of Aleppo, abu-al-Faraj (Bar Hebraeus, son of the Jew, 1226–1286), distinguished himself as a theological and historical writer in both Syriac and Arabic.

The finest talent of Moslem Syria of this period expressed itself through the medium of poetical composition. Two of its sons, abu-Tammam and al-Buhturi, achieved the distinction of becoming court poets to Abbasid caliphs. Abu-Tammam (about 804–850) was born in Hawran of a Christian father but embraced Islam and travelled widely before settling in Baghdad. He accompanied al-Mutasim in his raid on Amorium and wrote an ode to celebrate the victory. His claim to glory rests not only on his original compositions but also on his compilation — while snow-bound in a house with an excellent library — of *al-Hamasah*, a valuable anthology of the masterpieces of Arabic poetry from pre-Islamic days to his own time. Al-Buhturi (about 820–897) admired abu-Tammam and followed in his steps. In Baghdad he became the laureate of al-Mutawakkil and his successors. Typically, he employed his talent to extort remuneration from influential and wealthy personages under threat of changing his encomiums to lampoons. He was interested in wine and had a real ability to describe palaces, pools and wild animals — a rather rare feature in Arabic poetry.

In the non-poetical realm one man stands out, the theologian and jurist Abd-al-Rahman ibn-Amr al-Awzai. Born in Baalbek in 707, he flourished in Beirut, where he died in 774. Al-Awzai was noted for his learning, asceticism and moral courage, speaking out in disapproval of excessive harshness in the treatment of Christians, such as destroying their churches and homes, cutting down their trees and expelling the villagers from al-Munaytirah. The legal system worked out by this jurist was applied in Syria for about two centuries before it was supplanted.

PETTY DYNASTIES

THE first sign of internal decay in the Abbasid régime was the rise of the Turkish bodyguard after the death of al-Mamun in 833. Like the Janissaries in Ottoman history, this corps became too powerful for the caliph and at times held him in abject submission to its will. Except for short intervals thereafter Abbasid power declined steadily. As it disintegrated, petty dynasties, mostly of Arabian origin, were parcelling out its domains in the west, while others, mostly Turkish and Persian, were performing the same operation in the east.

First among these to affect Syria was the short-lived Tulunid dynasty (868–905). It was founded by a deputy governor of Egypt, Ahmad ibn-Tulun, whose father was a Turk sent from Bukhara as a present to al-Mamun. No sooner had the ambitious young man arrived at his post than he planned to take advantage of the distance that separated him from the central government and practise independence. On authorization from the caliph he increased his troops, reportedly to a hundred thousand, and marched against a rebel in Syria —the land of rebels against Abbasid rule. At the death of its governor in 877 he deemed the time ripe for full occupation. The Egyptian army marched through al-Ramlah in the south to Damascus, Homs, Hamah and Aleppo in the north without opposition. Only Antioch closed its gates and was reduced after a short siege. In 879/880 Ahmad proclaimed himself ruler of both lands.

This was a turning-point in the history of Egypt. It then and there embarked upon its career as an independent state, a position which it maintained with one important interruption for centuries to come. Syria throughout this long period went with Egypt, as it did in Pharaonic days. The old connection, severed about a thousand years before, was thus re-established. The land of the Nile profited by the change, at least to the extent of having its entire revenue spent within its territory, but the position of its Syrian adjunct was not improved.

A typical military dictator, Ahmad ruled with an iron hand. He built a powerful military machine on which he depended for the maintenance of his throne. Its core was a bodyguard of 24,000 Turkish and 40,000 Negro slaves from each one of whom he exacted an oath of allegiance. As if to justify his usurpation of power in the eyes of his subjects, he launched a programme of public works that had no parallel since Pharaonic days. He adorned his capital al-Fustat (Old Cairo) with magnificent buildings, including a hospital and a mosque which still bears his name. In Syria he fortified Acre and established a naval base there. So strong was the tower that topped its double wall that three centuries later it thwarted for almost two years the combined efforts of two Crusading monarchs and in 1799 it proved impregnable against the assaults of Napoleon's field artillery.

Ahmad was succeeded in 884 by his extravagant and dissolute twenty-year-old son Khumarawayh, who erected a splendid palace with a garden rich in exotic trees, an aviary and a zoological enclosure. Under him the Tulunid domain extended from Cyrenaica to the Tigris. The caliph al-Mutadid in 892 confirmed Khumarawayh and his heirs in the possession of this vast territory for thirty years in return for an annual tribute of 300,000 dinars. Khumarawayh's extravagance, including a fabulous dowry for a daughter who married al-Mutadid, left the treasury empty. He was murdered by his own slaves (895) and was succeeded by two sons in turn.

Their turbulent reigns were rendered more turbulent by

the advent of a militant extreme Shiite sect, the Carmathians. It was organized as a secret, communistic society, with initiation as a requisite for admission. Starting near Kufah about 890, the Carmathians became masters of an independent state on the western coast of the Persian Gulf. From these two centres they spread devastation in all directions. Throughout the Umayyad period Moslem Syria had followed the orthodox Sunnite line; but the imposition of the hated Abbasid régime had opened the way for the introduction of Alid doctrines which now prepared the people for Carmathian views. Just as in Byzantine Syria the people endeavoured to assert their nationality by espousing Christian doctrines considered heretical by Byzantium, so were they now ready to adopt ultra-Shiite, anti-Abbasid beliefs. The Carmathians defeated the Tulunid garrison and laid siege to Damascus in 901, reduced Homs, decimated Hamah and almost annihilated the population of Baalbek.

In 902 the caliph sent against the Carmathians an able general who, after defeating them and securing the allegiance of the Syrian vassals, set out for the conquest of Egypt. In 904 Khumarawayh's second son was assassinated and succeeded by an uncle, but the Abbasid general reached the Tulunid capital outside al-Fustat, razed it to the ground, cut off twenty Tulunid heads and carried the remaining male members of this house in chains to the imperial capital. In the following year the last Umayyad pretender on record unfurled the white flag in Syria and he too was captured and sent to Baghdad. The people who had once been described as acknowledging no other authority than that of the Umayyads had evidently at long last become demoralized and reconciled to alien rule.

The general who in the name of the Tulunids had defended Damascus against the Carmathians was a Turk named Tughj, whose son Muhammad managed to inherit the Tulunid legacy. After a brief interval of precarious

Abbasid sway in Egypt and Syria, Muhammad established himself at al-Fustat in 935 as the ruler of Egypt. Four years later the caliph bestowed on him the old Iranian princely title al-Ikhshid, just as in the nineteenth century an Ottoman sultan conferred on his Egyptian viceroy the Persian title khedive. Syria was then held by an adventurer called ibn-Raiq, who died in 941. Thereupon the viceroyalty of al-Ikhshid over Syria and Egypt, together with Mecca and Medina, was recognized by the caliph and the Buwayhid overlords of Baghdad. For centuries thereafter the fortunes of Hejaz were linked with those of Egypt. In 944 al-Ikhshid obtained from the imperial government hereditary rights for his family in the lands he acquired.

In the same year his authority was challenged by a new dynasty arising in northern Syria, the Hamdanids (944–1003). This family of Arabians had in the late ninth century seized the fortress of Mardin and had gradually extended their sway to Mosul and other parts of northern Mesopotamia. In 944 the most illustrious among them, Hasan, wrested Aleppo, Antioch and Homs from the Ikhshidid vassal. Hasan considered al-Ikhshid's death in 946 an opportunity to overrun all Syria, as Ikhshidid power passed to Muhammad's young sons. But the reins of government were held by a Negro eunuch named abu-al-Misk Kafur (musky camphor), who turned out to be an able regent. He defeated Hasan in two engagements and compelled him to recognize Egyptian suzerainty. After the boys' deaths Kafur himself reigned for two years over a state which included Egypt, Syria and part of Cilicia. He was the first Moslem ruler to achieve high eminence after rising from the lowliest slave origins.

Kafur was succeeded in 968 by an eleven-year-old Ihkshidid unable to cope with the problems of the day. The Hamdanids were threatening from the north, the resurgent Carmathians from the east and the Fatimids from the west. The Fatimid caliphate, which arose in Tunis in

909, had for years carried on secret correspondence with Alids and other sympathizers in Egypt. The opportunity was now obvious. In 969 the Fatimid army routed the Ikhshidid forces both in Egypt and at al-Ramlah; Egypt, Palestine and central Syria were incorporated in the emerging Fatimid empire.

The Ikhshidid dynasty (935–969), like its predecessor the Tulunid, had only an ephemeral existence. Both followed a pattern found in many other states which, in this period of disintegration, broke off from the imperial government. Both made lavish use of state moneys to curry favour with their subjects and thereby ruined the treasuries. Neither of them had any national basis in the land over which it tried to rule; neither could rely upon a strong coherent body of supporters of its own race among its subjects. Being intruders the rulers had to recruit their bodyguards, which were also their armies, from alien sources. Such a rule could be maintained only so long as the arm which wielded the sword remained strong.

Meanwhile Hasan al-Hamdani had consolidated his power in northern Syria and received the honorific Sayf-al-Dawlah (sword of state) from the Abbasid caliph, who sought thus to convey the impression that the recipient — in reality independent — was under his control. Sayf and his successors were tolerant Shiites and preserved the caliph's name in the Friday prayer. Sayf chose Aleppo for capital perhaps because of its ancient citadel and its proximity to the frontier fortresses which he intended to defend against the new wave of Byzantine inroads. For the first time since Amorite days, the northern metropolis became the seat of an important government. In it the new ruler erected a magnificent palace.

Sayf's domain covered northern Syria, a section of Cilicia and a large part of northern Mesopotamia. He even established a foothold in Armenia with the aid of Kurdish supporters; his mother was a Kurd. By marrying a daughter of al-Ikhshid he hoped to be left in peaceful possession of his territory; his principality consumed much of its time and energy struggling with the Byzantines. Sayf was the first after a long interval to take up the cudgels seriously against the Christian enemies of Islam. This Hamdanid-Byzantine conflict may be considered a significant chapter in the prehistory of the Crusades. As a warrior the Hamdanid prince had a worthy peer in the Byzantine emperor Nicephorus, with whom the historians record about ten engagements. Success was not always on Sayf's side. In 962 he even temporarily lost his own capital after a brief siege in which his palace, symbol of his glory, was destroyed. His death in 967 terminated a reign more noteworthy for its cultural brilliance than for its mundane achievements.

Sayf surrounded himself in his gorgeous palace with a circle of literary and artistic talent that could hardly be matched except by that of the Baghdad caliphs in their heyday. It comprised the renowned philosopher and musician al-Farabi, the distinguished historian of Arabic literature al-Isbahani, the eloquent preacher ibn-Nubatah, the philologist ibn-Khalawayh, the grammarian ibn-Jinni, the warrior-poet abu-Firas and, above all, the illustrious bard al-Mutanabbi.

Al-Mutanabbi (915–965) received his surname (prophecy claimant) because in his youth he claimed the gift of prophecy, attempted an imitation of the Koran and was followed by a number of admirers. The Ikhshidid governor of Homs cast him into prison, where he remained for almost two years and from which he went out cured of his prophetic illusion but not of his vanity, self-assertiveness and self-admiration, which accompanied him throughout his life. Born in Kufah, he roamed about in quest of a patron and settled in Aleppo as the laureate of Sayf-al-Dawlah; the two names have ever since remained inseparably linked. Outstanding among his odes are those depicting the glories of Sayf's campaigns against the Byzantines. It is a question whether or not those panegyrics did not contribute more than the exploits themselves to making Sayf the myth he is in Arabic annals. In them the poet appears as the consummate phrase-maker in the Arabic language. He later got into a dispute and deserted Aleppo for the court of Kafur, whom he first praised and later — disappointed in his hopes for high office — ridiculed in verses which almost every school child in the Arab world today commits to memory. In places the Mutanabbi style appears bombastic and ornate, the rhetoric florid and the metaphor overdone — but not to the Easterner. Such is the hold that this poet has had upon the imagination of generations of Arabic-speakers that he is still generally considered the greatest in Islam. In him and his two predecessors, abu-Tammam and al-Buhturi, Arabic poetry reached its full maturity. With few exceptions the decline after al-Mutanabbi was steady.

Of the rest of Sayf's circle two deserve special mention. Al-Isbahani (897–967) compiled the monumental *Kitab al-Aghani*, a twenty-volume treasury of Arab songs and anecdotes. His senior al-Farabi (870–950) was one of the earliest Moslem thinkers to attempt a harmonization of Greek philosophy and Islam. His system was a syncretism of Aristotelianism, Platonism and Sufism. He became in effect the intellectual ancestor of all other subsequent Moslem philosophers. In addition he was the greatest of all Arabic musical theorists.

Sayf was succeeded by his son Sharif, called Sad-al-Dawlah (967–991), but his authority was disputed by his cousin, the poet abu-Firas, who claimed Homs until he was slain. Internal discord enabled Nicephorus to capture Aleppo, Antioch and Homs (968) and to impose an ephemeral Byzantine suzerainty over the Hamdanid realm. Aleppo was lost to the Hamdanids only until 975, but Antioch remained in Byzantine hands for over a century (968–1084). Nicephorus's successor, John Tzimisces, in 974 reduced not only the coastal towns from Latakia to Beirut but such inland places as Baalbek. Warfare with the Byzantines continued sporadically throughout Sad's reign, but his son Said-al-Dawlah (991–1001) appealed for Byzantine aid against the Fatimids, then seeking to control all of Syria. The emperor Basil rushed with 17,000 men to Aleppo and the enemy withdrew for the time being, though later Said had to acknowledge Fatimid suzerainty. Being young he had over him a regent whose daughter he married. The regent now coveted the throne for himself and disposed of both his son-in-law and daughter by poison. For two years after that he held the regency in the name of the Fatimid caliphs over Said's sons. In 1003 he sent the two young princes to Cairo with the Hamdanid harem and appointed his own son co-regent. Thus ended the life-cycle of the Hamdanid dynasty, which did not differ in essence — except for its Arabian origin — from that of its two predecessors, the Ikhshidids and the Tulunids. A dominant leader carves out a principality for himself, is followed by incompetent successors; the state moneys are squandered; discord within and foes without bring the story to an end. In this case the munificence of Sayf in his patronage of science and art was the first great drain on the treasury.

UNDER FATIMIDS AND SELJUKS

THE Fatimid dynasty was the last of the medieval caliphates and the only major Shiite caliphate. Its name reflects the alleged descent of its founder and his successors from Ali and Fatimah, the daughter of Muhammad. We have already noted its establishment in Tunisia in 909 and the conquest of Egypt and much of Syria from the Ikhshidids in 969. For the next few years Syria was rent with warfare, not only between the Hamdanids in the north and the Fatimids in the south, but also involving the Carmathians, the Turks and the Byzantines. Damascus was occupied by Carmathians with Abbasid encouragement, and later by a Turkish general who used it as a base for a series of raids on the whole country. It was natural for the Turks and Carmathians to combine against their common foe.

In 977 the Fatimid caliph al-Aziz (975–996) took the field in person and inflicted a crushing defeat on the allied forces outside al-Ramlah. Al-Aziz extended his domain in Syria, especially along the coast, but failed to reduce Aleppo, mainly because of intervention by the Byzantines, who had just lost it to Sayf-al-Dawlah and were eager to take advantage of any opportunity to restore their authority in Syria. After this set-back al-Aziz devoted the rest of his reign, in so far as Syria was concerned, to consolidating his power in the south and central parts and imposing his suzerainty on the weakening Hamdanids in the north.

Under his rule there flourished in Fatimid Palestine one of the most original and capable of geographers, al-Maqdisi (946–about 1000). Born in Jerusalem (whence his name) under the Ikhshidids, he started at the age of twenty travels that took him through all Moslem lands except Spain, India and Sijistan. In 985 he embodied the information he thus gathered in a book based solidly on his personal observation and experience. Thanks to it and to the works of other geographers who began to flourish in this age, our knowledge of the economic and social conditions of tenth-century Syria reaches a height never before attained. No Latin or Greek geographer left us material comparable to this Arabic material in quality and quantity. Al-Maqdisi surveys trade, agriculture, industry and general education. He refers, among many other things, to iron ores in the 'mountains of Beirut', the abundant trees and hermits in Lebanon, the sugar and glassware products of Tyre, the cheese and cotton goods of Jerusalem and the cereals and honey of Amman. He characterizes Syria as a 'blessed region, the home of cheap prices, fruits and righteous people'.

On the whole al-Maqdisi and his contemporaries depict a people with an adequate standard of living and a satisfying, useful way of life, judged by the standards of the authors. Christians and Jews do not seem to have been worse off under the Hamdanids and early Fatimids than under the Abbasids. Most of the scribes and the physicians were still Christians. The Byzantines had been confined to Antioch; the Carmathians still irrupted occasionally but were not quite the menace they had been; the Turks had been checked for the time being. Steady immigration of bedouins from the Syrian Desert made the countryside turbulent, as they at last reached Lebanon and occupied the mountain slopes and the hidden valleys. But even for the heavily garrisoned cities this calm was brief and deceptive; times of trouble lay ahead.

Al-Aziz was succeeded by his son al-Hakim (996–1021), a blue-eyed boy of eleven whose behaviour was so freakish and irrational that he was deified in his lifetime by some and accused of psychopathic abnormalities by others and by later historians. In the second year of his reign a sailor from Tyre named Allaqah had the effrontery to declare his city independent and to strike money in his own name. For a time he defied the Egyptian army and with the aid of a Byzantine flotilla stood against the Egyptian fleet. But at last he had to surrender his besieged city and suffer flaying and crucifixion. His skin was filled with hay and exhibited in Cairo.

Al-Hakim revived the humiliating disabilities imposed by Umar II and al-Mutawakkil on Christians and Jews, who fared well under the other Fatimids. Although his mother and his vizir were Christians, al-Hakim reactivated earlier regulations requiring distinguishing garments and in 1009 added that when Christians were in public baths they should display a five-pound cross dangling from their necks, and Jews an equally weighty frame of wood with jingling bells. In the same year he demolished several Christian churches, including that of the Holy Sepulchre in Jerusalem. By way of implementing the koranic prohibition against wine, he ordered all grapevines uprooted. He invited those members of the tolerated sects who were unwilling to abide by his regulations to profess Islam or else emigrate to the Byzantine empire. Apparently in his time, almost four centuries after Muhammad, the Christians in Egypt and Syria were still fully as numerous as the Moslems.

Other edicts of al-Hakim show strange contradictions. He built an academy in Cairo only to destroy it with its professors three years later. He legislated against sexual immorality and went so far as to prohibit the appearance of women in the Cairo streets. He issued edicts against banquets and music and included certain dishes and chess playing. Like several other descendants of Ali, he was considered divine by extreme admirers. The first to offer him public divine veneration was a Persian called al-Darazi (the tailor), from whom the Druze sect took its name. Basic in the Druze system is the doctrine of the incarnation of the deity in human form, the last and most important mani-

festation being al-Hakim. Finding no response for this new
creed among Egyptians, al-Darazi migrated to a district at
the foot of Mount Hermon in Lebanon, where the hardy
freedom-loving mountaineers, evidently already impregnated
with ultra-Shiite ideas, were ready to give him a hearing.
Here he fell in battle in 1019 and was succeeded by his
rival Hamzah ibn-Ali, also a Persian.

When al-Hakim was assassinated two years later, probably as a result of a conspiracy by his own household,
Hamzah denied his death and proclaimed that he had gone
into a state of temporary occultation, whence his triumphal
return should be expected. Al-Muqtana, Hamzah's right
hand in the propagation of the new cult, at first addressed
epistles to potential converts from Constantinople to India,
with particular attention to Christians, but later enunciated
a new policy, that during the 'absence' of al-Hakim no
part of the religion should be divulged or promulgated — a
policy doubtless dictated by the desire for safety on the part
of a small heterodox minority struggling for existence.
Since then 'the door has been closed'; no one could be
allowed entrance or exit. The hidden imam idea had been
elaborately worked out, prior to the rise of Druzism, by a
number of ultra-Shiite groups.

Hamzah on behalf of al-Hakim absolved his followers of
the cardinal obligations of Islam, including fasting and
pilgrimage, and substituted precepts enjoining veracity of
speech, mutual aid among the brethren in faith, renunciation of all forms of false belief and absolute submission to
the divine will. The last precept, involving the concept of
predestination, has continued to be a potent factor in
Druzism, as in orthodox Islam. Another feature of this
cult is the belief in the transmigration of souls. The idea
came originally to Islam from India and received an incre-
ment of Platonic elements. The operation of the second
precept, enjoining mutual aid, has made of the Druzes an
unusually compact self-conscious community presenting

more the aspects of a religious fraternal order than those of a sect, and that despite the fact that the community itself is divided into two distinctly marked classes : the initiate and the uninitiate. The sacred writings, all hand-written, are accessible to the initiated few only and the meeting-places are secluded rooms on hills outside the villages, where Thursday evening sessions are held.

As they tried to gain a permanent footing in southern Lebanon, the Druzes found themselves in conflict with an already established Islamic heterodoxy, the Nusayriyah, whose followers were subsequently driven into northern Syria, their present habitat. The Druzes later spread into other rural districts, but were unable to thrive in any city. Some of them, as a result of Qaysite-Yemenite blood feuds, migrated in the early eighteenth century into Hawran in Syria. The influx was augmented by malcontents from Lebanon in the nineteenth century. In Hawran they now number about ninety thousand as against eighty thousand in Lebanon. Throughout their entire history they have shown remarkable vigour and exercised in Lebanese and Syrian national affairs influence quite disproportionate to their number.

The Nusayriyah were an Ismailite sect founded in the late ninth century. Not much is known about this religion, which is secretive in character, hierarchical in organization and esoteric in doctrine. Its sacred writings have not been exposed to the same extent as those of the Druzes, many of which came to light as a result of communal wars in the nineteenth century. Finding itself a small heterodoxy amidst a hostile majority, the cult chose to go underground. Like other extreme Shiites, the Nusayris deify Ali and are therefore sometimes referred to as Alawites, a name which became current after the French organized the mandated region centring on Latakia into a separate state under that name. The cult represents an imposition of extreme Shiite ideas on a pagan Syrian base. Its adepts must have passed directly from paganism to Ismailism with certain superficially Christian features, such as observation of Christmas and Easter. They have a three-class hierarchy of initiates, while the rest of the community constitutes the uninitiated mass. Unlike the Druzes, they admit no women into the initiated group. Their meetings are held at night in secluded places, giving rise to the usual charges brought against groups who practise their religion in secret. Today some three hundred thousand Nusayris, mostly peasants, occupy the mountainous region of northern and central Syria and are scattered as far as Turkish Cilicia.

The successors of al-Hakim, more interested in luxurious living than in state administration, were unable to maintain order at home or sovereignty abroad. In 1023 the chief of the Kilab bedouins, Salih ibn-Mirdas, wrested Aleppo from Fatimid control. The Mirdasid line held Aleppo, with varying fortunes, until 1079. They allied themselves with other Arab tribes: the Tayyi, who set al-Ramlah on fire in 1024, and the Kalb, who blockaded Damascus in 1025. Brigandage, highway robbery and lawlessness throve in the countryside, but Aleppo and other commercial cities prospered and their rulers grew fat on customs duties levied on merchandise.

The spirit of the age, with its political anarchy, social decay, intellectual pessimism and religious scepticism, was reflected in the poetry of al-Maarri (973–1057), of Maarrat al-Numan in northern Syria. Although blind he secured some education at Aleppo and twice visited Baghdad, where he probably came in contact with Hindus who converted him to vegetarianism. The remaining years of his life he lived as a bachelor in his native town, subsisting on the meagre proceeds earned by his lectures. Unlike the poets of his day al-Maarri did not devote his talent to eulogizing princes and potentates with a view to receiving remuneration; the ode he composed in his early career extolling Sayf-al-Dawlah was evidently never presented to the prince.

His later works embody his pessimistic, sceptical philosophy of life and his rational approach to its problems. In one epistle he peopled limbo with reputed heretics and free-thinkers enjoying themselves and discussing textual criticism. It was this treatise that had a stimulative effect on Dante's *Divine Comedy*. In another book he tried to imitate the Koran, a sacrilege in Moslem eyes. The philosophy advocated in this work is basically Epicurean. Al-Maarri was one of the few Arabic poets who rose above limitations of time and place to the realm of universal humanity.

Though the Fatimids had had difficulty in maintaining their precarious hold on Syria, first against Turks and Carmathians, then against Hamdanids and Byzantines, and later against Mirdasids and other bedouin assailants, their most formidable adversary did not appear on Syrian territory until 1070, by which time Fatimid rule had virtually collapsed because of rebellion in Egypt (1060). Sunnite Turkish Seljuks had pushed south from Turkestan to the region of Bukhara, embraced Islam there and continued their victorious drive until in 1055 their leader Tughril had forced the powerless Abbasid caliph to accept him as master instead of the Shiite Persian Buwayhids. Tughril assumed the title sultan, becoming the first Moslem ruler whose coins bear this title.

Under Tughril's nephew and successor Alp Arslan (1063–1072), the Seljuk empire was extended westward into Syria and Asia Minor. In 1070 Alp advanced against the Mirdasids in northern Syria and occupied Aleppo, leaving the Mirdasid governor as his vassal. The Turkoman general Atsiz pushed into Palestine and captured al-Ramlah, Jerusalem and other towns as far south as Ascalon, whose Fatimid garrison held out. In the following year Alp won a decisive victory over the Byzantines at Manzikert, north of Lake Van, and took the emperor himself prisoner. All Asia Minor then lay open to the Turks. Hordes of them rushed into Anatolia and northern Syria. Turkish generals penetrated as far as the Hellespont. With one stroke the traditional frontier separating Islam from Christendom was pushed four hundred miles west. For the first time Turks gained a foothold in that land — a foothold that was never lost.

Fragmentation of the vast sultanate soon followed. Asia Minor (Rum) was held by a cousin of Alp, Sulayman, who in 1077 established himself in Nicaea, not far from Constantinople. In 1084 the capital shifted south-east to Konya (Iconium). In the same year Antioch was recovered for Islam from the Byzantines by the Seljuks. Syria was in anarchy among Arabs, Seljuks, Turkomans and Fatimids until in 1075 Atsiz occupied Damascus. He exasperated its people by his exactions for two years before Alp Arslan's son Tutush took the city and killed him. At Malikshah's death (1079) Tutush became virtually independent. He took Antioch from the Byzantines (1084) and captured Aleppo (1094), but fell in battle in 1095. His holdings were split between his sons Ridwan at Aleppo and Duqaq at Damascus. The two amirs were soon involved in a family war, and a couple of years later Duqaq was forced to recognize the overlordship of his brother. In 1098 a brother-in-law of Tutush who held Jerusalem as fief surrendered it to the Fatimids.

Thus in 1097, when the Crusaders arrived in Syria after fighting their way across Seljuk Anatolia, they found Antioch under a Seljuk amir named Yaghi-Siyan, Aleppo under Ridwan and Damascus under Duqaq. The Fatimids held only a few ports — Acre, Tyre, Sidon, Ascalon — and were about to retake Jerusalem.

THE CRUSADES

On November 26, 1095, Pope Urban II delivered a fiery speech at Clermont in southern France urging the believers to 'enter upon the road to the Holy Sepulchre, wrest it from the wicked race and subject it' to themselves. Judged by its results this was perhaps the most effective speech in history. '*Deus vult*' (God wills [it]) became the rallying cry and was reiterated throughout Europe, seizing high and low as if by a strange psychological contagion.

The response, however, was not all motivated by piety. Besides the devout there were military leaders intent upon new conquests for themselves; merchants from Genoa and Pisa whose interest was more commercial than spiritual; the romantic, the restless, the adventurers ever ready to join a spectacular movement; the criminals and sinful who sought absolution through pilgrimage to the Holy Land; and the economically and socially depressed individuals to whom 'taking the cross' was more of a relief than a sacrifice. Other factors were involved: papal aid in pushing back the Moslems had repeatedly been solicited by the Byzantine emperor Alexius Comnenus, whose Asiatic possessions had been overrun by Seljuks almost as far as Constantinople. The pope viewed these importunities as providing an opportunity for healing the schism between Byzantium and Rome and establishing himself as head of Christendom.

By the spring of 1097 some hundred and fifty thousand men, mostly from France and adjacent lands, had responded. They set out overland for Constantinople, wearing as a badge the cross which gave them their name. Their route lay across Anatolia, then the domain of the Seljuks of Konya. They restored Nicaea to the Byzantines, defeated the Seljuk forces at Dorylaeum and proceeded south-east to the mountain barrier of the Taurus and Anti-Taurus.

Here the leaders started squabbling among themselves and planning local conquests each for himself. The first such ventures in Cilicia collapsed, but then Baldwin of Boulogne swung eastward into a territory occupied by Armenian Christians and early in 1098 set himself up as count of Edessa. Meanwhile the bulk of the Crusading army was pouring into northern Syria, its main objective, held by Seljuk amirs akin to those they had defeated in Anatolia. Antioch was the first Syrian city in their path, notable as the cradle of the first organized Christian church. They settled down confidently to a siege which proved unexpectedly long and arduous (October 2, 1097, to June 3, 1098). Attempts at relief by Ridwan of Aleppo and Duqaq of Damascus were repelled. At last treachery on the part of a disgruntled Armenian commander of one of the towers gave them access to the city.

No sooner, however, had the besiegers made their entry than they found themselves besieged. Karbuqa, a Seljuk adventurer who had wrested Mosul from its Arab rulers, arrived from his capital with reinforcements. The suffering from plague and starvation in the course of the twenty-five days that ensued was perhaps the worst ever experienced by Franks in Syria. Heartened by discovery of the 'holy lance' which pierced Christ's side, the Crusaders made a bold sortie which forced Karbuqa to withdraw. Bohemond, the shrewdest and ablest of all the Christian leaders, remained in charge of the newly acquired principality, Antioch and its territory. The Byzantine emperor expected the re-annexation of Antioch to his empire but was disappointed.

Also disappointed was Bohemond's rival Raymond of Toulouse, who pushed southward up the Orontes valley with his Provençals. After a futile siege of Arqah he was joined by Baldwin's brother Godfrey of Bouillon, who had followed the coastal route south. They struck the coast at

Tortosa and made contact with the Italian fleet. The re-united Crusaders avoided Latakia, which was being occupied by naval forces of the Byzantines, who had become alienated from the Latins. In Batrun the Crusaders established con-tacts with the Maronites, 'a stalwart race, valiant fighters', who provided greatly needed guides. Following Tripoli's precedent, the amir of Beirut offered money and a bountiful supply of provisions. The gardens of Sidon, where the Crusaders pitched their tents by the running water, pro-vided a welcome resting-place for a few days. Passing Acre, Caesarea and al-Ramlah, on June 7 they sighted their goal — Jerusalem.

The Crusaders then numbered some forty thousand, of whom about half were effective troops. The Egyptian garrison may be estimated at a thousand. At the end of a month's siege conducted by Godfrey, Raymond and Bohemond's nephew Tancred, the city was stormed (July 15) and its population was subjected to an indiscriminate slaughter. A third Latin state was set up under Godfrey, a devout leader and hard fighter. Allegedly reluctant to wear a crown of gold where Jesus had worn a crown of thorns, Godfrey chose the title 'defender of the Holy Sepulchre'. During his brief reign he defeated the Fatimid army near Ascalon, but this seaport with its Egyptian gar-rison remained a dangerous outpost and naval base. Jaffa and Haifa were occupied with naval aid from the Pisans and Venetians respectively. Tancred carved out a princi-pality in Galilee.

When Godfrey died his brother Baldwin (1100–1118) was summoned from Edessa and crowned king. Baldwin was the real founder of the Latin kingdom. His immediate task was to reduce the coast towns and thus ensure sea com-munication with the homeland and forestall hostile action by the Egyptian fleet. In the seamen of the Italian republics he found eager and greedy allies. These men insisted on a share of the booty, special quarters in the captured towns

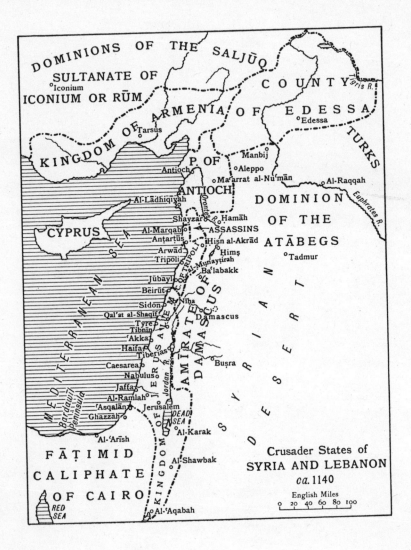

DOMINIONS OF THE SALJŪQ

SULTANATE OF
ICONIUM OR RŪM
○Iconium

COUNTY

OF EDESSA
○Edessa

KINGDOM OF ARMENIA
○Tarsus

TURKS

P. OF
Antioch○

Manbij○
○Aleppo
○Ma'arrat al-Nu'mān

○Al-Raqqah

ANTIOCH

DOMINION

Al-Lādhiqiyah○

OF THE

CYPRUS

Shayzar○ ○Hamāh

ATĀBEGS

Al-Marqab○
Antartūs○
Arwād○
Tripoli○

ASSASSINS

○Hisn al-Akrād
Himş○
○Tadmur

MEDITERRANEAN SEA

○Munaytirah
Ba'labakk○

Jūbayl○

Beirūt○

Niha○

Sidon○

Qal'at al-Shaqīf○
Tyre○
Tibnin○
'Akka○

○Damascus

Haifa○
Tiberias○

○Buşra

Caesarea○
Nabulus○

Jaffa○
Al-Ramlah○
'Asqalān○
Ghazzah○

Jerusalem○
DEAD SEA
○Al-Karak

SYRIAN DESERT

Bardawil Peninsula

○Al-'Arish

FĀṬIMID

CALIPHATE

○Al-Shawbak

OF CAIRO

Crusader States of
SYRIAN AND LEBANON
ca. 1140

English Miles
0 20 40 60 80 100

RED SEA
○Al-'Aqabah

under the jurisdiction of their own republics and the right of importing and selling merchandise without paying taxes. Arsuf and Caesarea were taken in 1101 with Genoese aid. Strongly walled Acre capitulated three years later as a result of attacks by Pisan and Genoese ships. In 1110 Beirut was besieged by land and sea for eleven weeks and then stormed. In the same year Sidon was taken with the aid of a Norwegian fleet of sixty ships. Baldwin extended his kingdom southward too, building a formidable fortress, Krak de Montréal, south of the Dead Sea (1115), to threaten the caravan route from Damascus to Egypt and Hejaz.

The Latin states to the north were likewise expanding. Raymond, who had had his eye on Tripoli ever since he passed there, returned after the capture of Jerusalem and commenced a siege which dragged on until 1109, four years after Raymond's death. Tripoli became the capital of a county, fourth and last of the Latin states. Latakia had been added in 1103 by Tancred to his captured uncle's principality of Antioch, and Apamea in 1106. Parts of Cilicia were also included in it from time to time.

During the reign of Baldwin II (1118–1131) the Crusader states reached their approximate maximum, and all three of the northern principalities — Tripoli, Antioch and Edessa — owed nominal allegiance to the king of Jerusalem. Their remarkable success must have inspired the Franks with confidence and an optimistic outlook. But in reality the prospects were not so bright. Except in the very north and south, the area was limited to the littoral — a narrow Christian territory set against a dark background of Islam. Not a town was more than a day's march from the enemy. Inland cities, such as Aleppo, Hamah, Homs, Baalbek and Damascus, were never conquered though occasionally assaulted. Tyre was taken in 1124 from the Fatimids. Within their own territories the Franks were spread thin. Even in Jerusalem and other occupied cities they never formed more than a minority. Clearly such exotic states could hold their own only as long as they received a constant supply of fresh recruits from home and the forces of opposition were not unified under strong leadership.

Their early good fortune in finding Syria divided among weak and mutually hostile amirs — some eager to appease the Franks and have them as allies — could not last indefinitely, but it did last for several decades. When Duqaq of Damascus died (1104), his young son's regent Tughtigin usurped power and passed it on after his death to his sons, who kept Damascus independent until 1154 by alternately fighting the Franks and making alliances with them. Ridwan's heirs at Aleppo were incompetent, and in 1117 the town passed into the hands of Il-Ghazi, a Turkoman who ruled Mardin. He was a redoubtable warrior against the Crusaders, but could never secure sufficient Moslem aid to do permanent damage.

In 1128 Aleppo was annexed by another warlike Turk, Imad-al-Din Zengi of Mosul. In subsequent years Zengi added Hamah, Homs and Baalbek to his realm, and in 1144 he wrested Edessa from the Franks. Its fall marks the beginning of the turn of the tide in favour of Islam. On the European side it provoked the so-called second Crusade (1147–1149). The usual classification of the Crusades, however, into a fixed number of campaigns is artificial, as the stream was somewhat continuous and the line of demarcation not sharply drawn. A more satisfactory division would be into first a period of Latin conquest extending to 1144; second a period of Moslem reaction inaugurated by Zengi and culminating in the brilliant victories of Saladin; and third a period of petty wars, coinciding roughly with the thirteenth century, in which the Ayyubids and the Mamluks figured and which ended in driving all Crusaders out of the land.

At Zengi's death (1146) the task of advancing the Islamic cause passed to his son Nur-al-Din Mahmud. The Crusade, led by Louis VII of France and Conrad III of Germany, failed miserably. More capable than his father, Nur-al-Din in 1154 wrested Damascus from the grandson of Tughtigin, thereby removing the last buffer between Jerusalem and Zengid territory, which now stretched from Mosul to Hawran. Realizing the decrepit condition of the Fatimids and the advantage of placing Jerusalem where it could be crushed between an upper and a lower millstone, Nur dispatched an able Kurdish general named Shirkuh to Egypt. Here he succeeded in 1169, through diplomatic and military victories, in persuading the Fatimid caliph al-Adid to appoint him vizir. Two months after his investiture Skirkuh died and his mantle fell on his brother's son Salah-al-Din Yusuf ibn-Ayyub (rectitude of the faith, Joseph son of Job), known to us as Saladin.

Saladin was born in 1138 of Kurdish parents at Takrit on the Tigris. When a year old he moved with the family to Baalbek, over which his father Ayyub had been appointed commander by Zengi. The youth, at first reluctantly, embarked on a military career devoted to the pursuit of three objectives: replacing Shiite with Sunnite Islam in Egypt, uniting Egypt and Syria under one sceptre and pressing the holy war against the Franks. The first proved to be the easiest to realize. As al-Adid lay on his deathbed in 1171, Saladin as vizir simply substituted in the Friday prayer the name of the contemporary Abbasid caliph al-Mustadi. Thus came to its end the Fatimid caliphate. Incredible as it may seem, the momentous change was effected without even 'the butting of two goats'. Thereby Saladin became the sole ruler of Egypt. The second ambition was realized in 1177 when his Syrian suzerain Nur-al-Din passed away. A few minor engagements snatched Syria from the hands of the eleven-year-old son of Nur-al-Din. With the first two goals attained, the third entered the range of possibility.

As adjuncts of Egypt, Cyrenaica and Hejaz immediately became parts of the newly rising Ayyubid domain. Saladin's elder brother Turan-Shah added Nubia and Yemen. In

1175 the Abbasid caliph at Saladin's request granted him a diploma of investiture over all these lands, thereby giving away what in reality was not his to give but what it was flattering to him not to refuse. The incorporation of upper Mesopotamia (except Mosul) rounded out the sultanate. Nur-al-Din's dream of enveloping the Franks and crushing them to death was becoming a reality through the achievements of his more illustrious successor.

At last Saladin was free to concentrate on 'the infidels'. The hour of peril for the Latin kingdom struck when, after a six-day siege, Tiberias fell and the Moslem army moved to cut off the Frankish forces under the stubborn and incompetent king of Jerusalem, Guy of Lusignan, at Hattin, overlooking the Sea of Galilee. There the battle was joined July 3 to 4, 1187. The heat was intense. Exhausted from the long march and crazed with thirst, the heavily armoured Franks were surrounded by lightly armoured Moslems and subjected to an incessant shower of arrows. Of the 20,000 knights and infantry only a few escaped; the rest were slaughtered or captured. Prominent among the captives was Guy of Lusignan, who was received as befitted his rank by the magnanimous and chivalrous sultan.

The destruction on the day of Hattin of the Frankish army, which comprised besides the capital's garrison contingents from the other states, sealed the fate of the Latin kingdom. After a week's siege Jerusalem capitulated on October 2. Saladin's treatment of the Frankish populace stood in sharp contrast to the treatment accorded the Moslems eighty-eight years earlier. Those who could ransom themselves individually did so; the poor were allowed forty days to collect a lump sum for ransom and the rest were sold as slaves. The lands of the evacuated Franks were purchased by troops and native Christians. From Jerusalem the tide of conquest continued, engulfing all the Frankish holdings except Tyre, Tripoli, Antioch and a few castles.

The Crusades

The loss of Jerusalem aroused Europe and inspired the 'third Crusade'. In it participated the three mightiest sovereigns of western Europe, Frederick Barbarossa of Germany, Philip Augustus of France and Richard the Lion-Hearted of England. Legend and history have collaborated to make this campaign, with Richard and Saladin as its chief heroes, one of the truly spectacular and romantic episodes in occidental and oriental annals.

Frederick took the land route and was drowned crossing a river in Cilicia. Discouraged, many of his followers returned home. Philip and Richard joined Guy in besieging Acre, which fell in July 1191 after a two-year siege which witnessed spectacular feats of valour on both sides. Included in the conditions of surrender were the restoration of the 'true cross', captured at Hattin, and the release of the garrison on the payment of 200,000 gold pieces. But the money was not paid in a month and the Lion-Hearted ordered the twenty-seven hundred captives slaughtered. After tedious but inconclusive skirmishing, peace was finally concluded in November 1192 on the general basis that the coast from Tyre southward belonged to the Latins and the interior to the Moslems and that the Christian pilgrims should not be molested. Palestine was partitioned. Richard bade Syria farewell and started for home, only to be captured and held for ransom by a Christian sovereign. Early in March of the following year Saladin died of fever, aged fifty-five. His tomb, still standing by the Umayyad Mosque, is one of the most revered shrines in Damascus.

More than a warrior and champion of orthodox Islam, Saladin was a builder and a patron of learning. Like his predecessor Nur-al-Din he founded schools, seminaries and mosques in both Egypt and Syria. The vast treasures of the Fatimid court which fell into his hands on the overthrow of the caliphate he distributed among his men, keeping nothing for himself. Nur-al-Din's estate was passed on intact to the deceased ruler's son. The estate Saladin himself left amounted to forty-seven dirhems and one gold dinar, but the memory he left is still a priceless treasure in the heritage of the Arab East. The memory of his chivalry is almost equally cherished in Europe, where it has touched the fancy of English minstrels as well as modern novelists.

With the death of the great hero of Islam the third period in Crusading history begins, that of dissension and petty wars covering a century. Throughout the thirteenth century European public sentiment remained indifferent to these campaigns. Most of these were commercially rather than religiously motivated and directed against Constantinople, Egypt and Tunisia rather than Syria. The Moslems too had lost the spirit of holy war, the unified leadership and the united domain. Saladin's brother al-Adil before 1200 acquired sovereignty over Egypt and southern Syria, but consistently tried to maintain cordial relations with the Franks in order to promote peace and trade with the Italian cities.

Only in Aleppo did Saladin's lineal descendants retain power. From al-Adil sprang Ayyubid branches which reigned in Egypt, Damascus and Mesopotamia. Other branches arose in Homs, Hamah and Yemen. In the course of the ensuing dynastic turmoils one after another of Saladin's conquests — Beirut, Safad, Tiberias, even Jerusalem (1229) — reverted to Frankish hands. Jerusalem was turned over by al-Adil's son al-Kamil (1218–1238) to Frederick II, king of Sicily, in accordance with a ten-year treaty in which al-Kamil was guaranteed Frederick's aid against his enemies, most of whom were Ayyubids. In 1244, however, al-Kamil's nephew al-Salih utilized a contingent of Turks dislodged by Genghis Khan to restore the city to Islam. In any event the Franks were in no position to capitalize on Moslem dissension. They themselves were in as bad a situation, with rivalries between Genoese and Venetians, jealousies between Templars and Hospitallers and quarrels among leaders. In these quarrels it was no more unusual for one side to secure Moslem aid against the other than it was for Moslems to secure Christian aid against other Moslems.

After the failure of the 'sixth Crusade' and his release from captivity in 1250, King Louis IX of France spent four years in Syria, where he fortified Jaffa, Caesarea, Acre and Sidon. Of all Crusading leaders, Louis was the noblest character and was later made a saint. A new and unexpected danger, however, was now threatening: Mongol hordes flooding northern Syria and advancing southward. Concurrently the Ayyubids were being supplanted by Mamluk rulers, to be discussed in the next chapter. The fourth Mamluk, Baybars (1260–1277), checked the first advance of the Mongols in Palestine, virtually destroyed the Armenian kingdom of Cilicia, recovered the Mongols' Syrian conquests, reunited Egypt and Syria and was then able to pursue the holy war. In addition to castles held by the military orders — Templars and Hospitallers — he regained Caesarea, Arsuf, Safad, Jaffa and even (1268) Antioch, where 16,000 people were put to the sword and 100,000 reportedly led into captivity. The city itself, with its ancient citadel and world-renowned churches, was given to the flames, a blow from which it has never recovered.

The fall of Antioch, second of the Latin states to be founded, had a demoralizing effect. A number of minor Latin strongholds were hastily abandoned. In 1271 the strong and strategically located Krak des Chevaliers, principal fortress of the Hospitallers and still the most admirably preserved of all Crusader castles, surrendered after a short siege. Similar mountain strongholds belonging to the Assassins, allies of the Hospitallers, were now reduced and truces were arranged with the great coastal fortresses, planted to control the maritime road and ports and to defend them against the fleet based on Egypt.

The Assassins were an extremist Ismailite order founded in 1090 and based on the fortress of Alamut in northern

Persia. Their name is derived from hashish (marijuana), the intoxicating hemp under the influence of which they supposedly committed their murders. The order was a secret organization headed by a grand master below whom stood priors followed by propagandists. Near the bottom were the devotees ready to execute at all cost the grand master's orders. The devotees made free and treacherous use of the dagger against Christians and Moslems alike; they made assassination an art.

About the same time that the Crusaders were entering Syria from the north-west the Assassins were entering it from the north-east. Their first important collaborator was the Seljuk amir Ridwan of Aleppo. Efforts to gain control of cities failed, as had the Druzes'. By 1140 they had acquired several strongholds in mountainous northern Syria, where between 40,000 and 60,000 obeyed the orders of the Syrian grand master at Misyaf. For thirty years, beginning about 1162, this high office was held by Rashid-al-Din Sinan. Assassins made two attempts on the life of Saladin and killed, among others, Raymond II of Tripoli and Conrad of Montferrat, titular king of Jerusalem. In 1172 Sinan sent envoys to the king of Jerusalem to discuss the possibility of conversion on the part of his men to Christianity. This was in line with the practice of dissimulation prescribed by ultra-Shiite tenets. Fearing the loss of tribute which the Assassins were then paying the Templars, these knights murdered the envoys. During his stay at Acre, Louis IX exchanged gifts with the current grand master, but the Assassins' power in the thirteenth century was less than in the twelfth. With Baybars' destruction of their fortresses, which for years had sheltered intrigue and murder, the Syrian Assassin power was for ever crushed.

The work begun by Baybars against the Franks was continued by his equally energetic and zealous successor Qalawun (1279–1290). The Hospitaller fortress al-Marqab yielded in 1285 and its defenders were escorted to Tripoli, the largest city still in Frankish hands. In 1289 Tripoli too fell and was levelled to the ground. Amidst preparations against Acre, the only place of military importance left, Qalawun died and was succeeded by his son al-Ashraf, who invested Acre for over a month, using ninety-two catapults, before he stormed it on May 18, 1291. He slaughtered its Templar defenders in violation of a safe-conduct he had granted them. The capture of Acre sealed the fate of the few remaining coastal towns. Tyre was abandoned on the same day and Sidon on July 14. Beirut capitulated on July 21 and Tortosa on August 3. Athlith, deserted by its Templars, was demolished a few days later. Only on the islet of Arwad off Tortosa were the Templars able to hold out for eleven years more. With Arwad's surrender the curtain fell on the last scene of the most spectacular drama in the history of the conflict between East and West.

Rich in picturesque and romantic incidents, the Crusades were rather disappointing in intellectual and cultural achievement. On the whole they meant much more to the West in terms of civilizing influences than they did to the East. They opened new horizons — industrial, commercial and colonial — before the eyes of Europeans. The states they built in Syria correspond to modern colonial acquisitions. The merchant or pilgrim rather than the returned soldier was the principal culture carrier. In the East they left a legacy of ill will between Moslems and Christians the effects of which are still noticeable.

Islamic culture in the Crusading epoch was already decadent in the East. For some time it had ceased to be a creative force. In science, literature, philosophy all its great lights had been dimmed. Moreover, the Franks themselves were on a lower cultural level. Nationalistic animosities and religious prejudices thwarted the free play of interactive forces between them and the Moslems and left them in no responsive mood. No wonder, then, that we know of only one major scientific work done from Arabic into

Latin throughout the whole period, a medical treatise by al-Majusi translated at Antioch in 1127 by a Pisan.   Another work translated in Antioch (1247) was *The Secret of Secrets*, a pseudo-Aristotelian treatise on occult science which had a wide vogue in the late Middle Ages.   Systematic hospitalization in the occident probably received a fresh stimulus from the orient, where Nur-al-Din's great hospital in Damascus led the way.   A number of hospices and hospitals, chiefly for lepers, began to appear in twelfth-century Europe.

In literature the influence was even slighter and more difficult to detect.   Stories, including some of Persian and Indian origin, were transmitted and appear strangely altered in the *Gesta Romanorum* and other collections.   Chaucer's *Squieres Tale* has an *Arabian Nights* antecedent; Boccaccio's *Decameron* contains a number of tales derived orally from oriental sources.   The Holy Grail legend preserves elements of undoubted Syrian origin.

In Syria the Franks learned the use of the crossbow, the wearing of heavier mail by knight and horse, the employment of the tabor and naker in military bands, the conveying of military intelligence by carrier pigeons and the use of fire for signalling at night.   They also acquired the practice of holding tournaments among knights wearing distinctive heraldic devices.   The double-headed eagle, the fleur-de-lis, the rosette and other emblems were borrowed from Moslem foes.   Many Mamluks bore names of animals, whose images they blazoned on their shields, as did their Christian imitators.   'Azure' and other heraldic terms have an Arabic origin.

The order of Templars, which, with that of the Hospitallers, was the Crusaders' nearest approach to harmonizing war and religion — an old achievement in Islam — followed in its organization a pattern similar to that of the Assassins. At the bottom of the Christian order stood the lay brothers, esquires and knights, corresponding to the associates, devotees and comrades.   The knight wore a white mantle with a red cross mark, the Assassin comrade a white mantle with a red cap. There was also an order of Arab chivalry which was reformed and patronized by the Abbasid al-Nasir (1180–1225). The initiate was also called comrade and wore distinctive trousers. Saladin's brother al-Adil and al-Adil's sons wore these trousers and may have belonged to the active Syrian branch of this order.

Most conspicuous among all Crusading remains in Syria are the many castles still crowning its hills. Then come the churches. In the churches the Franks employed the familiar Romanesque and Gothic styles but added Byzantine and Syrian motifs of decoration. The Church of the Holy Sepulchre and the Dome of the Rock were imitated in several ecclesiastical buildings of the 'round temple' type in England, France, Spain and Germany. Many of the Crusader churches have since been converted into mosques. Among these are the great cathedral of Tyre, the church at Sidon erected by the Hospitallers, the cathedral of Beirut and that of Tortosa, the most beautiful and best preserved of all. This structure, which was an object of pilgrimage, was begun in 1130 and housed a picture supposedly painted by Luke and an altar over which Peter allegedly celebrated the first mass.

For many generations before the Crusades pilgrims frequented the Holy Land and traders visited the eastern shores of the Mediterranean. The Crusading movement accelerated forces already in operation and popularized in Europe oriental products, some of which must have been previously known. The problem of tracing origins is further complicated by the fact that while the Syrian bridge was open for traffic two other bridges, the Sicilian and the Spanish, were in operation too, thus making it difficult to determine the exact route taken by any particular commodity.

While in Syria the Franks were introduced to or acquired a taste for certain native and tropical products with which the marts of Syria were then stocked. Among those products were sesame, millet, rice (*arizz*), lemons (*laymun*), melons and apricots, sometimes called plums of Damascus. The Syrian capital specialized in sweet scents and damask rose. Attars and fragrant volatile oils, of Persian origin, incense and other aromatic gums of Arabia, together with other spices, perfumes and sweetmeats became favourites. Cloves and similar aromatics, pepper and other condiments, alum, aloes and several drugs found their way into the European kitchen and shop. In Egypt ginger was added to the Crusader menu. More important than all these articles was sugar (*sukkar*), with the cane of which the Franks familiarized themselves on the Lebanese maritime plain. Arab traders had introduced sugar cane from India or south-eastern Asia, where it must originally have grown wild. Before the Crusades honey was the ingredient used by Europeans for sweetening foods and medicines. With sugar went a variety of soft drinks, sweetmeats and candy (*qandah*).

In matters of fashion, clothing and home furnishing new desires were likewise sharpened if not created. The Franks became convinced that not only native foods but native clothes were preferable. Men began to grow beards, wear flowing robes and cover their heads with shawls. Women wore oriental gauze ornamented with sequins and sat on divans, listening to the lute and rebab; they even veiled in public. Warriors, pilgrims, sailors and merchants returned with rugs, carpets and tapestries, which had been a fixture in Near Eastern homes from time immemorial. Fabrics such as damask (of Damascus), muslin (of Mosul), taffeta, velvet, silk and satin came to be appreciated as never before. Oriental luxuries became occidental necessities. Mirrors of glass replaced those of steel. The rosary, of Hindu origin, was used by Syrian Christians and then Sufi Moslems before it got into the hands of Roman Catholics. Pilgrims sent back home reliquaries of native workmanship which served as models for European craftsmen. Arras and other European centres began to imitate wares, rugs and fabrics of oriental manufacture. With cloth and metallic wares went dyestuffs and new colours such as lilac (*laylak*), carmine and crimson (*qirmizi*). Oriental work in pottery, gold, silver, enamel and stained glass was also imitated.

In the twelfth and thirteenth centuries maritime activity and international trade were stimulated to a degree unattained since Roman days. The introduction of the compass, of which presumably the Moslems made the first practical use, was a great aid in navigation. Before the Moslems the Chinese had discovered the directive property of the magnetic needle. Among the Europeans Italian sailors were the earliest users of the compass. The enhanced flow of trade created new demands, one of which was for ready cash on the part of pilgrim and Crusader. This demand helped to establish a money economy and increase the supply and circulation of currency. Banking firms were organized in the Italian city republics with branch offices in the Levant. The need was also felt for letters of credit. Gold coins with Arabic inscriptions were struck by the Latins. The first consuls reported in history were Genoese accredited to Acre in 1180. They presided over local Genoese courts, witnessed seal contracts, wills and deeds, identified new arrivals of their nationals, settled disputes and on the whole performed duties analogous to those of modern consuls in the Near East.

During the Crusades the periods of peace, it should be remembered, were of longer duration than the periods of war. Thus ample opportunity was provided for forging amicable bonds between Easterners and Westerners. Once the language barrier was removed the Frank must have discovered that after all the Moslem was not the idolater he was thought to be and that he shared in the Judaeo-Christian and Greco-Roman heritage of the European. We hear of many Crusaders who learned Arabic, but of no Arabs who spoke French or Latin. The tolerance, breadth of view and trend toward secularization which usually result from mingling of men of different faiths and cultures seem in this case to have accrued to the Western rather than to the Eastern society. On the social and economic level Christians and Moslems mixed freely, traded horses, dogs and falcons, exchanged safe-conducts and even intermarried. A new progeny from native mothers arose and was designated Pullani. Many modern Lebanese and Palestinians have inherited blue eyes and fair hair, while certain Christian families have preserved traditions or names suggesting European origins.

In his memoirs Usamah ibn-Munqidh (1095–1188) gives the clearest first-hand picture of interfaith association. A friend of Saladin, Usamah defended his picturesque ancestral castle on the Orontes, Shayzar, against Assassins and Franks. Never did this castle fall into Crusading hands. He himself fraternized with Franks in time of peace. To him the comparatively free sex relations among the Franks, 'who are void of all zeal and jealousy', were simply shocking. Their methods of ordeal by water and duel were far inferior to the Moslem judicial procedure of the day. Especially crude by contrast was their system of medication. Two members of a Frankish family at al-Munaytirah were properly treated by a native Christian physician until a European was summoned. The latter laid the ailing leg of one of the patients on a block of wood and bade a knight chop it off with one stroke of the axe. He then shaved the head of the other patient, a woman, made a deep cruciform incision on it and rubbed the wound with salt — to drive off the devil. Both patients expired on the spot. The native physician, himself the narrator of the story, concludes with these words: 'Thereupon I asked them whether my services were needed any longer, and when they replied in the negative I returned home, having learned of their medicine what I knew not before.'

The Crusades

In general, the effects of the Crusades on Syria were disastrous. The cities had been destroyed and the ports dismantled; all was ruin and desolation. Dissident Moslem elements, comprising Shiites, Ismailites and Nusayris, who then reportedly outnumbered the Sunnites and had on varied occasions compromised their loyalty by aiding Franks, were now decimated. Their remnant sought refuge in central Lebanon and the Biqa. The Mamluk al-Ashraf exacted from the Druzes outward conformity to Sunnite Islam, but the conformity did not last long. Baybars forced the Nusayris to build mosques in their villages, but he could not force them to pray in them. Instead, they used the buildings as stables for their cattle and beasts of burden. In pursuit of the 'scorched earth' policy Mamluk sultans methodically ravaged Lebanon. Shiites of the Kisrawan region were replaced by Kurds and Turkomans; Maronites from the north pushed on later to fill the vacancy. The defence of Beirut against recurring sea incursions was entrusted in 1294 by the sultans to amirs of the Buhtur family, one of whose members left us the most detailed account of the period. Lebanon then became less oriented westward; it assumed the general aspect that it has maintained till modern times. In fact, all Syria had in it by then almost every element of civilization it possessed until the early nineteenth century, when a fresh wave of Western ideas and cultural elements began to break on its shore.

Native Christians suffered no less than schismatic Moslems. A measure of hostility was engendered between the Syrian Christians and their Moslem neighbours that was seldom attained before and that is not yet entirely abated. The active help given the Crusaders by the native Christians led to ruthless reprisals which rarely discriminated between active collaborators and their innocent co-religionists. In Lebanon the Maronites were accorded by the Latins all the ecclesiastical and civil rights that pertained to members of the Roman Catholic church, though actual union was not effected until the eighteenth century. After Saladin's capture of Beirut (1191) thousands of Maronites migrated to Cyprus, where two thousand of their descendants still live, but those who stayed developed into what may be considered the national church of Lebanon. This church still retains its Syriac liturgy and its non-celibate priesthood, despite its ties to Rome. The 1952 census gives the number of Maronites in Lebanon as 377,544, more than any other religious body in that republic. Recent Maronite emigrants have carried their rite into Italy, France, North and South America, Australia and other parts of the civilized world.

The Armenian and Jacobite communities in the crusading period likewise entered into closer friendly relations than ever before with the Latins, but the *rapprochement* led to no union. Both of these churches, like the Coptic, are independent descendants of the Monophysite rite. The triumph of the church of the Syrians over those of Armenia, Egypt and Ethiopia was another conspicuous achievement of Syrian society and culture. All three used their respective vernaculars in their liturgies and survived primarily as vehicles of national spirit reacting against foreign domination. The Jacobite remnant in Syria and Lebanon, who prefer to be designated as Old Syrian, have a patriarchal seat at Homs. Those of them who in recent times joined the Roman Catholic Church form the Syrian Catholic church with its patriarchal seat in Lebanon. The Armenian Orthodox church has a similar Uniat offshoot.

The East Syrian church — called Nestorian by Roman Catholics as a stigma of heresy in contradistinction to those of its members who joined Rome as Uniats and became exclusively known as Chaldaeans — was not active in medieval Syria, as its patriarch had moved to Baghdad in 762 and its unparalleled missionary efforts had been directed eastward into Central Asia, India and China. Their cultural traces are still visible in the Syriac characters in which Mongol and Manchu were written and in the technique and decoration of bookbinding in Turkestan. The East Syrian church was represented at the beginning of the first World War by 190,000 members domiciled in and around the edges of Kurdistan. Those who survived drifted into Iraq and Syria and were given the appellation Assyrian chiefly by Anglican missionaries.

The East and the West Syrian churches with their ramifications did not comprise all Syrian Christians. There remained a small body which succumbed under the impact of Greek theology from Antioch and Constantinople and accepted the decrees of the Council of Chalcedon (451). Thereby this community secured orthodoxy and not only escaped excommunication but obtained protection, even patronage, from the state church and the imperial city. By way of reproach their opponents centuries later nicknamed them Melkites, royalists. Melkite ranks must have been recruited mainly from city-dwellers and descendants of Greek colonists. Gradually Greek replaced Syriac as the language of ritual and the Syriac liturgy gave place to the Byzantine. In the Crusading period the Melkite community suffered heavily. Their Syrian descendants maintain one patriarchate in Damascus and another in Jerusalem and are now known as Greek Orthodox. In recent years, strangely enough, 'Melkite' has been exclusively employed to designate Christians drawn from the Orthodox church and attached to Rome. Their patriarch maintains a residence in Egypt and another in Lebanon. At present they number about one-half of the Orthodox community, estimated at 230,000. The majority of the Greek Catholics and of the Greek Orthodox live in Syria rather than in Lebanon.

The spirit of holy war which animated the Mamluks in their counter-crusades seems, after its initial triumph, to have been canalized against Egyptian and Syrian Christians. Towards the end of his reign Qalawun issued edicts excluding his Christian subjects from governmental offices. In 1301 al-Nasir reactivated the old discriminatory laws requiring Christians and Jews to wear distinctive dress and refrain from horse and mule riding and padlocked many Christian churches. This wave of anti-Christian feeling is further reflected in the contemporaneous literature. Speeches, legal opinions and sermons inflamed popular antagonism. The writings of the Syrian theologian ibn-Taymiyah (1263–1328) embody the reactionary spirit of the age. Born in Harran, ibn-Taymiyah flourished in Damascus, where he lifted his voice high in condemnation of saint worship, vows and pilgrimage to shrines. His principles were later adopted by the Wahhabis, who today dominate the religious and political life of Saudi Arabia.

Another type of literature flourished now which may be termed counter-propaganda. It extolled the virtues of Jerusalem, recommended pilgrimage to it and insisted that Muhammad had proclaimed prayer in its mosque a thousand times more meritorious than in any other, excepting, of course, the two of Mecca and Medina. Alongside this genre arose a form of historical romance extolling the exploits — real or imaginary — of some Moslem hero. Saladin, Baybars and Antarah became the heroes of such romances. Antarah was a pre-Islamic poet-warrior, but his romance, judged by its latest historical allusions, was conceived in Syria in the early twelfth century. Story-tellers in the cafés of Cairo, Beirut, Damascus and Baghdad drawing their tales from it and the romance of Baybars attract larger audiences than when reciting tales from the *Arabian Nights*.

An interesting by-product of the Crusades was the initiation of Christian missionary work among Moslems. Convinced, by the failure of these wars, of the futility of the military method in dealing with Moslems, thoughtful men began to advocate concentration on peaceful methods. Raymond Lull (d. 1315), a Catalan ecclesiastic, was the earliest European to emphasize oriental studies as an instrument of pacific campaign in which persuasion should replace violence. He himself studied Arabic from a slave and taught it. With Raymond, the Crusading spirit turned into a new channel: converting the Moslem rather than expelling or exterminating him. The Carmelite order, still active in the area, was founded in 1154 by a Crusader in that country and named after one of its mountains. Early in the thirteenth century two other monastic orders, the Franciscan and the Dominican, were founded and their representatives were stationed in many Syrian towns. In the last years of that century Beirut had a large Franciscan church. In 1219 the founder of the Franciscan order, St. Francis of Assisi, visited the Ayyubid court in Egypt and held a fruitless religious discussion with al-Kamil. A Dominican bishop, William of Tripoli, wrote in 1270 one of the most learned treatises in medieval times on the Moslems, bringing out points in which Islam and Christianity agree and advocating missionaries rather than soldiers to undertake the recovery of the Holy Land.

AYYUBIDS AND MAMLUKS

WHEN Saladin died in 1193, the sultanate built by him, extending from the Nile to the Tigris, was partitioned among his heirs, none of whom inherited his genius. His son al-Afdal succeeded to his father's throne in Damascus, but in 1196 he was replaced by his uncle al-Adil of Egypt. In 1250 the Damascus branch was incorporated with that of Aleppo, only to be swept away after a decade by the Mongol avalanche of Hulagu. Saladin's second son, al-Aziz, followed his father on the Egyptian throne, but al-Aziz' son was supplanted in 1198 by the same al-Adil, who in both cases took advantage of the dissension among his nephews. It was these dynastic feuds which afforded the Franks an opportunity to regain some of their lost territory. Saladin's third son, al-Zahir, succeeded his father at Aleppo. Other branches were founded at Hamah, Homs, Baalbek and al-Karak (Krak de Montréal) and in Mesopotamia and Yemen.

Of the many Ayyubid branches the Egyptian was the chief. Several of this line held both Cairo and Damascus. One of them was al-Adil's grandson al-Salih Najm-al-Din, who died in 1249 leaving a widow Shajar-al-Durr (the tree of pearls). Formerly a Turkish or Armenian slave in the harem of the Abbasid caliph, Shajar had been freed by al-Salih after having borne him a son. For three months she kept the news of her husband's death a secret, pending the return from Mesopotamia of his son Turan-Shah, who soon lost the loyalty of his slaves (*mamluks*) and was murdered with the connivance of his stepmother. The daring and energetic woman thereupon proclaimed herself queen of the Moslems and for eighty days exercised sole sovereignty over the lands which had produced Zenobia and Cleopatra.

She even had coins struck in her name and had herself
mentioned in the Friday prayer.

Her former master the caliph addressed a scathing note
to the amirs of Egypt: 'If you have no man to rule you,
let us know and we will send you one'. They chose her
Turkish commander-in-chief, Aybak, sultan and she salvaged
a remnant of glory by marrying him. Aybak crushed the
legitimist Ayyubid party of Syria, who considered themselves
entitled to rule Egypt, and concentrated on eliminating
potential rivals, but he overlooked Shajar-al-Durr. On
hearing that Aybak (1250–1257) was contemplating another
marriage, the queen had him murdered at his bath after a
ball game. Her turn then came. Battered to death with
wooden shoes by the slave women of her husband's first
wife, her body was cast from a tower in the citadel of Cairo.

Aybak was the first of the Mamluk sultans. This unusual
dynasty was drawn from the Ayyubids' slave bodyguard, a
military oligarchy in an alien land. When one of them died,
often it was not his son who succeeded him but a slave or a
mercenary of his who had won distinction and eminence.
Thus the bondman of yesterday would become the army
commander of today and the sultan of tomorrow. For almost
two and three-quarter centuries the slave sultans dominated
by the sword one of the most turbulent areas of the world.
Generally uncultured and brutal, they nevertheless endowed
Cairo with some architectural monuments of which it still
rightly boasts. Two other services to the cause of Islam
were rendered by them: they cleared Syria of the remnant
of the Crusaders and they definitely checked the redoubtable
advance of the Mongol hordes of Hulagu and of Timur
(Tamerlane). Had they failed to do so, the entire subsequent history of south-western Asia and Egypt might have
been different.

Originally purchased in the slave markets of Moslem
Russia and the Caucasus to form the personal bodyguard of
the Ayyubid al-Salih, the first Mamluks started a series

which is divided into two rather dissimilar dynasties, called Bahri (1250–1390) and Burji (1382–1517). The Bahris received their name from the Nile (Bahr al-Nil), on an islet in which their barracks stood. They were mostly Turks and Mongols; the Burjis were largely Circassians. Their rise was followed a decade later by the advent of the Mongols. Once more Syria became a battlefield of two contending powers.

Fresh from the destruction of the caliphate of Baghdad and the Assassin nest of Alamut, the Mongol horde under Hulagu, grandson of Genghis Khan, made its ominous appearance in northern Syria in 1260. The first victim was Aleppo, where fifty thousand people were put to the sword; Hamah suffered a similar blow. Damascus was besieged. Latin Antioch became a Mongol satellite. Louis IX and the pope thought an alliance with the invaders would help in the struggle against the Moslems. Shamanism was the official religion of the newcomers — as it was of their cousins the Turks — but among them were some Christian descendants of converts by early Syrian missionaries. It was a Christian general, Kitbugha, who overran and devastated most of Syria. The reigning Mamluk was Qutuz (1259–1260), an ex-slave who had displaced Aybak's son and executed Hulagu's envoys. In a battle at Ayn Jalut (Goliath's spring), near Nazareth, Baybars led the vanguard under Qutuz and administered a crushing defeat to the intruders. Kitbugha fell and the remnant of his army was pursued and chased out of Syria. In recognition of his military service Baybars expected to receive Aleppo as a fief but the sultan disappointed him. On the way homeward from Syria a fellow-conspirator addressed the sultan and kissed his hand while Baybars stabbed him in the neck. The murderer succeeded his victim.

Fourth in the series, Baybars (1260–1277) was the first great sultan, the real founder of Mamluk power and the victor over both Mongols and Crusaders. He was also a great administrator responsible for canals, harbour improvements, swift postal service and public works — renovation of mosques including the Dome of the Rock, restoration of citadels such as that of Aleppo and establishment of philanthropic endowments. His mausoleum at Damascus is now the library of the Arab Academy, which boasts one of the oldest manuscripts on paper (880).

A second Mongol invasion in 1280 was met by another Turkish ex-slave sultan, Qalawun (1279–1290), who seized power after two sons of Baybars had reigned briefly. After defeating at Homs the numerically superior invaders, reinforced by Armenians, Georgians and Persians, Qalawun proceeded with the reduction of Crusader fortresses — a task completed in 1291, as previously mentioned, by his son al-Ashraf. Another son, al-Nasir, was defeated in 1299 by a third Mongol host, which proceeded to devastate northern Syria. Early in 1300 the invaders occupied Damascus, utterly destroying a large part of the city. By 1303 the Egyptian army was strong enough to defeat the Mongols south of Damascus and to expel them permanently from the stricken land. The Mamluks had beaten the most persistent and dangerous enemy Syria and Egypt had to face since the beginning of Islam. As in the case of the Crusades, the Mongol invasions had disastrous consequences for the minorities. The Druzes of Lebanon, whose 12,000 bowmen harassed the Egyptian army on its retreat before the Mongols in 1300, were brought to a severe reckoning. The Armenians saw their unhappy land vengefully devastated by al-Nasir, who also made his own Christian and Jewish subjects suffer.

Al-Nasir was followed in a period of forty-two years (1340–1382) by twelve descendants, none of whom distinguished himself in any field of endeavour. The last among them was a child whose reign was first interrupted and then terminated by a Circassian, Barquq. Barquq founded the second Mamluk series, called Burji after the towers of the citadel in Cairo, where they were first quartered as slaves. With the exception of two Greeks the Burjis were all Circassians. They rejected even more emphatically than their predecessors the principle of hereditary succession. Turn-over was rapid and natural death exceptional. The reign of Qait-bay (1468–1495) was the longest and perhaps the most successful. The new régime was no improvement on the old. Corruption, intrigue, assassination and misrule continued to flourish. Several of the sultans were inefficient and treacherous; some were immoral, even degenerate; most were uncultured. Not only the sultans were corrupt but the amirs and the entire oligarchy, and the situation in Egypt was duplicated in Mamluk Syria.

The Mamluk administrative system continued that set up by the Abbasids and Fatimids, while the half-dozen provinces followed the divisions under the Ayyubid branches. Provincial governors, originally slaves of some sultan, represented the military as opposed to the learned class. Generally independent of one another, each maintained a court reproducing on a small scale, that of Cairo. Animosities and disturbances in the federal capital were often reflected in the provincial ones. The change of a Mamluk sultan usually provoked a rebellion on the part of a governor in Damascus or some other Syrian province. Western Lebanon remained under its native Buhturid amirs. Because of its historic background, Damascus, where Baybars often held his court, took precedence over other Syrian cities. One of its governors, Tangiz (1312–1339), as regent over Syria brought water to Jerusalem and restored the tower of Beirut, where he also built hostels and public baths. After an unusually long and beneficent reign he fell into disgrace and was put to death in a prison in Alexandria.

Almost the entire Mamluk era was punctuated with periods of drought, famine and pestilence. Earthquakes added their quota to the general devastation. Owing to these calamities and Mamluk misgovernment, the population of Egypt and Syria was reduced to an estimated one-third of its former size. The economic difficulties were compounded by exorbitant tax burdens. Such necessities as salt and sugar, as well as horses and boats, were heavily taxed. Some sultans monopolized certain commodities and manipulated prices to their advantage. Others debased the currency and contributed to the inflationary spiral. As the people became impoverished, the rulers waxed rich. Without an abundance of wealth the sultans could not have erected the lavish architectural monuments which still adorn Egypt and Syria.

Some of the economic loss was offset by an increase in trade. The concessions offered by al-Adil and Baybars to Venetians and other European merchants stimulated exchange of commodities. Syrian silk shared with perfumes and spices first place in the export trade. Glass and manufactured articles stood next on the list. Damascus, Tripoli, Antioch and Tyre were among the leading centres of industry. In the bazaars of Aleppo, Damascus and Beirut one could buy ivories and metal-work, dyed cloth and carpets. The neighbourhood of Beirut produced olive oil and soap, as it does today. Syrians did not depend entirely on foreigners for their export trade. As early as Saladin's day their merchants took up residence in Constantinople, where the emperor built a mosque for them and their Egyptian colleagues in reciprocation for privileges enjoyed by Byzantine merchants in Syria and Egypt. No other foreign merchants were permitted permanent residence in the Byzantine capital.

A German clergyman who sojourned in Syria from 1336 to 1341 was most favourably impressed by the signs of prosperity in Damascus and described Acre as 'exceeding neat, all the walls of the houses being of the same height and all alike built of hewn stone, wondrously adorned with glass windows and paintings, while all the palaces and houses in the city were not built merely to meet the needs of those who dwelt therein, but to minister to human luxury and

pleasure'. He goes on to say: 'At every street corner there
stood an exceeding strong tower, fenced with an iron door
and iron chains. All the nobles dwelt in very strong castles
and palaces along the outer edge of the city. In the midst
of the city dwelt the mechanic citizens and merchants, each
in his own special street according to his trade.'

With remarkable dexterity the feudal chiefs of Lebanon
maintained their power by co-operating with successive
overlords and by offering military service to each in turn —
Fatimids, Franks, Ayyubids and Mamluks. In the struggle
between Mamluks and Mongols the Buhturid amirs at times
had representatives in both camps, to ensure that they would
be on the winning side no matter which it was. Mount
Lebanon was still partly wooded, with wild beasts frequent-
ing its slopes. Wild fruits and edible plants attracted
ascetics and hermits of both faiths, but penetration by Arab
tribes was reducing their solitude.

Despite its political turmoils and economic vicissitudes
Syria enjoyed under the Ayyubids a flourishing era of
artistic and educational activity. The hospital built in
Damascus by Nur-al-Din continued to prosper on an en-
dowment which yielded fifteen dinars daily. It was staffed
with wardens who kept a record of the cases and expenses
and with physicians who attended the patients and prescribed foods and free medicines. An Egyptian official
recorded a visit he paid this institution around 1428 accompanied by an amiable Persian pilgrim who, attracted by
the comforts accorded the patients, feigned illness and
was admitted. On feeling his pulse and examining him
thoroughly, the head physician realized there was nothing
wrong with the gentleman but nevertheless prescribed fat-
tened chickens, fragrant sherbets, fruits, savoury cakes and
other delicacies. When the time came, however, he wrote
a new prescription: 'Three days are the limit of the
hospitality period'.

This hospital was equipped with a library and served as

a medical school. There is evidence to show that physicians, pharmacists and oculists were examined and given certificates before being allowed to practise their professions. In the manuals for the guidance of officials responsible for law enforcement, their duties with respect to phlebotomists, cuppers, physicians, surgeons, bone-setters and druggists are clearly set forth, indicating a certain measure of state control. Ibn-al-Nafis, a Syrian physician 'who would not prescribe medicine when diet sufficed', in a commentary on ibn-Sina contributed a clear conception of the pulmonary circulation of the blood three centuries before the Spaniard Servetus, to whom the discovery is usually credited. The only major Arabic medical works of the thirteenth century were treatises by two Syrian oculists. One of them, Khalifah ibn-abi-al-Mahasin of Aleppo, was so confident of his surgical skill that he did not hesitate to remove a cataract from a one-eyed man. To this century too belongs the most distinguished Arabic historian of medicine, Ahmad ibn-abi-Usaybiah of Damascus. He compiled biographies of some 400 Arab and Greek physicians and scientists. All these men, however, lived in the late twilight of Islamic science.

Saladin and his heirs continued Nur-al-Din's interest in building schools and mosques. It was Saladin who introduced from Syria into Egypt the dervish 'monastery' and the collegiate mosque to inculcate orthodox Sunnism and combat the widely held Shiite doctrine. In Jerusalem he built a hospital, a school and a monastery all bearing his name. The Ayyubid school of Syrian architecture was continued in Mamluk Egypt, where it is still represented by some of the most exquisite monuments Arab art ever produced. Strength, solidity and excessive decoration characterize this school. Its decorative motifs assume infinite grace on its durable material of fine stone. In the thirteenth century Egypt received fresh Syro-Mesopotamian influences through refugee artists and artisans who had fled Damascus, Baghdad and Mosul during the Mongol invasions. The influence is apparent in schools, mosques, hospitals, dervish monasteries and palaces. The ornamentation of Ayyubid and Mamluk monuments enhanced their architectural beauty. Among the Ayyubid innovations was a tendency towards elaboration in detail, greater elegance of proportion and increase in the number of stalactites. There was also a breakaway from the tradition of the plain square towers. In the Bahri Mamluk period the elaborate type of minaret evolved from the Ayyubid. The finest minarets, however, belong to the Burji period, in which Arab architecture — as represented in the mosques — achieved its greatest triumphs.

Exquisite specimens of iron-work, copper-work, glassware and wood-carving have come down to us from the Ayyubid-Mamluk age. Especially noteworthy among copper utensils are vases, ewers, trays, chandeliers, perfume burners and Koran cases — all with rich decoration of a vigour and 'sureness of touch that make it not only a delight to the eye but also . . . a delight to the intelligence'. Damascus was especially noted for its 'gold-like' basins and ewers inlaid with figures, foliage and other delicate designs in silver. Bronze ornaments from doors of mosques bear witness to the good taste of the age. Wood-carvings with floral and geometrical designs indicate freedom from the sterile formulas of Fatimid art. A thirteenth-century bottle survives as one of the oldest specimens of enamelled glass, while mosque lamps prove that Syria was still ahead of any European land in the technique of glass manufacture.

Intellectually, the entire Ayyubid-Mamluk period was one of compilation and imitation rather than of origination. Nevertheless Damascus and Cairo, especially after the destruction of Baghdad and the disintegration of Moslem Spain, remained the educational and intellectual centres of the Arab world. The richly endowed schools in these two cities served to conserve and transmit Arab science and learning.

In Sufism certain significant developments took place.

Ayyubid Aleppo was the scene of the activity of an extraordinary Sufi, al-Suhrawardi (1155–1191), founder of the doctrine of illumination and of a dervish order. According to this doctrine light is the very essence of God, the fundamental reality of all things and the representative of true knowledge, perfect purity, love and goodness. Clearly such theories combine Zoroastrian — more especially Manichaean — Neo-Platonic and Islamic ideas. The conception of God as light is stressed in the Koran. Intoxicated with his mystical fervour, young al-Suhrawardi so incensed the conservative theologians that on their insistence he was starved or strangled to death on orders from the sultan. Another illuminationist Sufi, ibn-Arabi (1165–1240), left his native Spain on a pilgrimage to Mecca in 1202 and thereafter made Damascus his home. A pantheistic philosopher, ibn-Arabi is considered the greatest speculative genius of Islamic mysticism. He recognized the inner light as the one true guide and influenced such Christians as Raymond Lull and Dante.

In literature Syria of the Ayyubid-Mamluk period could boast an array of geographers, biographers, historians and encyclopaedic scholars without peer in Islamic history. Yaqut (1179–1229), originally a Greek slave, wrote a masterful geographical dictionary at Aleppo, as well as a monumental dictionary of learned men. Ibn-Khallikan (d. 1282) was, for many years, chief judge of Syria, as well as compiler of the finest Moslem collection of biographies. He took pains to establish the correct orthography of names, fix dates, trace pedigrees, ascertain the significant events, and on the whole produce as accurate and interesting portrayals as possible. A continuation of this work was penned by al-Kutubi (d. 1363) of Aleppo. A more prolific biographer was al-Safadi (1296–1363), treasurer of Damascus and author of a thirty-volume work in the extant part of which the lives of some fourteen thousand rulers, judges and literati are portrayed.

Syria

Among Syrian historians of the period the most important are abu-Shamah (1203–1268), chronicler of the careers of Nur-al-Din and Saladin, and abu-al-Fida (1273–1332), Ayyubid ruler of Hamah and continuator of the great ibn-al-Athir (d. 1234). Abu-al-Fida made a worthy contribution to geography too; he argues for the sphericity of the earth and the loss or gain of one day as one travels around it. His contemporary Shams-al-Din al-Dimashqi (d. 1326/7) wrote a cosmographical treatise rich in physical, mineral and ethnic data. Another Damascene, ibn-Fadl-Allah al-Umari (d. 1349), produced a travel book and an epistolary manual for administrators and diplomats. The two leading historians of the period, the Egyptian al-Maqrizi and the Tunisian ibn-Khaldun, are connected with Syria. Al-Maqrizi (1364–1442) was of Baalbekan ancestry and held a professorship in Damascus. His teacher was ibn-Khaldun (1332–1406), who, in 1401, accompanied the Burji sultan Faraj to Damascus and was received as an honoured guest by Timur. Ibn-Khaldun's prolegomena, the first volume in his comprehensive history, entitles him to the distinction of being the greatest philosopher of history Islam produced. In his attempt to interpret historical happenings and national traits on economic, geographic, physical and other secular bases, ibn-Khaldun had no predecessor in Islam and remains without a worthy successor.

The onslaught on Syria by Timur Lang (Tamerlane) was the last and most destructive of the Mongol invasions. Timur spread havoc and ruin throughout south-western Asia until Syria lay prostrate beneath his feet. For three days in October 1400 Aleppo was given over to plunder. Its citadel was perhaps for the first time taken by storm, the invader having sacrificed of his men enough to fill the moat with their corpses. Some twenty thousand of the city's inhabitants were slaughtered and their severed heads piled high. The city's priceless schools and mosques built by Nurids and Ayyubids were for ever destroyed. The

routing of the advance forces of Faraj opened the way to
Damascus. Its citadel held out for a month. In violation
of the capitulation terms the city was plundered and committed to the flames. Thirty thousand of its' men, women
and children were shut up in its great mosque, which was
then set on fire. Of the building itself only the walls were
left standing. The cream of Damascene scholars, craftsmen,
artisans, armourers, steel workers and glass manufacturers
were carried away to Timur's capital, Samarkand, there to
implant these and other minor arts. This was perhaps the
heaviest blow that the city, if not the whole country, ever
suffered. Timur crushed the Ottoman army at Ankara in
1402, but died two years later. His successors exhausted
themselves in internal struggles, making possible the recon-
stitution of the Ottoman power in Asia Minor and later
the rise of the Safawid dynasty in Persia.

Rivalry between the Mamluk and the Ottoman sultanates
asserted itself in the second half of the fifteenth century.
Hostilities did not break out till 1486, when Qait-bay con-
tested with the Ottoman Bayazid II the possession of Adana,
Tarsus and other border towns. Selim I (1512–1520)
destroyed the Safawid army and occupied Mesopotamia.
He charged that the Mamluk Qansawh al-Ghawri (1500–
1516) had entered into treaty relations with the Safawid
shah against him and had harboured political refugees.
Qansawh moved northward under the pretext of acting as
an intermediary between the two contestants. He sent a
special envoy to Selim, who shaved his beard and sent him
back on a lame donkey with a declaration of war.

The Ottoman and Mamluk armies clashed on August
24, 1516, north of Aleppo. The seventy-five-year-old
Qansawh fought valiantly but hopelessly. He could not
depend upon the loyalty of his Syrian governors nor could
his troops match the redoubtable Janissaries with their
superior equipment. Khair Bey, the treacherous governor
of Aleppo, who was entrusted with the command of the left

wing, deserted with his men at the first charge. The Turkish army employed artillery, muskets and other long-range weapons which the Egyptian army, comprising bedouin and Syrian contingents, was unfamiliar with or disdained to use, clinging to the antiquated theory that personal valour is the decisive factor in combat. In the thick of battle Qansawh was stricken with apoplexy and fell from his horse. Selim's victory was complete. In the citadel of Aleppo he found Mamluk treasures estimated in millions of dinars. In mid-October he moved on to Damascus. Syria passed quietly into Ottoman hands, there to remain for four full centuries. Its people, as on many a previous occasion, welcomed the new masters as deliverers from the old. Egypt was subdued in January 1517 and Hejaz, with its two holy cities, automatically became a part of Selim's empire. A new era began for the Arab world : the era of domination by the Ottoman Turks.

TURKISH PROVINCE

The dynasty which in 1516 so abruptly overran the lands of the Arabs was no upstart. Beginning modestly about 1300 as a petty Turkish state in western Asia Minor, the Ottomans had gradually taken over all Anatolia from the other heirs of the Seljuks, had penetrated into Thrace and made Adrianople their capital and had entirely recovered from Timur's catastrophic incursion. In 1453 they conquered Constantinople and liquidated the pathetic remnant of the Byzantine empire. Their next conquests drove westward into the Balkans and eastward into Transcaucasia, Mesopotamia and Safawid Persia. The sudden stab southward into Syria and Egypt was apparently unpremeditated, an opportunist assault which led to an unexpected though not unwelcome accretion of territory, wealth and power for Selim I and his successors, all twenty-seven of whom were his direct descendants.

The Ottoman empire attained its height under Selim's son Sulayman I the Magnificent (al-Qanuni, the lawgiver, 1520–1566). Sulayman added most of Hungary, Rhodes and North Africa — except Morocco — to his realm. For a century the borders remained almost stationary, but then a gradual decay set in. Provinces were detached or achieved autonomy; the authority of the Sublime Porte crumbled and in 1922 dissolved utterly. Syria was among the last to benefit from this trend, however, remaining firmly under Turkish rule until the first World War, four centuries after it had toppled so unceremoniously into Ottoman hands. Lebanon, as will be indicated, was somewhat more fortunate during these centuries, but still was never able completely to shake off the sultans' authority.

On his return from the conquest of Egypt, Selim lingered long enough in Syria to consolidate his position and organize the new domain. For purposes of taxation he empowered a commission to draw up a *cadastre* of the whole land, reserving much of the fertile Biqa plain and the rich valley of the Orontes to the crown. The Mamluk procedure of farming out tax collection to the highest bidder was, of course, retained. The Hanafite rite of jurisprudence, preferred by the Ottomans, was given official status in Syria. After a brief period of turbulence the land was divided into three provinces (*vilayets* or *pashaliks*) — Damascus, Aleppo and Tripoli — under Turkish governors or pashas.

Lebanon, however, with its hardy Druze and Maronite mountaineers, deserved a different treatment. Expediency dictated that its native feudal lords be recognized, especially since the real danger came from Egypt and Persia. Selim confirmed Fakhr-al-Din al-Mani of al-Shuf (south-east of Beirut) and the other Lebanese amirs in their fiefs, allowed them the same autonomous privileges enjoyed under the Mamluks and imposed on them a comparatively light tribute. Fakhr-al-Din was recognized as the leading chieftain of the mountain. Thereafter the Ottoman sultans dealt with their Lebanese vassals either directly or through a neighbouring Syrian pasha. As a rule these vassals acted independently, transmitted their fiefs to their descendants, offered no military service to the sultan, exercised the right of life and death over their subjects, exacted taxes and duties and at times even concluded treaties with foreign powers.

The Buhturid amirs, who had remained loyal to the Mamluks, were apprehended and jailed by the virtual viceroy, Jan-Birdi al-Ghazali, who as governor of Damascus had followed his colleague Khair Bey of Aleppo in deserting Qansawh at the critical juncture. Al-Ghazali sent the heads of several Arab chieftains and rebellious bedouins to Constantinople, but at Selim's death in 1520 he discarded his professed new loyalties and proclaimed himself in the Umayyad Mosque an independent sovereign, struck coins in his own name and tried to induce his former colleague Khair Bey, whom Selim had rewarded with the vice-royalty of Egypt, to follow his example. But Aleppo did not openly support al-Ghazali and Sulayman sent against him an army which, on January 27, 1521, destroyed the Syrian rebels and killed al-Ghazali. The punishment which Damascus and its environs received was even more severe than that meted out earlier by Timur. About a third of the city and its villages was utterly destroyed. Ever since then the name of the Janissaries has been associated in the Syrian mind with destruction and terror.

Ottoman political theory considered the conquered peoples, especially the non-Moslems, human flocks to be shepherded for the benefit of the conquerors, the descendants of Central Asian nomads. As such they were to be milked, fleeced and allowed to live their own lives so long as they gave no trouble. Mostly peasants, artisans and merchants, they could not aspire to military or civil careers. But the herd needs watchdogs. These were recruited mainly from war prisoners, purchased slaves and Christian children levied as a tribute and then trained and brought up as Moslems. All recruits were put through a rigorous system of training in the capital covering many years. They were subjected to keen competition and careful screening; the mentally bright among them were further prepared for governmental positions and the physically strong for military service. The toughest were drafted into the infantry corps termed Janissary. The governing and the military class in the empire came at first almost exclusively from this source. Grand vizirs, vizirs, admirals, generals, provincial governors were once slaves and so remained. Their lives and property were always at the disposal of their sultan master, who never hesitated to exercise his right of ownership. This left the Ottoman house as the only aristocracy in the empire, wielding absolute power in the administration of the state and for its defence.

The subject peoples were classified according to religious affiliation. From time immemorial Near Eastern society has been stratified in terms of belief rather than of race and within the religious community the family rather than the territory has been the nucleus of organization. Hence in the people's minds religion and nationality were inextricably interwoven. Each of the religious groups of the Ottoman empire was termed a millet. The two largest millets were those of Islam and the Greek Orthodox. Armenians and Jews were also classified as millets. According to this system all non-Moslem groups were organized into communities under religious heads of their own who also exercised certain civil functions of importance. This amounted to a provision for the government of subject minorities.

The Ottoman governor was no improvement on his Mamluk predecessor, who likewise was recruited from the slave class. Besides, he was farther removed from the central government and therefore freer from its control. But that did not make much difference, as corruption in the capital was as rife as in the provinces. Governors bought their appointments there and entered upon their duties with the main desire of promoting their own interests. Not a few returned to Constantinople to face execution and confiscation of property. Exploitation went hand in hand with instability. Turn-over was rapid, so governors had to extort their profits with brutal haste. At times pashas engaged in bloody conflicts against one another with utter disregard of the central government. Occasional visits by Janissaries added to the misery of the people, most of whom, however, were manifestly resigned to their fate. The general attitude seems to have been one of passivity, frustration, distrust of leadership and pessimism as to the result of effort. The old spirit of rebellion which had often flared under Abbasid and Fatimid misrule was by this time apparently dead.

Clearly the dark ages which began under Seljuk Turks were getting darker under Ottoman Turks. While Europe was entering upon its age of enlightenment, Syria was groping in Ottoman darkness.

Occasionally reforms were introduced by able grand vizirs or bold sultans, but all remained merely ink on paper because of obstruction and opposition by Janissaries, corrupt officials, local collaborators and powerful conservative theologians. Even after the destruction of the Janissaries in 1826, reform rescripts could not be effectively implemented and the old corrupt and inefficient system persisted far into the modern period, which for Syria and Lebanon began about 1860.

Neither the political nor the ethnic structure of Syria was seriously affected by the Ottoman conquest. The only radical change in the Ottoman period was incidental and involved the desert tribes, which migrated into the Syrian Desert from Arabia. In this last great bedouin immigration were included such currently prominent groups as the Shammar and the Anazah, of which the Ruwalah are a major branch. Turks came and went as officials but there was no Turkish colonization of the land. At heart they and their Syrian subjects always remained strangers to one another. A few thousand Moslem Circassians drifted into northern Syria and Transjordan after the Russo-Turkish war of 1877, and several thousand Armenian refugees found a haven in Lebanon after the first World War. Arabic remained the language of the people. It borrowed only a few Turkish words, mostly relating to politics, army and food.

Syrian economic life underwent a steady decline for which Ottoman maladministration, however, was not entirely to blame. The Ottoman conquest of the Arab East coincided with changes in the international trade routes that left that region economically insignificant. The discovery of America and of the Cape of Good Hope route to India deprived the Arab world of its intermediate position between

India and Europe and of the resultant profits levied on transit merchandise. The Mediterranean, hitherto a middle sea, no longer held that position; it had to wait three and a half centuries, till the opening of the Suez Canal, before it could resume its place as a highway and a battlefield.

Syrian merchants had therefore to depend more upon overland trade. As the terminus of the route leading to Baghdad and Basrah, Aleppo began to flourish as a centre of internal trade for the empire and of international trade between Europe and Asia. It eclipsed for the time being Damascus, as the ports of Alexandretta and Tripoli eclipsed Beirut. In fact it remained until the mid-seventeenth century the principal market of the entire Near East. A sizable Venetian colony grew in Aleppo. Their consular reports refer to arrivals at both Aleppo and Damascus of caravans with spices from India. Spices were in special demand for preserving meat in those pre-refrigeration days.

Venetian traders in the Syrian cities and ports soon had competitors — first French, then English. A 1740 Franco-Turkish treaty put not only French pilgrims to the Holy Land but all other Christians visiting the Ottoman empire under the protection of the French flag. These concessions served as the basis of the later French claim to protect all Catholic Christians of Syria. Besides Aleppo the French had settlements (factories) at Alexandretta, Tripoli, Sidon, Acre and al-Ramlah. They and their English rivals tried to satisfy the Western taste for Eastern luxuries promoted during the Crusades. The list of native products was headed by silk from Lebanon, cotton from Palestine, wool and oil. Competition with sea traders was keen but the Portuguese insistence on high, almost monopolistic, prices gave the traders in Syria their chance. No enduring benefits evidently accrued to Syria from this new development in its trade, which was largely in European hands. The population of the land continued on its downward course in numbers as in prosperity.

On the heels of European businessmen came missionaries, teachers, travellers and explorers. The door was thus opened to modern influences, one of the most pregnant facts in the history of Ottoman Syria. The missionaries were Jesuits, Capuchins, Lazarites and members of other Catholic orders. Their activity was centred in the native Christian communities and resulted in the founding of the Uniat churches — Syrian and Greek — in the seventeenth and eighteenth centuries. Syria was, however, much less exposed to Western influences than was Lebanon, and less affected by them throughout the Ottoman period.

Intellectually the period was one of sterility. Oppressive rule, high taxation, economic and social decline are not conducive to creative or original work in art, science or literature. The era of compilation, annotation, abridgment and imitation which had its beginnings centuries before continued with fewer and poorer productions. Throughout the Ottoman age no Syrian poet, philosopher, artist, scientist or essayist of the first order made his appearance. Illiteracy was widespread, almost universal. Judges were appointed whose mastery over the written word was deficient. The few intellectuals who developed tended to be attracted to Constantinople, there to become fully Ottomanized. Damascus was the centre of some mediocre intellectual activity until about 1700. It was there that al-Maqqari of Tlemcen compiled between 1628 and 1630, from material brought with him from Morocco, the voluminous work considered the chief source of information for the literary history of Moslem Spain.

The first press with Arabic characters in the East made its appearance in 1702 at Aleppo through the initiative of a patriarch, Athanasius, who wavered between Orthodoxy and Catholicism. The Gospels (1708) were among the first books printed in this press, which may have come from Wallachia, and which followed by 188 years the Arabic press at Fano (Italy), the first of its kind in the world, probably a reflection of papal missionary zeal. The output of the Aleppo press and those which soon sprang up in Lebanon was mostly religious and linguistic, supplementing the work of the schools. Slowly but surely the implementation for embarking on a new cultural life was being forged.

Meanwhile the history of Ottoman Lebanon had followed a different path. With the Ottoman conquest the Manid amirs began to replace the Tanukhs as masters of central and southern Lebanon. To the north of them were other feudal families, which competed for power without regard to the Ottoman overlords. The sultans cared little who ruled in Lebanon as long as tribute was paid regularly and in full, provided domestic disorder and foreign intrigue did not exceed reasonable limits. As Druzes and Maronites the Lebanese were mostly subject to their own laws administered by the religious heads of their respective communities under the millet system. That Lebanon under its local feudal lords fared better than Syria under its Turkish governors is indicated by the increase in its population through natural causes and immigration. The comparative safety and stability it enjoyed attracted Sunnites and Shiites from the Biqa and Baalbek, Maronites from the Tripoli district and Druzes from the south and south-east. The struggle for power on the local and national levels, by peaceful and forceful methods, occupied no small part of the time and energy of the feudal amirs and the leaders of these rival groups. Punitive expeditions kept the reckless in line, and outstanding leaders were often killed by jealous compatriots or Ottoman agents.

Manid power reached its zenith under Fakhr-al-Din II (1590–1635), the ablest and most fascinating figure in the history of Ottoman Lebanon. Fakhr-al-Din wrested control of the northern portion from his father-in-law and brought under his sway the Shiites of Baalbek and the bedouin chiefs of the Biqa and Galilee. He allied himself with a rebellious Kurdish governor of Aleppo and set himself up as an autonomous ruler. His southward expansion brought under his command castles which since Crusading days had dominated strategic roads and sites. The acquisition of the rich Biqa increased his income enough to enable him to organize a trained disciplined army, with a core of professional soldiers, to supplement the old irregulars whose chances of standing against Janissaries were nil. The income left was enough to employ spies in his rivals' and enemies' courts and to bribe Ottoman officials. Another source of revenue was the trade he encouraged especially with the Florentines, whose ships offered Lebanese silk, soap, olive oil, wheat and other cereals a lucrative foreign market. In 1608 the lord of Lebanon signed with Ferdinand I, the Medici grand duke of Tuscany, whose capital was Florence, a treaty containing a secret military article clearly directed against the Ottomans. Thereupon the sultan, prompted by the Turkish governor of Damascus, resolved to take action against his audacious vassal and put an end to his separatist and expansionist policy.

An army from Damascus was unable to surmount the mountain barrier, but the appearance of a fleet of sixty galleys to blockade the coast prompted a prudent retirement. Fakhr-al-Din spent the years from 1613 to 1618 in instructive travels in Italy and Sicily but was disappointed in his hope of returning home at the head of an expeditionary force provided by the European powers and the pope. On his return to Lebanon he re-established his rule and even extended his realm. In 1624 the sultan acknowledged Fakhr-al-Din as lord of the Arab lands from Aleppo to the borders of Egypt, under Ottoman suzerainty. This diminutive man, whose enemies described him as so short that if an egg dropped from his pocket to the ground it wouldn't break, was the only one able to maintain order, administer justice and insure regular taxes for himself and the sultan.

During his remaining eleven years Fakhr-al-Din was free to pursue his ambitious dream of modernizing Lebanon.

In his public and private projects he employed architects, irrigation engineers and agricultural experts he brought from Italy. Documents show that he invited missions from Tuscany to instruct the Lebanese farmer in improved methods of tilling the soil and made requests for cattle to improve the local breed. He embellished and fortified Beirut, where he built an elaborate residence with a magnificent garden. In this period the Capuchin mission entered Sidon and established centres in Beirut, Tripoli, Aleppo, Damascus and in certain villages of the Lebanon. The Jesuits and Carmelites entered the country about the same time. Fakhr-al-Din was on friendly terms with European missionaries, merchants and consuls, all of whom enjoyed the capitulations initiated by Sulayman. Consular reports show he protected European merchants in Sidon against pirates. Throughout his career he had Maronite counsellors and was sympathetic to Christians. Though he 'was never known to pray, nor ever seen in a mosque', he probably professed Islam openly and practised Druzism privately.

Fakhr-al-Din's prosperity, military might and negotiations with Europeans once again aroused the sultan's suspicions. In 1633 the governor of Damascus was sent against him with a vast army supported by a fleet. The amir's subordinates began to desert him, his son fell in battle and his Italian allies ignored his pleas for aid. He fled to the mountains and hid for months in an almost inaccessible cave, but was at last discovered and led in chains to Constantinople, where he and his three sons were held as hostages. News that his relatives and followers were flouting authority doomed the hostages and they were beheaded in April 1635. The independent greater Lebanon of which he dreamed and which he successfully initiated was not to be fully realized until 1943.

Lebanon entered upon a period of anarchy following the death of Fakhr-al-Din. The Manids were persecuted by rival families and Ottoman governors and by 1697 the family was extinct. They were succeeded by their relatives by marriage the Shihabs, freely elected by the Lebanese notables at a national conference. The Shihabs' ancestors were related to the Prophet's family. Evidently the Lebanese spirit of home rule was not entirely dead. Turkey, herself in danger of being destroyed by European powers, was content so long as the taxes were guaranteed. The Shihabs held the reigns of government until 1841, using the old techniques: bribing Ottoman officials, rising against weak sultans, playing one chief or one party against another and thus maintaining their hold on the mountain, though they never adopted the Druze creed of their people. Yamanite opposition was crushed in 1711 and the feudal system was reorganized with Shihab partisans at the helm. New family alignments developed as Druzes and Maronites contended for power.

Palestine came into prominence in the mid-eighteenth century under a bedouin governor, Zahir al-Umar. Zahir took Tiberias, Nablus, Nazareth and Acre, which he fortified, made his residence and used for exporting silk, cotton, wheat and other Palestinian products to foreign markets. A benevolent dictator, Zahir stamped out lawlessness, encouraged agriculture and assumed a tolerant attitude towards his Christian subjects. His financial obligations to the Ottoman government he regularly met, for he realized that to the government it made no great difference who the agent was, Turk or Arab, so long as the cash was forthcoming. His downfall resulted from an alliance with an Egyptian rebel and dependence on a Russian fleet which helped him to take Sidon in 1772. The governor of Damascus, the Shihab amir of Lebanon and a Turkish squadron combined to blockade him in Acre, where his death was encompassed by Turkish gold.

Zahir was succeeded at Acre by a Bosnian ex-slave called Ahmad Pasha al-Jazzar (the executioner). Al-Jazzar made his small state strong and prosperous, extended its borders and in 1780 was appointed governor of Damascus. He ruled as virtual viceroy of Syria and arbiter of Lebanese affairs, with no major set-back until his natural death in 1804, a record almost unique in the annals of Ottoman Syria. The high-water mark in al-Jazzar's career was attained in 1799, when he checked the advance of Napoleon. The French invader had conquered Egypt and marched triumphantly along the Palestinian coast until he reached the gates of Acre. With the aid of the English fleet under Sir Sidney Smith, al-Jazzar successfully defended Acre from March 21 to May 20, when Napoleon was forced to retreat with an army decimated by plague. The lord of Acre ruthlessly cut down his enemies and rivals and terrorized Syria and Lebanon, where his name still lives as a synonym of cruelty. Yet he sponsored the election of Bashir II al-Shihabi (1788–1840), one of the ablest and most constructive rulers of Ottoman Lebanon.

Bashir's position as governor-general of Lebanon was at first precarious. His predecessor's sons were actively conspiring against him and his patron al-Jazzar was turning against him for failing to support him in the struggle against Napoleon. Forced to retire, he fled in 1799 to Cyprus on one of Sidney Smith's ships. The British then became his friends. After a few months' absence he returned to crush his domestic foes and consolidate his domain. The Biqa was re-attached to Lebanon, the desires of the Damascus governor notwithstanding. Bashir's policy towards the Turks was now one of firmness and friendliness. Early in 1810, when the Wahhabis of Nejd, emerging from the desert, burst through the Syrian frontier and were threatening the settled tracts, Bashir was there with 15,000 Lebanese to help to drive them back. He began to play an important rôle in Syrian affairs and even in disputes between rival governors of Damascus and Tripoli. This, however, forced another period of exile on him (1821–1822), which he this time spent in Egypt. There he struck up a friendship with Muhammad

Ali, viceroy of the country and founder of its royal family.

When, a few years, later Muhammad Ali launched his campaign against Turkey through Syria, Bashir cast his lot with him. The Egyptian viceroy had expected — by way of compensation for the services he had rendered his Turkish suzerain on the battlefields of Greece and Arabia — the addition at least of Syria to his viceroyalty. But his expectation was not fulfilled. Lebanese troops stood side by side with the Egyptians in the siege of Acre in 1831. Thanks to Bashir's co-operation the task of Ibrahim Pasha, son of Muhammad Ali and commander of the Egyptian expedition, was rendered comparatively easy. Ibrahim captured Damascus, routed the Turkish army at Homs, crossed the Taurus and struck into the heart of Anatolia before being forced to withdraw by England, Austria and Russia. In Syria his régime was ended in 1841. Muhammad Ali's ambition to establish an empire of Arab lands with himself at its head turned out to be a daydream. As yet there was no foundation in the consciousness of the people for such a state. On the expulsion of Ibrahim the Turks called Bashir to account. He went to Malta and died in Constantinople in 1850.

The Lebanon of Bashir prospered no less than that of Fakhr-al-Din. Bashir built roads, renovated bridges and set Beirut on its way to becoming what it is today, the gateway to Lebanon and Syria. The city had been avoided by the Manids and earlier Shihabs partly because of its exposure to piratical and other hostile attacks. Both Bashir and Fakhr-al-Din envisaged a greater Lebanon which would embrace with the mountain the coastal towns and the eastern plain. Both encouraged foreign trade relations. Both welcomed political refugees and religious minorities. Bashir offered refuge to a number of Druze families from Aleppo and to Greek Catholics. He was doubtless a Christian but did not consider it expedient to profess his faith. If

Fakhr-al-Din was the first modern Lebanese, Bashir was the second. Anecdotes extolling his equity, sternness, wisdom and ability are still told and retold around fireplaces.

In 1840 another Shihab named Bashir, who had taken part in the rising of the Lebanese against Ibrahim Pasha when he tried to disarm and overtax them, and who had co-operated with the Ottomans and the British in expelling him, was appointed governor of Lebanon. The Ottomans were then carrying out a policy of centralization and Ottomaniza-tion and became more than ever convinced that the only way of keeping the mountain under control was to sow the seeds of discord and stir up hatred between Christians and Druzes. The civil strife thus engendered began in 1841 and culminated in the massacre of an estimated 11,000 Christians in 1860, with an additional 4000 perishing of destitution. This massacre brought about European inter-vention, culminating in the occupation of Lebanon by a French army. Further European influences followed, bringing with them the fresh breeze of modern civiliza-tion.

The first introduction of Western culture to Lebanon, however, must be dated to 1584, when Pope Gregory XIII founded in Rome a seminary to train Maronite students for clerical careers. This unique educational institution en-abled the brightest Christian youths to fit themselves either to return to their homeland to occupy high ecclesiastical positions or to remain in Rome to teach and write. Gradu-ates included teachers of Syriac and Arabic, compilers and translators of the Bible and distinguished scholars like al-Samani (Assemani, 1687–1768), to whose efforts the Vatican library owes many of the finest manuscripts in its oriental collection. The researches of al-Samani on these manu-scripts in Syriac, Arabic, Hebrew, Persian, Turkish, Ethiopic and Armenian, for the sake of which he undertook two trips to the East, were embodied in his voluminous *Bibliotheca Orientalis*, still a major source of information on the churches

of the East. It was the work of these Rome-educated
Maronite scholars that made modern Europe for the first
time fully conscious of the importance of Near Eastern
languages and literatures, especially in their Christian
aspects.

INTELLECTUAL AND NATIONALIST
STIRRINGS

THE dawn of the nineteenth century found Syria, like its neighbours, deep in its dark ages. The black-out, though interrupted by a decade of enlightened and tolerant Egyptian occupation ending in 1841, was soon resumed. Egypt under Muhammad Ali (1805–1848) was the first Arabic-speaking land to establish vital cultural contact with western Europe. Not only did the Ottoman Turks deliberately cut themselves off from cultural intercourse with the West, but they denied their subjects that opportunity at the crucial time when Europe was passing through the eighteenth-century enlightenment and the industrial revolution. They neither joined nor allowed others to join the caravan of progress that Europe was heading. The only major technical element permitted to pierce the Ottoman curtain was the military one, which was of no avail to Syrians and other Arabs.

Down to the mid-nineteenth century Syria had, therefore, remained medieval in all the varied aspects of life. The family followed the old extended patriarchal type, dominated by the grandfather or the oldest male member, in contrast to the small biological type consisting of parents and unmarried children. Learning, what there was of it, was almost the monopoly of theologians, mostly of the conservative obscurantist variety. Industry operated on the low domestic level and was carried on with looms and simple hand tools. The economy was provincial and business partnership was largely confined to members of the same family. Science, in the modern sense, was non-existent. Quacks practised medicine, at best with the aid of yellow-leafed texts of Avicenna (ibn-Sina) and other Arab physicians of a thousand years' vintage. Barbers served as dentists and grocers as pharmacists. But by the early twentieth century the whole picture was on the way to a radical change.

The point of departure may be fixed in 1860 when, as a result of the communal wars in Lebanon, which had spread to Damascus, public-spirited Europeans hastened to the aid of the afflicted in the area. Some of the work was intended for immediate relief, some for enduring value. The French military intervention in Lebanon, resulting in the granting of autonomy to the mountain under a Christian governor-general and the aegis of the then six great European powers, made of that land a chief centre for receiving cultural influences and radiating them to the entire adjoining area. Another international development of an entirely different nature, the opening of the Suez Canal to world traffic in 1869, helped to end the physical and intellectual isolation — and with it the stagnation — of the entire region and to restore it to its traditional rôle as the link connecting the three historic continents.

In the newly constituted Lebanon philanthropic and educational agencies could operate in a more congenial atmosphere. They thrived. Catholic missionaries needed no introduction to the area, some of them having been in operation on a limited scale since the benevolent days of Fakhr-al-Din al-Mani. Before the end of the nineteenth century these Capuchins had founded parishes in Antioch and Beirut and maintained houses in Aleppo and three Lebanese villages. Another Catholic mission, the Lazarist, had started work in Damascus as early as 1755 and twenty years later had founded a school for boys that is still in operation. This was the oldest modern school in the city. In the early stages such institutions were, as one would expect, patronized by Christians only.

Protestant activity was not slow to vie with Catholic. Following the war of 1860 the German Deaconesses of Kaiserswerth established a centre at Sidon, transferred later to Beirut, for orphan training, hospital nursing and higher education. The same year saw the British Syrian Mission enter the field with the establishment of schools for boys and girls in Damascus, Beirut, Baalbek and other towns. Their Training College for girls in the Lebanese capital is still a going concern.

Of far greater importance was the advent of American educators, teachers, preachers and physicians whose work culminated in the founding of the Syrian Protestant College (1866), now the American University of Beirut. The French were quick to follow with their Université Saint-Joseph (1874), both still leading institutions in the Near East. Through these two institutions Syrian higher education entered upon a new era in its evolution. Through their schools of medicine the art of healing belatedly entered its scientific age. Graduates of these universities became leaders of thought, science and literature not only in Syria-Lebanon but throughout the eastern Arab world. They founded the earliest literary and scientific magazines, organized the first learned societies, established the most modern schools and produced the most up-to-date books. Their influence has not abated. To implement their educational work the Americans had, as early as 1834, established in Beirut a printing-press, one of the first adequately equipped to print in Arabic. Nineteen years later the French, more particularly the Jesuit order, followed with the Imprimerie Catholique connected with their Beirut university. Both presses are still in operation.

Soon native schools began to deviate from the traditional conventional methods of instruction and follow Western models. French and English were introduced into the curriculums. Textbooks, scientific treatises, plays, novels began to be translated first from French and then from English to satisfy the new needs of the knowledge-starved youth. By the early twentieth century a new crop of writers, authors, poets, *littérateurs* and scientific workers had been raised and was beginning to inch its way slowly to the front, receiving its stimulation from the living present rather than the dead past. Through their pens the Arabic language, rusty with age and given to the expression of traditional unprogressive thought, received a fresh polish and an injection of new life which started it on its way to becoming a vehicle capable of expressing the finest shades of scientific thought and the most delicate sentiments of the human heart. In this it repeated its experience in Baghdad under Harun al-Rashid and al-Mamun, when it rose to meet the challenge of the new day with its translations from Syriac, Greek and Persian. In both instances it embarked upon a new career of adequate and effective expression for a newly enlightened generation.

The impact of modern ideas — secular, scientific, democratic, naturalistic — played havoc with old traditions, cherished beliefs and venerated institutions. It caused tension and brought about conflicts in the social order. This was indeed a period of transition and, like all such periods, a time of stress and strain. Old ties were loosening; conventional loyalties were changing; and accepted scales of value were being rearranged. How to reconcile the old with the new became and remained the major problem. Hitherto society had consisted of but two classes: one of landowners, aristocrats, ecclesiastics and the well-to-do and another of farmers, peasants, manual workers and the poor. Any in between were of no consequence. But now a fresh middle class of physicians, teachers, lawyers, writers and other professionals, together with a new variety of businessmen, emerged and began to exercise telling influence. With the disruption of the social order the family institution, with its time-honoured loyalties and virtues, began to show cracks in its structure. This was, however, true only in urban settlements. By the early twentieth century women were demanding and receiving a large measure of freedom. Sons were seeking wives of their own choice and when married were moving into domiciles of their own.

Syria

Meantime an economic transformation was going on, less violent but no less radical. In it no deeply rooted emotions were involved as in the case of the social and spiritual transformation. Hitherto agriculture had been largely of the subsistence, rather than the commercial, type. The average farmer concerned himself with the necessary produce for his family. The craftsman likewise operated on a narrow scale, his customers being his neighbours or fellow-townsmen. The typical city merchant was his own buyer, salesman and bookkeeper. Neighbourliness, personal relationship, characterized most economic dealings as it did social ones. But with the improved methods of sea and land transportation and the intrusion of foreign merchants and goods, this pattern yielded to change. Factory-made textiles from Manchester, machine-made articles from Paris and, later, line-produced commodities from New York and Detroit invaded the market. Before such an onslaught the primitive local industry stood helpless. The public developed a new taste for fashionable clothes, alcoholic drinks, soft beverages, cigars and cigarettes, candies and bonbons which the native market was incapable of producing. Village and town handicraft, unable to adjust itself to the new situation, dwindled or vanished. Urban population increased. Beirut, which started the nineteenth century with about 5000 inhabitants, ended it with some 120,000; Damascus ended it with 170,000. He among the city merchants who had the foresight and intelligence to adopt new techniques in his business survived, thrived and achieved membership in the rising influential class. In the old society the discrepancy between the two existing classes, though genuine, was not so apparent as in the new society. Now the *nouveaux riches* could and did display their riches in the form of shining jewellery bedecking their wives and daughters, Paris-tailored clothes worn on festive occasions, exotic foods and drinks — none of which were available before. As the rich became richer, the poor felt poorer.

The improved economy called for quicker and better means of communication. In 1863 a highway connecting Beirut with Damascus was opened by a French company. It operated a diligence service. With this highway as the main artery a network of roads finally linked the principal towns of Syria-Lebanon. Horse-drawn carriages began to roll. In 1894 another French company inaugurated a Beirut-Damascus-Hawran railroad. This trunk was later extended into Turkey, Iraq and Hejaz. For the first time remote villagers and desert-dwellers were brought within the range of modern civilization. At the turn of the twentieth century Syria-Lebanon was acknowledged to be the most civilized province of the Ottoman empire. Autonomous Lebanon was admittedly the best governed sanjaq.

Increased knowledge, improved sanitation and the mounting rise in the standard of living resulted in an increased population. In 1840 the estimated population of Syria-Lebanon was a million and a quarter, a fraction of what it was in Roman days. In 1900 it reached four million. Pressure from the increase and the urge to escape from Ottoman oppression found a safety-valve in emigration into Egypt. The bulk of the emigrants were Christian Lebanese who sought a new home in British-occupied Egypt. Before 1890 this was the only land to which migration was officially allowed by the Ottomans, who still considered it a part of their empire. There educated Syrians and Lebanese found a wider and more rewarding field for their activity. The British governments of Egypt and the Sudan welcomed to their employment especially those educated in American and British schools. Other emigrants established themselves as editors of magazines and newspapers, writers, interpreters and teachers and became known as the founders of the school of journalism and writing still dominant in the Arab East.

As the wave of migration swelled it splashed and reached the Americas, where at present there is hardly a good-sized town in the north or south which does not claim at least one Lebanese or Syrian family. In the New World, western Europe and Australia the immigrants engaged in business pursuits. All started from scratch. Many became leaders of trade and industry in their respective communities; some amassed fortunes considered impressive by world standards. Few returned home for permanent residence. Thus did these descendants of Aramaeans and Phoenicians write a new chapter in the history of international trade worthy of their ancestors. Remittances to the folks back home bolstered the economy of the old homeland. Their Arabic newspapers in Cairo, New York, São Paulo, Buenos Aires and other places, together with their private correspondence and return visits, reinforced the principles of secularism, self-determination and nationalism already in operation there.

From time immemorial the outlook on life throughout the Near East was religious and mystical. Everyday happenings were given a providential interpretation. An epidemic of smallpox, a plague of locusts, a crop failure was considered literally an act of God. With the advance of science, however, a more critical, more rational view was introduced. Consequently religious sanctions began to lose their hold. Even the canon law of Islam, basically God-given, felt the impact of secularization. Attempts to modernize it began with the sultans before the mid-nineteenth century, but proved to be premature. Before the end of the century new commercial and maritime codes following French models were promulgated and adopted in all provinces.

Of all the secular ideas introduced from the West the most potent were political: self-determination, democracy and nationalism. The three marched side by side. Of the trio nationalism was undoubtedly the most dynamic. Political awakening, with its urge to throw off foreign domination and assert independence, was bound to follow the intellectual awakening. It was Revolutionary French thought that contributed the new concepts of liberty, equality and fraternity.

These and cognate ideas found their earliest expression — as was to be expected — in the writings of Syrian and Lebanese residents of Egypt, several of whom were condemned *in absentia* to death by the oppressive régime of Abd-al-Hamid (1876–1909). One of the first Arabic writers to address himself to the subject of liberty and equality, defining and characterizing them, was a Christian Aleppine, Faransis al-Marrash (1836–1873). Another Aleppine, a turbaned Moslem, Abd-al-Rahman al-Kawakibi (1846–1906), authored a most devastating treatise on the 'characteristics of dictatorship and the evils of oppression'. In 1870 a Christian Beiruti, Butrus al-Bustani, issued a literary magazine carrying for its motto : 'Love of country an article of faith' — a novel concept in a brand-new expression. Orthodox Islam considered the country of the believer not that delimited by geographical or political lines, but the entire area where Moslems lived. The Moslem's was a religious, not a territorial, homeland. Another writer, Adib Ishaq, a Damascene living in Egypt, was one of the first to use and give currency to a new term *watan* in the sense of fatherland. The term for nationalism (*qawmiyah*) did not acquire vogue until the second and third decades of the twentieth century.

Though basically the modern concept of nationalism, in the sense of loyalty to a political unit that transcends all other loyalties including the religious, is in conflict with the theory of Islam as a religious fraternity, the idea developed from faint beginnings to become an all-penetrating element in the life of Moslems from Morocco to Iraq. Its earliest expression took the form of an all-embracing Arab nationalism based on language and culture rather than on religion. Its earliest voice was that of a Christian Lebanese, Ibrahim al-Yaziji who, in a secret session of a Syrian learned society held in Beirut in 1868, recited a fiery original poem in which he exhorted: 'Arise, ye Arabs, and awake'. That verse was passed on from mouth to mouth to become the bugle-call for a Pan-Arab movement. The spark immediately touched off fire in Egypt. Starting from a wide base the new movement was soon to suffer fragmentation. As the political aspects developed they became diversified and localized. In Egypt, where opposition to British occupation became the chief concern, a provincial — Egyptian — type gradually developed. In Syria, Arab nationalists had to concentrate their efforts first against Ottoman rule and then against the French mandate and to that extent part company with the general movement of Pan-Arabism. An anaemic Syrian nationalism developed. In Syria, as in Egypt, the young generation was thus torn between a grandiose Pan-Arab loyalty and a provincial one called forth by the realities of existing conditions. In all cases a powerful weapon adopted from the Western arsenal was therewith directed against the West. The experience of Egypt and Syria was repeated in Lebanon and Iraq as well.

With the firm establishment of nationalism and the urge for independence as a ruling passion in life the first chapter in the history of modern Syria was concluded. The half-century beginning in 1860 carried it from its medieval slumber to the dawn of an age of enlightenment and self-assertion. But a serious interruption was in store. A dark cloud was looming on the horizon — the cloud of world war.

WAR, OPPRESSION AND PESTILENCE

ONE bright July day in 1908 the world was startled by the news that the long tyrannical rule of Abd-al-Hamid was approaching its end. A *coup* staged by officers in his own army had been successful. It was the work of the Committee of Union and Progress, the striking arm of a secretly organized society, known as the Young Turks, which had had its inception years before at Geneva through the activity of students and youthful reformers and was later moved to Paris. It aimed at a constitution with an elective parliament and the building up of a homogeneous democratic state. Wily Abd-al-Hamid reacted favourably, restored the parliament of 1876, ordered the abolition of espionage and censorship and the release of all political prisoners. A wave of jubilation spread over the Arab world. In Damascus, Beirut, Aleppo, Jerusalem and other towns the new measures were hailed with fireworks, bonfires and eloquent orations. It was the dawn of a new day. Ottoman utopia lurked round the corner. Syria sent delegates to the parliament. Its nationalists founded in Constantinople the Arab-Ottoman fraternity to promote the new cause. But the sultan had no more intention of preserving this democratic paraphernalia of 1908 than that of 1876. The early constitution had been drafted by one of the most liberal-minded Turks of his day, Midhat Pasha, then grand vizir and later governor of Syria. Caught staging with reactionaries a counter-revolution in April 1909, Abd-al-Hamid was replaced by his doddering brother, Muhammad Rashad. Authority lodged in the hands of a military triumvirate of the committee.

With more zeal than experience the new régime embarked upon a policy of centralization of power, Ottomaniza-

tion of the diversified elements of the empire and repression
of all non-Turkish nationalism. To this end they prohibited
all societies formed by non-Turkish groups. Arab nationalists
were driven underground. Impetus was given to the de-
centralist and the separatist wings around them. A group
of Syro-Palestinian and Lebanese students and emigrants in
Paris organized the Young Arab Society aiming at securing
Arab independence from Turkish rule. But the Arab
Congress which it sponsored there in 1913, and which was
attended by twenty-four delegates from Syria, Lebanon and
Iraq, including two Lebanese from New York, called simply
for home rule and the recognition of Arabic as the official
language. It also warned against meddling by European
powers. Secret societies mushroomed in Damascus, Baghdad
and Cairo. Arab officers in the Turkish army formed their
own cells. Lack of communication facilities made it difficult
to co-ordinate or integrate the work of the separate organiza-
tions. With these developments the Young Turks were
unable to cope. Their domestic troubles were complicated
by foreign ones of even more serious nature. When war
broke out in August 1914 the Constantinople régime cast
its lot with the Central Powers.

Late in that year Jamal Pasha, a member of the trium-
virate, arrived at Damascus as governor-general of Syria-
Lebanon-Palestine and commander-in-chief of the fourth
Ottoman army. The area was considered dangerously anti-
Ottoman with strong pro-Arab leanings and with the
Christians of Lebanon entertaining pro-French sympathies.
Jamal lost no time in abolishing Lebanon's autonomy and
launching a policy of intimidation, deportation, torture and
suppression of all nationalist activity. He inaugurated a
reign of terror before which earlier ones paled and earned
the sobriquet al-Saffah (bloodshedder). At Alayh, 'bride
of Lebanese summer resorts', he instituted the following
summer a military court which summarily sentenced, even
condemned to death, suspects and nationalist leaders. Those

sentenced to death were hanged in public squares in Damascus and Beirut. Membership in one of those societies on the black list; charges proffered by personal enemies or jealous rivals; sympathy with the French as revealed by the seized archives of the Beirut consulate; and above all, espousal of the Arab cause upheld by al-Sharif Husayn of Mecca — any of these was enough to bring the alleged criminal before the military tribunal. The Sharif in 1916 unfurled the banner of rebellion against the Young Turks, declared himself 'king of the Arabs' and entered into secret communication with Arab nationalists outside Hejaz. On May 6 of that year Jamal sent fourteen Moslems and Christians in Beirut and seven in Damascus to the gallows. The day is still commemorated as 'martyrs' day' in both cities, and the sites are called 'martyrs' squares'.

By way of preparation for the ill-conceived attack on the Suez Canal Jamal imposed military conscription, requisitioned beasts of burden and summoned the populace to provision his troops at a time when they could hardly provision themselves. The Allied blockade by sea and land was becoming tighter and its effects were beginning to tell. The entire area became a paradise for all kinds of disease germs — malaria, typhus, typhoid and dysentery. Contaminated soldiers spread all sorts of maladies. A plague of locusts in the spring of 1915 veiled the sun and added its quota to the economic misery. Whatever drugs were available were hardly enough to meet the military demands. Evidence goes to show that in the case of Lebanon a deliberate effort was made to starve and decimate the people. About a hundred thousand are estimated to have been lost out of its four hundred and fifty thousand population. But for remittances and aid from the United States, some of which was side-tracked by local authorities, casualties would have been heavier.

While the people were passing through these agonizing experiences the Allied Powers were planning the parcelling out of their lands among themselves. The secret Sykes-Picot agreement of May 1916, whose contents were first divulged by the Bolsheviks in Russia, divided the Fertile Crescent between Britain and France. In October of the preceding year Henry McMahon, British high commissioner in Cairo, recognized in the name of Great Britain the independence of the Arabs within certain boundaries defined by the Sharif to include the Fertile Crescent and accepted with certain vague reservations. The Sharif had assumed the leadership of the Pan-Arab movement. On November 2, 1917, Lord Balfour made his famous declaration that the British Government 'views with favour the establishment of a national home in Palestine for the Jewish people' — whatever that may mean. Seven days later a joint Anglo-French declaration, emanating from the general head-quarters of their expeditionary force at Cairo, assured the people that the goal envisaged by these two powers was 'the complete and final liberation of the peoples who have for so long been oppressed by the Turks, and the setting up of national governments and administrations that shall derive their authority from the free exercise of the initiative and choice of the indigenous populations'. These promises echoed the doctrine of self-determination previously enunciated by President Woodrow Wilson and his insistence that the post-war settlement should be based upon 'the free acceptance of that settlement by the people immediately concerned'. By Armistice Day, November 11, 1918, Allied troops under General Allenby, supported by Arab troops under Faysal, son of King Husayn, had occupied Syria-Lebanon-Palestine. In pursuance of their newly enunciated doctrine of self-determination the Allied leaders at the Peace Conference of Versailles in 1919, where Faysal repre-sented his father in arguing the Arab case, agreed to send a commission to Syria. But only the United States sent its King-Crane Commission, England, France and Italy having failed to act. In its report, which was not made public until

1922, the commission declared that the consensus of opinion in Syria insisted on independence, repudiating the mandate form of tutelage but overwhelmingly favouring assistance provided by the United States or, failing that, by Great Britain, but not by France. Lebanon by a majority also favoured independence, called for a Greater Lebanon from Tripoli to Tyre, unrelated to Syria and receiving assistance from France. On Palestine the commission recommended that the Zionist programme be reduced, Jewish immigration limited and the idea of converting Palestine into a Jewish commonwealth abandoned.

By then the San Reı.ıo (Italy) conference had partitioned the Ottoman empire (April 1920), giving France the mandate over Syria and Lebanon and Great Britain the mandate over Palestine and Iraq. The dream of Arab unity was shattered. Four months later Turkey signed the treaty of Sèvres (France) renouncing all rights to the mandated territory. The mandate institution was a novel one in political relations generally ascribed to the initiative of General Smuts of South Africa and President Wilson. All four mandates — Syria, Lebanon, Palestine and Iraq — were classified as class A under the League of Nations. The covenant acknowledged these communities as having reached a stage of development where their existence as 'independent nations can be provisionally recognized subject to the rendering of administrative advice and assistance by a Mandatory until such time as they are able to stand alone'. Further, the covenant reiterated the Wilsonian doctrine that the wishes of the people concerned were to be a principal consideration.

UNDER THE FRENCH MANDATE

EARLY in June 1920 Faysal, who had become the symbol of Syrian aspirations, returned to Damascus from his second trip to Europe fully convinced that England and France were in no mood to accept a fully independent status for Syria. More than that, he had agreed with Georges Clemenceau to accept assistance in administrative, financial and technical affairs. But an over-enthusiastic Syrian congress, convened at Damascus, rejected (March 8) this mild form of mandatory tutelage and proclaimed Faysal king over an expanded Syria 'in its natural boundaries' 'from the Taurus to Sinai'. In the congress Syria and Palestine were adequately represented, but not Lebanon. On July 14 the French high commissioner Henri Gouraud, one-armed hero of the Marne, addressed an ultimatum to King Faysal demanding unconditional acceptance of French authority and shortly afterwards moved his forces upon Damascus. The seasoned troops had no difficulty in scoring a victory at Maysalun against a handful of hastily assembled, poorly trained Syrian soldiers. Faysal left the country and was later installed by the British as king over Iraq, where his grandson, until 1958, ruled. On September 1, 1920, Greater Lebanon was declared by Gouraud.

Syria itself presented well-nigh insurmountable difficulties. It was at perhaps the lowest ebb in its history politically, economically, socially and spiritually. It had no developed institutions for self-rule, no proper implementation for democratic procedure, and its people had no experience in parliamentary affairs or modern civil service. The mandatory was from the outset confronted with the task of literally creating administrative and judiciary organs of state, repairing roads, establishing public education on a systematic basis and developing the natural resources.

Slowly the mandatory established comparatively modern administrative machinery, carried on land registration, organized an educational system, encouraged archaeological researches, gave fellowships for study in France especially in such neglected fields as art, set up a department of public health and sanitation and developed public security. Modern codes of law were promulgated. The customs were organized jointly with Lebanon, whose capital Beirut remained the chief port of entry for the entire hinterland. Public works, including roads, were not carried out on as large a scale as in Lebanon. But on the whole the government's energies were directed to political rather than economic problems and the people themselves concentrated on the political struggle.

They felt that mandatory administration differed more in theory than in practice from colonial rule. To them French control was more direct and more hateful than that exercised by the Turks. The first three high commissioners, Henri Gouraud (1919–1923), Maxime Weygand (1923–1925) and Maurice Sarrail (1925), who were also commissioners to Lebanon and commanders-in-chief of the armed forces, were military generals who had distinguished themselves in the World War. For aides they drew largely upon the reservoir of officers with colonial experience in Africa. Repeated attempts to reach a compromise between nationalist aspirations and French rule failed. A draft constitution submitted in August 1928 by an elected constituent assembly was rejected by the commissioner and the assembly itself was dissolved. Until 1930 the country was governed without a constitution. Even the one then promulgated was drawn up by the commissioner himself but embodied much material, with reservations, from the one submitted by the assembly. Potential separatist movements — regional and religious — were given a chance to be actualized and the old-time principle of 'divide and rule' was applied. The country was divided into four states: the state of Damascus, the state of Aleppo, that of the Druzes in Hawran and that of the Alawites centring on Latakia.

A larger dose of French culture was administered than the people would tolerate. The French language was emphasized at the expense of Arabic. Repressive measures were taken against nationalists. Shukri al-Quwatli, future president of the independent Republic, Faris al-Khuri, future prime minister, Salih al-Haffar, also prime minister-to-be, and other leaders of thought and action were, at some time or other, banished or jailed. Restrictions were placed on personal liberties to the exasperation of the population, who started to vent their discontent in strikes and local uprisings culminating in the general revolt of 1925. Sparked by Druzes, the revolt soon spread into Damascus, Aleppo, Hamah and other places and continued until the autumn of 1927, when the capital was subjected to a bombardment by artillery and aircraft which left scars on it for years to come. In face of the outburst of world-wide indignation the French replaced the high commissioner by a civilian, Henri de Jouvenel, whose attempt to negotiate peace terms were unsuccessful. Equally unsuccessful were the efforts of his successors. In January a nationalist congress met at the capital, formally condemned the French policy and issued a Pan-Arab manifesto.

The late 1930's were marked with even greater resentment because France, in violation of the terms of the mandate charging it with safeguarding the integrity of the territory entrusted to its care, granted Turkey privileges in the Sanjaq of Alexandretta and finally ceded it in June 1939 to become incorporated in the Turkish Republic. The Turks had a sizable minority in the Sanjaq. This was the price — paid at Syria's expense — to win Turkey over to the Anglo-French side in the great war which was developing.

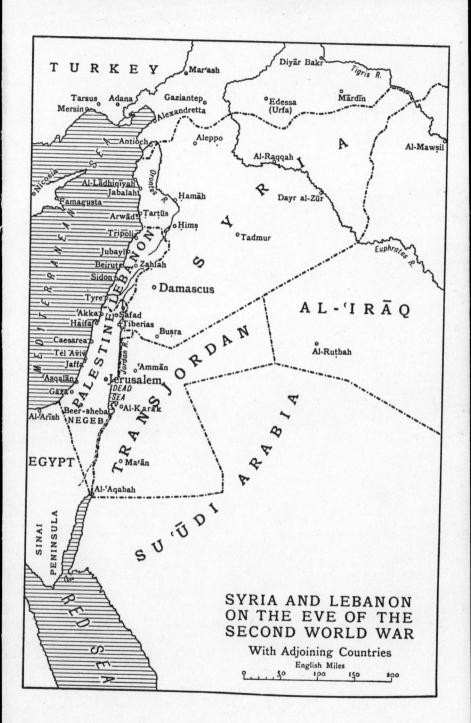

SYRIA AND LEBANON
ON THE EVE OF THE
SECOND WORLD WAR

With Adjoining Countries

English Miles

0   50   100   150   200

Under the French Mandate

The second World War was infinitely kinder to Syria and the Syrians than the first. German propaganda, though intensive and at times effective, resulted in no overt hostility on the part of Syrians, as it did in the case of Iraqis. Fearing the Axis Powers' penetration and fully appreciating the rebellious condition of Palestine due to Zionist infiltration, the French and British took the necessary preventive measures against intensifying native discontent and distrust. Their increased troops required large supplies of foodstuffs and necessitated building new roads, repairing old ones and undertaking other public enterprises, all of which gave added employment to local workers. Transit trade increased. The Middle East Supply Centre, established at Cairo, planned for the whole extended area, rationed wheat, rice, meat, drugs and other necessities of life, helped to increase local production, dealt effectively with the situation resulting from shipping shortage and on the whole not only succeeded in averting need and epidemics but contributed to a measure of prosperity. Meantime several merchants and industrialists amassed fortunes through hoarding and other means.

On the political side, however, retrogression rather than progression marked the scene. In May 1939 Gabriel Puaux, high commissioner since early 1938, renounced in the name of his government the Franco-Syrian treaty which had been negotiated as early as 1936. He then proceeded to re-establish the mandatory régime on a firmer basis. Martial law was declared. With France's surrender to the Axis he pledged loyalty to the Vichy government and closely collaborated with the German commission sent to Syria-Lebanon. British and Free French troops had then to open hostilities for the recovery of the land. On June 8, 1941, their troops entered Syria from the east and the south and forced the Vichy commander-in-chief in Syria and Lebanon to ask for terms, thus cancelling German attempts to obtain control of these territories. Georges Catroux was appointed by the chief of the Free French, General de Gaulle, as commander of the troops of the Levant, delegate general and plenipotentiary. On the day of the invasion of Syria by Allied troops General Catroux had proclaimed to the Syrian people that he was sent 'to put an end to the mandatory régime and to proclaim you free and independent'. The United Kingdom government also declared that 'they support and associate themselves with the assurance of independence given by General Catroux on behalf of General de Gaulle to Syria and Lebanon'. On September 16 Catroux formally announced Syria's independence and eleven days later its new government formally proclaimed its status as an independent state. But all this was more nominal than real. There was little change in personnel and less in methods. No constitutional life was established until August 1943 when a newly elected chamber chose the nationalist leader Shukri al-Quwatli as president of the Republic. The national government sought to gain possession of the powers and prerogatives of independent rule. It inaugurated legations in Paris, London, Moscow and Washington and later in other capitals.

But points of dispute soon arose. Chief among them was the disposition of the so-called common interests involving matters of concern (such as customs) to both Syria and Lebanon. Then there were the 'special troops', locally recruited from Syrian and Lebanese levies, trained and integrated with the army of occupation. France then demanded a new treaty giving her a privileged position in the country, which the Syrians categorically rejected. As late as May 1945, when Syria objected to the admission of new French troops and broke off relations with France, the army of occupation repeated its performance of eighteen years earlier and bombarded Damascus with aircraft and field guns. The day was May 29; delegates from all over the world were holding at San Francisco the charter meeting of the United Nations. No worse day could have been chosen. The shock was universal. The British intervened and restored order. By the end of the year France and Britain had agreed to consult about evacuating their troops from both Syria and Lebanon. The admission of both states to the United Nations on April 12, 1945, implied international recognition of the termination of the mandate. Twenty days before that Syria had signed the pact of the newly created Arab League, whose other members were Egypt, Iraq, Lebanon, Saudi Arabia, Transjordan and Yemen. Under pressure from the United Nations the evacuation of Syria was at last completed on April 17, 1946; that of Lebanon on December 31, 1946. A public square in Damascus and a national holiday commemorate 'the day of evacuation'. Self-government then became completely established.

INDEPENDENT REPUBLIC

SYRIA embarked upon its career as a fully independent state under its president Shukri al-Quwatli with hope and aspiration but with no rosy path in sight. It soon found itself beset with a multiplicity of thorny problems, both internal and external. There was first its relation with its twin sister Lebanon, with which it shared the common interests of tariff and customs duties, concessionary companies, the administration of antiquities and the guarding of the common frontier. With Turkey it wished to settle the problem of Alexandretta, now the province of Hatay. *Vis-à-vis* Jordan it faced the question of Greater Syria long and ardently advocated by King Abdullah. In 1946 the king declared that in furthering this project he was motivated not by dynastic interests but rather by the ideal of a Pan-Arab state nucleated around a joint Syria-Palestine unit. An influential Syrian group favoured the plan. Another, the People's Party, advocated the Fertile Crescent project, sponsored by Iraq, which would bring Syria, Iraq and Jordan into one entity as a preliminary step towards the realization of a Pan-Arab union. Iraqis could claim that their king as the son of Faysal was entitled to both thrones; but their treaty relations with Great Britain made Syrians hesitate.

Different from all these groups and distinct by itself was the Syrian Nationalist Party, which preached the doctrine that there was such a thing as a Syrian nationhood independent of and unrelated to Arabism. Syria, in their definition, included Lebanon. The organization was authoritarian in its administration, aggressive and determined in its propaganda, and soon won converts mainly from among the educated youth. Its founder, a Lebanese Christian who had lived in Brazil, was condemned to death by the Lebanese government on the ground of conspiring against its security. The party then went underground. Last but not least was the Zionist problem, which had grown out of its narrow dimensions and assumed international importance. Syria could not tolerate the thought of an intrusive Zionist state created at the expense of a territory not only contiguous to it but considered part of it. Within Syria's own boundaries there were those who favoured one or the other of the proposed projects, but against Zionism the feeling was intense and unanimous.

Of all these problems the Zionist was the most pressing. The situation in Palestine was gradually getting out of hand. A state of terrorism bordering on anarchy began to prevail as the Jewish Agency absorbed authority from the British mandatory and flooded the land with new recruits from abroad, mostly young and potential fighters for Zionism. When the general assembly of the United Nations on November 29, 1947, approved the partition plan for Palestine guerrilla warfare broke out. The majority vote for partition was secured at the last minute by manœuvring and intensive lobbying by United States agents at Lake Success and by wire-pulling from Washington — all in response to Jewish pressure. Arab anti-Western feeling now began to include the United States. As the United Nations had no means of enforcing the partition or establishing security and as the British troops withdrew, the Zionists achieved military superiority over the Palestine Arab 'liberation army' and on May 14, 1948, proclaimed the state of Israel. It was immediately recognized by the United States and Russia. Members of the Arab League, including Syria, moved against the new state but their disorganized, inadequately equipped and poorly trained troops, with the exception of Jordan's Arab Legion, made such a poor showing that they had in February 1949 to sign an armistice with Israel.

Syria

Throughout, the domestic situation in Syria was moving from bad to worse. As under the mandate, the people's thought and energy continued to be canalized in political and military channels to the neglect or detriment of other aspects of life. Finances passed into a disastrous condition. Currency, still tied to the French franc, remained unstable. As prices soared, sales dipped. The military performance in Palestine was humiliating. An expansionist Israel posed a threat to the safety of Syria. The mirage of an Arab union was dimmed beyond recognition. The time was ripe for a change in government.

In the silent night of March 30, 1949, a *coup d'état* was hatched by an army group headed by Colonel Husni al-Zaim. Al-Quwatli and some of his ministers were held under detention until they signed their resignations. Therewith was effected the first in a series of three military coups which punctuated the remaining nine months of the year. Al-Zaim introduced progressive, even radical reforms. He gave women of elementary education electoral rights and brought the privately endowed charitable institutions (*waqfs*) under state control. He ordered a curfew, enforced censorship of the press and closed the frontiers. A 15 per cent tax was ordered on all industrial concerns and made retroactive to 1940. The Arabian American Oil Company (Aramco) was granted wayleave for its proposed Trans-Arabian Pipe Line (Tapline). A modern commercial law was adopted. The Syrian dictator took Kemal Atatürk for model. The colonel promoted himself to field-marshal and ordered a richly ornamented bâton from Paris. Suspicion spread that he had French leanings. His fall was as abrupt and dramatic as his rise.

On August 14 another group of officers, led by Colonel Sami al-Hinnawi, forced their way into al-Zaim's residence and that of his prime minister, apprehended and summarily shot them, to save the country, in the words of the communiqué, from the tyrant who had abused his authority, wasted public funds and restricted personal liberty. Al-Hinnawi's régime was even shorter than his predecessor's and much less productive. On December 19 a third *coup* engineered by Colonel Adib al-Shishakli, chief of staff, overthrew the Hinnawi régime because 'it plotted against the republican régime in conjunction with foreign elements'. Al-Hinnawi favoured union with Iraq and the 'foreign element', the supposed villain, in this case was Great Britain, Iraq's ally. The seventy-four-year-old Hashim al-Atasi, elected shortly before that as provisional president of the Republic, was retained. In due course al-Shishakli gathered the reins of the executive power into his own hands.

Conditions did not greatly improve under the new régime. The rupture of the Syro-Lebanese customs union (March 1950) severed the last economic link with its closest neighbour. Lebanon pursued its time-honoured policy of free trade and open market, while Syria embarked upon a protective tariff policy. The Lebanese frontier was closed to Syrian exports. Syria was the greater economic sufferer. It planned to improve the port of Latakia and the roads leading from and into it. The asylum given Syrian political refugees in Lebanon was a constant source of friction. On the Syrian-Israeli border clashes were intensified. The main issue was whether Israel had the right to extend its drainage work in the Lake Huleh swamps to the upper reaches of the Jordan, included in the demilitarized zone between the two states. Appeals to the United Nations by both sides were frequent but the results often unsatisfactory. Anti-Western feeling was intensified, especially since Israel was receiving arms and financial support from Great Britain, France and the United States.

The national defence item climbed higher and higher in the Syrian budget. The government refused American aid 'with strings attached to it'. There was no immediate source to tap for bolstering the shaky economy. Long-range projects were headed by the draining of the Ghab swamps on the Orontes, which would reclaim and irrigate 200,000 acres at a $280,000,000 cost, provide hydro-electric power for new industry and exterminate disease-bearing insects. Other major drainage and irrigation projects involved the Euphrates, the Khabur and the Yarmuk rivers on a five-year plan adopted in 1955 at an estimated cost of about $200,000,000. By decree some 4,000,000 acres of state domain lands were distributed among a number of agricultural co-operative settlements. Trade agreements with Lebanon ended the deadlock. Water, electricity and communication companies in Damascus and Aleppo were nationalized. In June 1953 al-Shishakli promulgated a draft constitution modelled to a limited extent after that of the United States. It featured an elective president in whose hands lodged executive power, a chamber of deputies with legislative function and a supreme court.

At a time when the Shishakli régime seemed secure, undercurrents swelled to undermine it. Four years were not enough to reconcile or eliminate opposition. The Arab Liberation Party, a Shishakli creation and the only one allowed to operate, proved to be a broken reed. Business strikes, student demonstrations, political disturbances gained more momentum as the year 1954 passed into 1955. The imprisonment of twelve opposition leaders, some of whom had held the highest positions in the government, and the rushing of troops to crush uprisings in Jabal al-Duruz produced the opposite results. At last, when the Aleppo garrison declared its rebellion and threatened to march against the capital, al-Shishakli yielded. He offered his resignation and fled to Saudi Arabia and later to Paris, where he still is. The aged Atasi, ousted by the dictator in 1951, was restored to power by the army. He replaced the Shishakli constitution with that of 1950. On September 6 Shukri al-Quwatli, who had fled to Egypt during the Zaim *coup*, returned to accept the chamber of deputies' election as president of the Republic. A five-year military rule inscribed a circle which took it back to its starting-point. It was tested and proved wanting. Civilian control with constitutional authority was resumed.

Under al-Quwatli Syria pursued the ideal of Arab unity through *rapprochement* with Egypt and Saudi Arabia. Hostile to Israel, unfriendly towards Turkey, alienated from Lebanon and more recently from Iraq, she felt isolated and vulnerable. By history, geography and tradition, Iraq would have been a natural partner of Syria. But the signing by Iraq of the Baghdad pact (February 1955) allied it with Turkey and the West. Both Egypt and Syria then considered the Arab League security pact as no longer effective and the two bound themselves by a new defence treaty. The treaty established unity of command and covered training, equipment and other phases of military organization and activity. On the East-or-West issue Syria and Egypt saw eye to eye. Saudi Arabia was determined in its opposition to dealings with Russia.

The avowed policy of Syria under al-Quwatli was that of 'neutrality': rejection of foreign pacts and readiness to receive arms from any source that offered them 'with no strings'. Russia and her satellites expressed willingness to accommodate. Early in 1956 the Syrian government recalled its delegation seeking a thirty-million-dollar loan from the International Bank for Reconstruction and Development. It signed a trade and payment agreement with Rumania to export cotton, tobacco, hides, textiles and olive oil for Rumanian timber, dyes, chemicals, medicines, agricultural engines and other machinery. Similar agreements followed with Hungary, Bulgaria and Czechoslovakia. Cultural missions were exchanged with Russia and Communist China. The cultural agreement with Russia involved exchange of specialists in science, art, education and scholarships. Eight of the thirty participant countries in the Damascus third international fair (September 1956) belonged to the Communist bloc. In the 1957 fair Great

Britain, France and the United States were conspicuous by their absence.

Syrian-Israeli tension continued unabated. Border incidents became more serious. An Israeli raid on a Syrian army post at the northern corner of the Sea of Galilee (December 11, 1955) killed thirty-six Syrians against six Israelis and, following a United Nations security council report, elicited from the three great Western powers a censure in 'strong and unequivocal terms'. But in effectiveness this censure was no stronger than an old-time poultice on a cancerous area. The continued aid to Israel from the West — particularly from the United States — the festering wound of the nine hundred thousand Palestinian refugees, the policy of France in North Africa, an increase in border clashes with Turkey intensified hostility to the West as it accelerated *rapprochement* to the East. All this urged intensified military preparedness. Plans for constructing air-raid shelters, for introducing military training into secondary and trade schools and for strengthening border defences were hastily laid and carried out. On August 12, 1956, a nation-wide draft of civilians including women was announced.

Any hope of reconciliation with the West was shattered when on October 30, 1956, Israel's invasion of Egypt was seconded by an Anglo-French one. Syria rallied to the support of her ally. Army officers blew up the Iraq Petroleum Company's pipe-lines in her territory and repairs were allowed only after withdrawal of all foreign forces from Egypt, despite the loss of a major element in the country's national income. The triple attack on Egypt and its failure to achieve its purpose raised the stature of Gamal Abdel Nasser (Jamal Abd-al-Nasir) from that of a national Egyptian hero to an international Arab one ; it placed him in a niche by himself, a symbol of resistance to Western aggression and a champion of the Pan-Arab cause. To the Moslem masses throughout south-western Asia the Egyptian president became an idol.

Russia also threatened to help Egypt with 'volunteers'. Earlier in the summer its foreign minister had paid a visit to Egypt and Syria, and when President al-Quwatli was repaying the visit to Moscow he was assured by President Klimenti Y. Voroshilov at a reception in his honour of Soviet readiness 'to supply Syria with the necessary assistance to overcome as rapidly as possible the vestiges of colonialism', and in doing so 'the Soviet Union claims no privileges or advantages for itself'. On two following occasions, when Syria accused Turkey of intending aggression, Russia warned of her readiness to support the Syrian side. Thus did the Soviet Union seek and find common ground for identifying her interests with those of Syria and the rest of the Arab world: hostility to the three great Western powers, arms against Israel and sympathy with the Pan-Arab movement. It was its policy that won friends, not its ideology. Officially the Communist party remained banned in Syria, as it was in other Arab states, though one seat in the parliament was held by its leader. As late as the autumn of 1957 al-Quwatli was still declaring: 'Had it not been for Israel, we would not have felt the need for new weapons; and were it not for the unrelenting preferential treatment of Israel by the United States, we would not have been introduced to new Russians.'

On the other hand, the Eisenhower doctrine offering aid and protection to any Near Eastern country that sought it against Communist threat fell flat and was rejected outright by the Syrian government (June 1957). The tripartite agreement of May 1950 among Great Britain, France and the United States to take immediate action against any Arab state or Israel violating the frontier lacked implementation, as did the avowed policy of 'equal friendship to both sides' declared by Secretary of State John Foster Dulles on his return from a trip to the troubled area. The downward curve in Syrian-American relations hit bottom when on August 13, 1957, military authorities 'uncovered' in Damascus 'an American plot to overthrow Syria's present régime'.

Advantage was taken of the announcement to reshuffle, in favour of the leftist side, some high officers in the army. Three American embassy officials were ousted. In retaliation the United States expelled the Syrian ambassador and one of his Washington aides. Shortly after that Syria, backed up by Russia, accused Turkey of massing troops on her Syrian border, and Premier Nikolai Bulganin warned that 'the Soviet Union cannot remain indifferent' to 'the report about Turkish troops' concentration on Syria's border'.

For two years Syrians and Egyptians have been considering the possibility of political union as a first step towards a Pan-Arab one. It was high time to take decisive action and consummate the merging of the two states into one. Exchange of visits and views among high officials, meetings of joint deputies' committees and of ministers' commissions and other relevant measures were now expedited. The groundwork was laid for a draft constitution. On the first of February 1958 the merger of the two into the United Arab Republic, with President Nasser as its head, was proclaimed at Cairo. The new Republic would have one flag, one army and one people. Other Arab states were invited to join. The kingdom of Yemen responded and opened negotiations. Those of Iraq and Jordan, under two young cousin kings, reacted by a merger of their own which was named the Arab Federation. Saudi Arabia stayed on the fence. Lebanon declared that it would neither interfere in its neighbours' internal affairs nor countenance interference on their part in its affairs.

The stage was set for a new act in the drama of Arab history. The signing of the birth certificate of the United Arab Republic inscribed the title of the first scene, in which the rôle to be played by Syria belongs to future history.

INDEX

NAMES AND PLACES

259

Index

Beersheba, 12
Beirut, 2, 6, 17, 19, 35, 61, 78, 87, 89,
    92, 104, 111, 159, 166, 169, 178,
    181, 186, 189, 191, 195, 196, 198,
    204, 205, 218, 222, 229, 230, 232,
    233, 235, 237, 239, 243
Bel, 87
Belisarius, 104, 106
Ben-Hadad, 44
Benjamin, tribe, 47
Berbers, 120, 129, 131, 134, 139, 141
Bethlehem, 102
Beth-shean, 56
Bible, 45, 92, 99
Biqa, al-, 12, 32, 38, 61, 77, 152, 214,
    220, 221, 224
Bisharri, 20
Black Stone, 125
Boccaccio, 190
Bohemond, 177
Bolsheviks, 240
Bordeaux, 104, 134
Bosporus, 96
Brazil, 251
British Government, 240
British Syrian Mission, 230
Bronze Age, 29
Buddhism, 99
Buenos Aires, 234
Buhtur, 195
Buhturi, al-, 158, 166
Bukhara, 120, 130, 160, 174
Bulganin, 258
Bulgaria, 255
Bulgars, 133
Burjis, 202, 204
Bustani, al-, 235
Buwayhids, 174
Byblus, 33, 35, 37, 38, 53, 54, 61, 111
Byzantine empire, 34
Byzantine Syria, 97, 101, 162
Byzantines, 52, 63, 106, 120, 121, 128,
    151, 154, 165, 167 ff., 174 ff.
Byzantium, 96, 107, 108, 112, 121,
    133, 153, 162, 176

Cadiz, 36
Caesarea, 88, 97, 102, 104, 110, 111,
    178, 181, 187
Cairo, 167, 170, 198, 200, 201, 203,
    204, 208, 234, 240, 247

Callinicus, 121
Cambyses, 52
Canaan, 34, 46
Canaanite, 31
Canaanites, 2, 32, 33, 36, 38, 46, *see*
    Phoenicians
Cape of Good Hope, 217
Cappadocia, 133
Capuchins, 219
Caracalla, 92, 94
Carchemish, 40, 43, 50
Carmathians, 162, 163, 168, 169, 174
Carmelites, 222
Carthage, 36, 104, 120
Caspian Sea, 20
Cassius, 75
Catholicism, 132
Catroux, 247, 248
Caucasus, 102, 201
Central Africa, 140
Central Asia, 2, 17, 32, 120, 128, 134,
    196
Central Powers, 238
Ceylon, 128
Chalcedon, 100, 121, 197
Chalcolithic, 28 ff.
Chaldaeans, 40, 43
Chaldaeans, Uniats, 196
Charles Martel, 134
Chaucer, 190
China, 84, 104, 127, 135, 196, 255
Chinese, 193
Chosroes I, 104, 105
Chosroes II, 105
Christ, 96, 99, 100, 108, 144
Christian Europe, 133
Christian Fathers, 91
Christian Lebanese, 233
Christian Syrians, 2
Christianity, 1, 38, 62, 65, 91, 92,
    96 ff., 106, 155, 188, 199
Christians, 89, 93, 102, 109, 115, 123,
    139 ff., 146, 153 ff., 159, 169 ff.,
    184, 188, 189, 194, 195, 198, 218,
    226
Church Fathers, 101
Church of the East, 100
Cilicia, 36, 63, 75, 100, 120, 163, 164,
    173, 177, 181, 185
Cilician Gates, 121
Circassians, 204, 217

Index

263

Index

265

Index

Index

Index

THE END